What makes Shakespeare's late plays so special? Through detailed analyses of key passages, Kate Aughterson shows how these plays portray a world of political intrigue, familial chaos and crisis, which teeters continually into tragedy: a world we can recognise today.

Part I of this engaging study:

- provides stimulating close readings of extracts from *The Tempest, The Winter's Tale, Cymbeline* and *Pericles*
- examines major topics, such as openings, endings, familial roles, stage properties, spectacle and song
- offers suggestions for further work and summarizes the methods of analysis.

Part II supplies essential background material, including:

- detailed accounts of Shakespeare's literary and historical contexts
- samples from important critical works and performances.

With a helpful Further Reading section, this illuminating volume is ideal for anyone who wishes to appreciate and explore Shakespeare's late plays for themselves.

Kate Aughterson is Principal Lecturer and Academic Programme Leader for English Literature at the University of Brighton. She is the author of *Webster: The Tragedies* and *Aphra Behn: The Comedies*, both also in the *Analysing Texts* series.

Analysing Texts is dedicated to one clear belief: that we can all enjoy, understand and analyse literature for ourselves, provided we know how to do it. Readers are guided in the skills and techniques of close textual analysis used to build an insight into a richer understanding of an author's individual style, themes and concerns. An additional section on the writer's life and work and a comparison of major critical views place them in their personal and literary context.

ANALYSING TEXTS

General Editor: Nicholas Marsh

Published

Jane Austen: The Novels   *Nicholas Marsh*
Aphra Behn: The Comedies   *Kate Aughterson*
William Blake: The Poems   *Nicholas Marsh*
Charlotte Brontë: The Novels   *Mike Edwards*
Emily Brontë: Wuthering Heights   *Nicholas Marsh*
Chaucer: The Canterbury Tales   *Gail Ashton*
Daniel Defoe: The Novels   *Nicholas Marsh*
Charles Dickens: David Copperfield/Great Expectations   *Nicolas Tredell*
John Donne: The Poems   *Joe Nutt*
George Eliot: The Novels   *Mike Edwards*
F. Scott Fitzgerald: The Great Gatsby/Tender is the Night   *Nicolas Tredell*
E. M. Forster: The Novels   *Mike Edwards*
Thomas Hardy: The Novels   *Norman Page*
Thomas Hardy: The Poems   *Gillian Steinberg*
John Keats: *John Blades*
Philip Larkin: The Poems   *Nicholas Marsh*
D. H. Lawrence: The Novels   *Nicholas Marsh*
Marlowe: The Plays   *Stevie Simkin*
John Milton: Paradise Lost   *Mike Edwards*
Shakespeare: The Comedies   *R. P. Draper*
Shakespeare: The Histories   *John Blades*
Shakespeare: The Late Plays   *Kate Aughterson*
Shakespeare: The Sonnets   *John Blades*
Shakespeare: The Tragedies   *Nicholas Marsh*
Shakespeare: Three Problem Plays   *Nicholas Marsh*
Mary Shelley: Frankenstein   *Nicholas Marsh*
Webster: The Tragedies   *Kate Aughterson*
Virginia Woolf: The Novels   *Nicholas Marsh*
Wordsworth and Coleridge: Lyrical Ballads   *John Blades*

Further titles are in preparation

Shakespeare: The Late Plays

KATE AUGHTERSON

BLOOMSBURY ACADEMIC
LONDON • NEW YORK • OXFORD • NEW DELHI • SYDNEY

BLOOMSBURY ACADEMIC
Bloomsbury Publishing Plc
50 Bedford Square, London, WC1B 3DP, UK
1385 Broadway, New York, NY 10018, USA
29 Earlsfort Terrace, Dublin 2, Ireland

BLOOMSBURY, BLOOMSBURY ACADEMIC and the Diana logo
are trademarks of Bloomsbury Publishing Plc

First Published 2013 by PALGRAVE MACMILLAN

Reprinted by Bloomsbury Academic

Copyright © Kate Aughterson 2013

Kate Aughterson has asserted her right under the Copyright,
Designs and Patents Act, 1988, to be identified as the author of this work.

All rights reserved. No part of this publication may be reproduced or transmitted in any form or by any means, electronic or mechanical, including photocopying, recording, or any information storage or retrieval system, without prior permission in writing from the publishers.

Bloomsbury Publishing Plc does not have any control over, or responsibility for, any third-party websites referred to or in this book. All internet addresses given in this book were correct at the time of going to press. The author and publisher regret any inconvenience caused if addresses have changed or sites have ceased to exist, but can accept no responsibility for any such changes.

A catalogue record for this book is available from the British Library.

A catalog record for this book is available from the Library of Congress.

ISBN: HB: 978-0-2303-6862-0
PB: 978-0-2303-6863-7
ePDF: 978-1-1373-7564-3
ePub: 978-1-3503-1028-5

To find out more about our authors and books visit
www.bloomsbury.com and sign up for our newsletters.

To Molly, who loves the chorus 'like Shakespeare'

Contents

General Editor's Preface x

A Note on Editions xi

Introduction: Ways of Reading 1
   Analysing Shakespeare's Late Plays 1
   Language 2
   Drama and Performance 4

PART 1: ANALYSING SHAKESPEARE'S LATE PLAYS

1 **Openings** 9
   Analysis: *The Winter's Tale*, 1.1.1–43 10
   Analysis: *The Tempest*, 1.1.1–68 16
   Conclusions 24
   Methods of Analysis 27
   Suggested Work 28

2 **Turning Points: Tragedy and Comedy** 30
   Analysis: *The Winter's Tale*, 3.2.1–147 30
   Analysis: *The Tempest*, 3.3.1–110 43
   Conclusions 52
   Methods of Analysis 54
   Suggested Work 55

3 **Endings** 57
   Analysis: *The Winter's Tale*, 5.3.8–155 57
   Analysis: *Pericles*, Scene 22, ll.21–65 67
   Analysis: *The Tempest*, 5.1.319–338 70
   Analysis: *Cymbeline*, 5.4.436–486 73
   Conclusions 76
   Methods of Analysis 79
   Suggested Work 79

4	**Fathers, Sons and Husbands**	**81**
	Analysis: *Cymbeline*, 1.1.110–54	81
	Analysis: *The Winter's Tale*, 1.2.152–209	86
	Analysis: *The Winter's Tale*, 4.4.378–438	91
	Analysis: *The Tempest*, 1.2.388–422	95
	Analysis: *The Tempest*, 2.1.100–133	98
	Analysis: *The Tempest*, 4.1.13–33	99
	Conclusions	101
	Methods of Analysis	103
	Suggested Work	104
5	**Mothers, Daughters and Wives**	**106**
	Analysis: *The Winter's Tale*, 4.4.97–135	106
	Analysis: *The Winter's Tale*, 5.1.34–75	110
	Analysis: *The Tempest*, 3.1.48–91	113
	Analysis: *The Tempest*, 5.1.165–184	117
	Analysis: *Pericles*, Scene 19, ll.47–150	119
	Conclusions	124
	Methods of Analysis	126
	Suggested Work	126
6	**Masters, Servants and Slaves: Society and Politics**	**129**
	Analysis: *The Tempest*, 1.2.306–364	129
	Analysis: *The Tempest*, 2.1.141–162	135
	Analysis: *The Tempest*, 2.2.41–75 and 154–182	137
	Analysis: *The Winter's Tale*, 2.3.95–157	140
	Analysis: *The Winter's Tale*, 4.4.724–747	145
	Conclusions	147
	Methods of Analysis	149
	Suggested Work	150
7	**Stage Properties**	**152**
	Analysis: *Cymbeline*, 2.2.1–51	152
	Analysis: *Pericles*, Scene 5, ll.155–204	158
	Analysis: *The Winter's Tale*, 3.3.1–56	162
	Conclusions	166
	Methods of Analysis	167
	Suggested Work	168

8 **Spectacle and Theatricality**   170
   Analysis: *Cymbeline*, 5.3.124–214   170
   Analysis: *The Winter's Tale*, 4.1.1–32   177
   Analysis: *The Tempest*, 4.1.57–142   181
   Conclusions   189
   Methods of Analysis   191
   Suggested Work   191

9 **Music and Song**   193
   Analysis: *Cymbeline*, 4.2.258–282   193
   Analysis: *The Winter's Tale*, 4.3.1–30   196
   Analysis: *The Winter's Tale*, 4.4.219–233   198
   Analysis: *The Winter's Tale*, 4.4.257–317   200
   Analysis: *The Tempest*, 1.2.374–404   204
   Analysis: *The Tempest*, 5.1.88–94   207
   Analysis: *The Tempest*, 3.2.114–24   208
   Conclusions   210
   Methods of Analysis   211
   Suggested Work   211

General Conclusions to Part I   214

PART 2: THE CONTEXT AND THE CRITICS

10 **Shakespeare's Literary Career**   219

11 **Jacobean Contexts**   233
    The Political and Social Context of the Late Plays   240

12 **Sample Critical Views and Performances**   248
    Northrop Frye   249
    Leonard Tennenhouse   251
    Janet Adelman   256
    Gabriel Egan   259
    Performances   261

Further Reading   268

Index   273

General Editor's Preface

This series is dedicated to one clear belief: that we can all enjoy, understand and analyse literature for ourselves, provided we know how to do it. How can we build on close understanding of a short passage, and develop our insight into the whole work? What features do we expect to find in a text? Why do we study style in so much detail? In demystifying the study of literature, these are only some of the questions the *Analysing Texts* series addresses and answers.

The books in this series will not do all the work for you, but will provide you with the tools, and show you how to use them. Here, you will find samples of close, detailed analysis, with an explanation of the analytical techniques utilised. At the end of each chapter there are useful suggestions for further work you can do to practise, develop and hone the skills demonstrated and build confidence in your own analytical ability.

An author's individuality shows in the way they write: every work they produce bears the hallmark of that writer's personal 'style'. In the main part of each book we concentrate therefore on analysing the particular flavour and concerns of one author's work, and explain the features of their writing in connection with major themes. In Part II there are chapters about the author's life and work, assessing their contribution to developments in literature; and a sample of critics' views are summarised and discussed in comparison with each other.

Some suggestions for further reading provide a bridge towards further critical research.

Analysing Texts is designed to stimulate and encourage your critical and analytic faculty, to develop your personal insight into the author's work and individual style, and to provide you with the skills and techniques to enjoy at first hand the excitement of discovering the richness of the text.

NICHOLAS MARSH

A Note on Editions

References to act, scene and line numbers in all the plays are to the Oxford Shakespeare Editions, which are published as separate plays by Oxford University Press in the World's Classics Series.

Stage directions in these editions conflate ones from the 1623 folio text with editorial additions (the usual custom); for ease of reading stage directions in square brackets in the extracts here are those added by editors.

Introduction: Ways of Reading

Analysing Shakespeare's Late Plays

The plays of Shakespeare's late career, spanning the period roughly 1608–1612, have been the focus of fierce critical and theatrical debate. Are they the acme of a brilliant career, or the signs of a playwright who has lost his way and his audience? Are they about the Jacobean political world or Shakespeare's own aesthetic biography? Are they comedies or tragedies? What plays are included in the denomination 'late' anyway? This book focuses mainly on extracts from *The Winter's Tale* and *The Tempest*, with supplementary ones from *Cymbeline* and *Pericles*, the four plays most commonly denominated 'the late plays': you could also consider *Antony and Cleopatra*, *Henry VIII* and *The Two Noble Kinsmen* alongside them.

This book will help you decide some of the answer to these questions yourself: but it will do so by returning to the texts themselves, and engaging in close textual and theatrical analysis. It is only through such close analysis that any rigorous understanding of the plays can evolve, and it is only then that you can begin to debate and answer some of the conundrums about them. Before we move into the plays themselves, it is useful to outline some of the analytical terms and approaches we will be using to discuss the texts.

Language

Verse, Metre, Rhythm and Rhyme

These plays use a combination of verse and prose. The former is usually unrhymed, consisting of a ten-beat (syllable) line, in which there are usually five stressed syllables and five unstressed (de *dum*, de *dum*, de *dum*, de *dum*, de *dum*). This is sometimes known as **blank verse**. Each pair of syllables is called a **foot**. A ten beat line with five stresses is known as a **pentameter** (from the Greek meaning, five feet). Where the stresses fall in this alternating rhythm, we call it an **iambic pentameter**, often described as the natural rhythm of spoken English. 'Goodbye' usually stresses the second syllable, not the first. Shakespeare's blank verse is a consummate example of the flexibility of this metre, which enables variation of emphasis within feet and within lines. Actors and audience can use the rhythm as proxy indicators of emotion and stage directions: for example, where the foot carries the emphasis in the first syllable and not the second (what is known as a **trochaic foot**), the speed of delivery alters, and so does the meaning of the line, and where there are two stresses in a foot (a **spondee**), the emphatic delivery intensifies emotion.

Shakespeare varies the standard ten-beat model in at least three ways in the late plays. For example, in Leontes' first main soliloquy (1.2.183–205) he uses all four variations in a single speech.

First, Shakespeare frequently varies the way the stresses work within a line, where there are some feet that are trochees and some that are iambs, and occasional ones that are spondees (two stresses in a foot). For example, the first four syllables of Leontes' first jealous outburst, 'Inch-thick, knee-deep, o'er head and ears a forked one!' (1.2.184) are all equally stressed, forming a strong drum beat of two spondees as the opening two feet of this speech.

Second, the number of syllables per line can vary. In short lines, the rhythmic break acts as a stage direction to the actor or director: something is expected to happen here. In this same speech he uses one short line of four beats ('Go to! Go to!' l.180), a pause of six beats suggesting time for an emotional and physical response to Hermione's exit. Longer lines of 12 or 13 beats (for example, 'And many a man there is, even at this present', l.190) can contain six stresses, or simply feel too long, and produce a sense of emotional stuttering, drawing attention to the cluttered line.

Thirdly, lines which look visually like more than ten beats, when spoken sound like a ten beat line through elisions or accentual beat, or the presence of a feminine ending. Leontes claims 'From east, west, north, and south be it concluded', a line of 11 syllables: but the last three syllables contain only one stress on the middle syllable of 'concluded', creating a final foot which has only one stress. The overall sound of the five stressed iambic pentameter dominates. A final foot with three beats may have this emphasis; or an **anapaestic** (two unstressed followed by one stressed) or **dactylic** (stressed followed by two unstressed) foot, and if it ends on two unstressed beats, is known informally as a feminine ending.

These variations enable Shakespeare to write verse which is fluid and makes characters sound responsive to the different situations and emotions in which they find themselves, whilst retaining an overall coherence and elegance.

Pauses, stops and continuous speech are an integral part of how rhythm works. In this book I have used common descriptive terms for these within the verse. Pauses in the midst of a line are called **caesura**. Where a line's end coincides with the end of a sentence, we use the term **end-stopped**, and where the end of a line does not mark the end of the sentence or subclause, we term it a **run-on line**.

Like many of his contemporaries, Shakespeare occasionally uses rhyme in his verse, sometimes in alternate lines, and sometimes as a **rhyming couplet** (when two adjacent lines rhyme). These often occur at the ends of scenes, or at the end of a key character's speech. The natural symmetry of a couplet enables it to both summarise and point forward, or condense two paradoxical ideas in one expression.

Prose is used frequently in these plays for a variety of purposes and registers, occasionally for whole scenes and sometimes interspersed with verse. It is crucial to note where Shakespeare does this because it is a good indicator for the reader and performer of a directorial change of pace, character, tone or place.

Imagery

Throughout this book we will comment on and analyse the imagery of various extracts. What is imagery and how does it work? Imagery is a word or a group of words which self-consciously creates an image or picture for the purpose of comparing one thing or idea to something else. When Prospero says to Ferdinand, 'The strongest oaths are straw / To th'fire i'th' blood' (4.1.2–3), he is not talking about literal fire-making, or straw men, but the heat of passion in the blood.

There are several different kinds of imagery discussed in the book, but it is worth flagging up the two most common. The first is **metaphor**. A metaphor is an image which claims identity rather than just comparison with the idea, thing or concept to which it is referring. The example just quoted is an example of a metaphor: Prospero uses it as a way of imagistically warning Ferdinand in a way direct speech may not achieve. When analysing how a metaphor works, we look at both the literal meaning of the image (lighting a fire) and the concept or thing to which it is compared (passion). These two parts of a metaphor are called respectively the **vehicle** (the literal image) and **tenor** (the end meaning).

The second most frequent image is a **simile**. A simile is an image which explicitly compares itself to something else, using 'like' or 'as' to signal the comparison. Ariel comments on Ferdinand's grief: 'With hair up-staring,—then like reeds, not hair,—'(1.2.213), in a simile because the comparison is explicit. In a simile both tenor and vehicle are simultaneously present: in a metaphor the vehicle is what we see and the tenor is what we intuit from the surrounding context.

The third type of image is **metonymy**. A metonymy is a particular type of metaphor where the vehicle is linked by sense or logic to the tenor. The most common example of this is to use the word 'sail' to refer to a whole ship.

Drama and Performance

In this book we talk about the play text as both a dramatic structure and as a performance and performance text, using the text to envisage it in three dimensions on stage. There are a number of hints in the text which help us to do this: explicit and implicit stage directions, stage positioning, scenic structure, scenic and character juxtapositioning, dialogue, iconography, and musical directions. In addition, some formal critical terms are used to help understand the theatrical nature of the plays, and these are defined below.

Peripeteia is a Greek term used in Aristotle's *Poetics*, meaning the change or reversal that often happens towards the end of a play which precipitates its final closure. It can also mean 'turning point' in the plot, action or narrative, after which the fortunes of a character or particular course of action are irretrievably changed.

Blocking is the arrangement of characters on and about the stage during a scene.

Deus ex machina is a term originating from Greek drama when a God (*deus*) literally used to emerge from above the stage, lowered by a crane (*ex machina*) at the end of the play in order to produce effective dramatic closure.

Meta-theatricality literally means 'above' or 'beyond' the theatrical, and is used to refer to elements of the play which self-consciously reflect on, or ask the audience to reflect on, the fictional status of the play or actor.

PART 1
ANALYSING SHAKESPEARE'S LATE PLAYS

1

Openings

The opening of a text is our first entry into the story's fictional world: and in a play the opening scene or prologue additionally gives us a visual and oral entrance into this world. Equally, in a play which will last at the most three hours, it is crucial that the opening catches the audience's attention. This is why plays often open in the middle of some action or conversation, so the audience is plunged immediately into the characters' world and setting. Drama depends upon forward moving action and each individual scene is integral to the action and plot. Even an opening scene is never 'just' an introduction: it is imagistically and structurally critical. Of course all audiences require time to settle into a play before their attention is fully engaged, and some openings are prologues to the main action. In Shakespeare's time, there was often music or clowning prior to the performance, and this functioned as an experiential transition between arrival at the playhouse and immersion into the play. The play's opening cannot therefore be dismissed as mere introduction to later more important or significant events. We must pay full attention from the beginning, because Shakespeare gives us key clues both to the forthcoming action, to character and perspective, and implicit directions to the actors about who to be and how to perform.

If we look at the text of the play and imagine it as if it were being performed, it helps remind us that theatre is a three-dimensional art, in which words on the page are only a part of the overall meaning. We must consciously consider how these words work in a theatrical space. How do these actors move across the stage as they speak (or don't speak)? How do costume and lighting (if any) affect our interpretation, and are these indicated by stage directions or dialogue? What is the relationship between audience and actors, and how is it figured in the text? How does this scene relate to those that follow? How is the relationship between characters visualised on stage? And how do answers to these questions help us understand the rest of the play?

This chapter will look at the opening scenes to *The Tempest* and *The Winter's Tale* and discuss and assess their unique entrances into the play-worlds they represent. We shall focus on content, style and performance as our entry point into our own journey into the world of Shakespeare's late plays.

Analysis: *The Winter's Tale*, 1.1.1–43

Enter Camillo and Archidamus

ARCHIDAMUS	If you shall chance, Camillo, to visit Bohemia on the like occasion whereon my services are now on foot, you shall see, as I have said, great difference betwixt our Bohemia and your Sicilia.	
CAMILLO	I think, this coming summer, the King of Sicilia means to pay Bohemia the visitation which he justly owes him.	5
ARCHIDAMUS	Wherein our entertainment shall shame us; we will be justified in our loves. For indeed—	
CAMILLO	Beseech you,—	10
ARCHIDAMUS	Verily, I speak it in the freedom of my knowledge. We cannot with such magnificence—in so rare—I know not what to say. We will give you sleepy drinks, that your senses, unintelligent of our insufficience, may, though they cannot praise us, as little accuse us.	15
CAMILLO	You pay a great deal too dear for what's given freely.	
ARCHIDAMUS	Believe me, I speak as my understanding instructs me and as mine honesty puts it to utterance.	
CAMILLO	Sicilia cannot show himself over-kind to Bohemia. They were trained together in their childhoods,	20

	and there rooted betwixt them then such an affection, which cannot choose but branch now. Since their more mature dignities and royal necessities made separation of their society, their encounters, though not personal, have been royally attorneyed with interchange of gifts, letters, loving embassies, that they have seemed to be together, though absent, shook hands, as over a vast, and embraced as it were from the ends of opposed winds. The heavens continue their loves.	25

30 |
ARCHIDAMUS	I think there is not in the world either malice or matter to alter it. You have an unspeakable comfort of your young prince Mamillius. It is a gentleman of the greatest promise that ever came into my note.	
CAMILLO	I very well agree with you in the hopes of him. It is a gallant child, one that, indeed, physics the subject, makes old hearts fresh. They that went on crutches ere he was born desire yet their life to see him a man.	35
ARCHIDAMUS	Would they else be content to die?	
CAMILLO	Yes, if there were no other excuse why they should desire to live.	40
ARCHIDAMUS	If the King had no son, they would desire to live on crutches till he had one.	*Exeunt*

This opening scene (at 43 lines) is short compared to Shakespeare's other plays: excluding prologues, only *Twelfth Night* and *Macbeth* have shorter opening scenes. It is also in prose, unlike the majority of the rest of the play. These two features immediately suggest a distinctive opening: but of what kind? What is happening here?

The two characters are courtiers from Bohemia and Sicilia respectively, each advisers to their monarchs; they are alone on stage, perhaps in the main presence chamber, prior to the entry of the main dignitaries and visitors and the larger state occasion we witness in the next scene. This scene feels like a prologue to something that is *about* to happen, an almost off-stage ushering into the on-next scene's onstage action, an incidental and informal conversation. This interpretation only acknowledges part of the scene's dramatic function, and nothing of its effect. Any opening scene must perform this illusion of ushering an audience from its world into the world of the play's characters: here Camillo and Archidamus take us in a very particular way into the political world we are about to enter more fully. It is a contemplative scene, both men at ease and relaxed, talking about their shared knowledge of the past. They are both conscious of their status (they each serve their respective kings), and of the fragility of political power and states. We learn whether we trust their insights and judgements and how to see the play's key characters.

The play opens with a hypothetical 'If', as the visitor, Archidamus, invites Camillo to visit him in Bohemia. This social commonplace between two minions to powerful men innocently floats the idea of comparison between the two monarchs and the two nations. When Archidamus says 'see... the great difference betwixt our Bohemia and your Sicilia' (ll.3–4), does he refer to nation or monarch, or both? And does he suggest that Bohemia is better or just different? The doubling of linguistic referents echoes our doubled understandings: is this an innocent exchange or a political minefield? The occasion lends their language and mode of dialogue an informality, even if some of the content retains elements of courtly convention. Prose is usually a mode reserved for comedic scenes and baser characters in Shakespeare's plays. However, here the characters are both high-born advisers. The lack of formal metrical structure conveys orally the sense of informality and of escape from the formal aristocratic public world about which they are talking. Language echoes the opening's dramatic situation: this is an insider's informal view of the world we are about to enter, and we have been let in by the back door. The courtiers' ease with each other is conveyed through the delivery of the dialogue: they switch topics quickly, they interrupt each other (at lines 9 and 10) without anger, as though they know each other well, and they share past memories and an intimate consideration of the young prince. Both reiterate that they are speaking 'in... freedom' (ll.11 and 17), and 'honesty' (l.19) enhancing the atmosphere of frank and jovial autonomy, suggesting honesty and truth-telling is important in their worlds. The relationship between the men is not quite equal: Archidamus defers to Camillo (perhaps because he is the guest), tends to ask more questions, and Camillo has more words in total. How far are these initial assumptions and feelings borne out by the rest of their dialogue?

Their banter of mutual self-deprecating courtly flattery is friendly. Archidamus uses the conventional modesty-topos and insists that Bohemia cannot entertain with the 'magnificence' of Sicilia and will therefore have to ply future guests with 'sleepy drinks' to make their memories 'unintelligent of our insufficience' (l.14). However, Archidamus's opening 'If you shall chance' introduces risk and uncertainty through the hypotheticised opening and the language of hazard, which echoes insistently and incrementally through the scene. The relationship here is not only that between two private individuals, but also between two monarchs and two nations.

Their fond account of the two monarchs establishes an idyllic past of intertwined childhoods ('there rooted betwixt them then such an affection', l.23). Yet even as they rehearse this shared history, the two men move forward to more recent pasts and to a future as yet unwritten. Camillo's language becomes both more awkward and more legalistic when he talks about recent history. The longest sentence of the opening scene is the most convoluted: 'Since their more mature dignities and royal necessities made separation of their society, their encounters though not personal, have been royally attorneyed with interchange of gifts, letters, loving embassies, that they have seemed to be together, though absent, shook hands over a vast and embraced, as it were, from the ends of opposed winds' (ll.23–30). This sentence marks a shift away from the hypothetical and the past to the present. It begins with a conjunction, and has frequent qualifying subclauses ('their encounters, though not personal'; 'together, though absent', 'as over a vast', 'as it were'), which both partly contradict the main clause and simultaneously suggest scrupulous clerkly accuracy. Whilst apparently claiming the monarchs are very close, and decrying the fact that they have not seen each other for years, he describes their meetings as 'attorneyed with interchange of gifts' (l.26). Shakespeare's transformation of the noun 'attorney' into a verb ensures we notice its eruption into the sentence: the meaning suggests unconsciously that their relationship is now managed by lawyers not by personal connection. Two subordinating conjunctions introduce key words ('not personal' and 'absent') which stand as sentry commentaries on the whole speech, and proleptically echo into future events in Sicilia. Two other subordinating interjections introduce imagery: 'as over a vast' and 'as it were, from the ends of opposed winds'. By both using the word 'as' to make a comparison, and searching for two comparisons, Camillo begins to suggest an uncertainty about how to describe the men's current relationship.

Finally, this sentence exhibits a characteristic overloading of subjects to verbs (consistent with proliferating subclauses). The conversion of the adjective 'vast' to a noun function, and the noun 'attorney' to a verb, suggests verbally a world where objects and things dominate: where both action and nuanced description are reduced to objects or things. This linguistic effect echoes Leontes' epistemological confusion in the next scene, when he sees Hermione's actions 'prove' her a strumpet. The rhetorical effect of the longest sentence is a covert sentence on the men's lack of communication.

There is a nicely balanced tension here as the two courtiers blithely claim their master's boundless love ('I think there is not in the world either malice or matter to alter it', ll.32–3), whilst audience and actor trip on the ambiguities inherent in the sentence's description and delivery. This tension between what is literally said (and hoped for) and the structure, grammar and metaphorical notsaid is often called 'dramatic irony'. However, such a labelling can often mask a scene's theatrical power. Here are two senior political advisers genuinely celebrating a political meeting between two old friends: but inadvertently in the process of discussing their joy and hopes, unconsciously and insidiously alerting the audience to a vague sense of threat. It only becomes irony in retrospect, when we know the misreading and betrayals. In the moment of enactment it is two characters exhibiting joy, loss and hope: through their language and delivery Shakespeare enables the actors to signal unconscious insights into the political minefields between two men and two countries.

Neither man names their master, nor talks directly of their current meetings, but move from idealisation of their remote pasts, through the evasive description of why they have not met personally, on to celebration of the young prince Mamillius (the only person named here). The heightened praise ('greatest promise', 'gallant child') echoes what he symbolises: 'physics the subject, makes old hearts fresh' (37–8). Camillo's medicinal metaphor, extended into the image of be-crutched old men desiring a longer life to see Mamillius as king, is taken up literally by Archidamus. At one level his question ('would they else be content to die?') is an innocent joke (for who after all wants to die?) However, Camillo's answer ('Yes; if there were no other excuse why they should desire to live') suggests a serious anomie at the heart of the Sicilian political state. If political subjects have no desire to live without Mamillius, what kind of state is it? Archidamus's response, whilst witty and connotative of Christian themes (without a son all would be living half lives waiting for a saviour), also suggests a current political state of disabled inaction.

Politics is both absent and present here: the subjects of the conversation, the rulers, are off stage. Their main advisers are their representatives and proxies present here. Yet their language, both verbal and bodily, suggests a tentativeness about the future and the immediate past. The present is not mentioned at all: only an idyllic past and a possible idyllic future in the next generation. This absence establishes a tension. First, about what is going to happen next, and establish a 'present', and second about its nature given the ambivalences inherent in Camillo's images, grammar and delivery.

Archidamus is the last, as he is the first, to speak (and does not speak again in the play): the scene framed by the stranger / visitor to the court. The scene's structure thus dramatically emphasises the outsider view as key to the opening's dramatic effect. As he began, so also he ends on a hypothetical statement, echoing forward into the next scene. The horrific idea ('If the king had no son...') on which the scene ends literally falls like a prophetic curse on to the entrance of the partying, laughing characters arriving for the next scene. The opening scene, whilst spoken apparently whimsically and nostalgically by two old courtiers, conveys larger and wider truths about the world of the play than the characters themselves know. Already the audience is alert to verbal and dramatic nuances: the directors and actors have picked up on their doubled cues, and the gaps in the characters' accounts of the present are opened and ready for a crisis to appear before us.

Let us now move on to read the opening of *The Tempest* with this same alertness to linguistic and performance detail.

Analysis: *The Tempest*, 1.1.1–68

A tempestuous noise of thunder and lightning heard.
Enter a Shipmaster and a Boatswain

MASTER	Boatswain!	
BOATSWAIN	Here, master. What cheer?	
MASTER	Good—speak to th' mariners. Fall to't yarely, or we run ourselves aground. Bestir, bestir!	*Exit*

Enter Mariners

BOATSWAIN	Hey, my hearts! Cheerly, cheerly, my hearts! Yare, yare! Take in the topsail. Tend to th' master's whistle. [*To the storm*] Blow, till thou burst thy wind, if room enough!	5

Enter Alonso, Sebastian, Antonio, Ferdinand, Gonzalo, and others

ALONSO	Good boatswain, have care. Where's the master? [*To the Mariners*] Play the men.	10
BOATSWAIN	I pray now, keep below.	
ANTONIO	Where is the master, bos'n?	
BOATSWAIN	Do you not hear him? You mar our labour. Keep your cabins—you do assist the storm.	
GONZALO	Nay, good, be patient.	15
BOATSWAIN	When the sea is. Hence! What cares these roarers for the name of king? To cabin; silence! Trouble us not.	
GONZALO	Good, yet remember whom thou hast aboard.	
BOATSWAIN	None that I more love than myself. You are a councillor; if you can command these elements to silence, and work the peace of the present, we will not hand a rope more—use your authority. If you cannot, give thanks you have lived so long, and make yourself ready in your cabin for the mischance of the hour, if it so hap. [*To the Mariners*]—Cheerly, good hearts! [*To the courtiers*]—Out of our way, I say.	20 25 *Exit*
GONZALO	I have great comfort from this fellow. Methinks he	

	hath no drowning mark upon him—his complexion is perfect gallows. Stand fast, good Fate, to his hanging, make the rope of his destiny our cable, for our own doth little advantage. If he be not born to be hanged, our case is miserable.	30
		Exeunt

Enter Boatswain

BOATSWAIN	Down with the topmast! Yare! Lower, lower! Bring her to try with main-course. [*A cry within*] A plague upon this howling! They are louder than the weather or our office.	35

Enter Sebastian, Antonio, and Gonzalo

	Yet again? What do you here? Shall we give o'er and drown? Have you a mind to sink?	
SEBASTIAN	A pox o' your throat, you bawling, blasphemous, incharitable dog	40
BOATSWAIN	Work you then.	
ANTONIO	Hang, cur, hang you whoreson, insolent noisemaker! We are less afraid to be drowned than thou art	
GONZALO	I'll warrant him for drowning, though the ship were no stronger than a nutshell and as leaky as an unstanched wench.	
BOATSWAIN	Lay her a-hold, a-hold! Set her two courses off to sea again; lay her off!	50

Enter Mariners wet

MARINERS	All lost! To prayers, to prayers! All lost!	*Exeunt*
BOATSWAIN	What, must our mouths be cold?	
GONZALO	The King and Prince at prayers, let's assist them, For our case is as theirs.	
SEBASTIAN	I'm out of patience.	
ANTONIO	We are merely cheated of our lives by drunkards. This wide-chopped rascal—would thou mightst lie drowning	55

	The washing of ten tides!	*Exit Boatswain*
GONZALO	He'll be hanged yet,	
	Though every drop of water swear against it	
	And gape at wid'st to glut him.	
	A confused noise within	
	'Mercy on us!'—'We split, we split!'—'Farewell,	60
	my wife and children!'— 'Farewell, brother!'	
	—'We split! we split! we split!'	
ANTONIO	Let's all sink wi' th' King.	
SEBASTIAN	Let's take leave of him.	*Exit with Antonio*
GONZALO	Now would I give a thousand furlongs of sea for	65
	an acre of barren ground—long heath, brown furze, any-	
	thing. The wills above be done, but I would fain die a dry	
	death.	*Exit*

This scene shares with *Macbeth* the accolade of being Shakespeare's most dramatic opening: we are plunged *in medias res* into the centre of a subtropical storm, with its associated panic, noise, and life-and-death decisions. It is frequently played with spectacular sound and visual effects, which drown out the sound of the actors' voices. However, it is clear if we read the text carefully that we need to hear what is said. This scene crucially establishes ideas and perspectives on the future action. What actually happens on stage?

The opening stage direction ('*A tempestuous noise of thunder and lightning heard. Enter a Shipmaster and a Boatswain*') emphasises the audience's aural senses: we hear the storm before we see the mariners. 'Tempestuous' noise implies an experience more overwhelming than a usual storm. A feeling of multi-sensory immersion is reiterated in other stage directions. For example, '*enter Mariners wet*' brings physical theatre onto stage, and both '(*a cry within*)' and the '*confused*' (l.59) voices off stage articulating anonymous cries of despair act as dissonant chorus to the visual and verbal stage action. From the beginning, the scene and play announce themselves as a discordant multi-sensory disturbance.

The ship is a microcosm of a larger world, but an enclosed and potentially claustrophobic world as a disaster strikes. As such it shares the features of other disaster-dramas which intensify all experiences and relationships, particularly the accelerating time-frame, the shouted linguistic delivery, and the personality clashes. This scene is one of the first such scenes in western literature.

The scene is only 68 lines, but there is a lot of action within this space of about two or three minutes of performed time. The action is telegraphed both by the swift coming and going of characters, and the situation. The movement of characters on to stage within these 68 lines tell us how busy the stage space is made to be. There are seven definable separate scenic 'moments', of separate conversations which flow or bump into the next one, within the scene. The overall scene is structured like this:

Lines	Characters present / newly entered	Exits	Content
1–4	Master and Boatswain	Master (l.4)	Orders to change the ship's direction to avert grounding
5–8	Mariners [enter] and Boatswain		Order to change tack
9–27	Alonso, Sebastian, Antonio, Ferdinand, Gonzalo (and 'others') [entered], Boatswain	Boatswain (l.27)	King demands to see the master: Boatswain tries to manage courtiers and sailors
28–33	Alonso, Sebastian, Antonio, Ferdinand, Gonzalo (and 'others')	all courtiers (l.33)	Gonzalo ironically commends Boatswain
34–7	Boatswain [enter] and mariners		Orders to mariners on managing sails
38–57	Sebastian, Antonio and Gonzalo [enter] and Boatswain and mariners	Boatswain (l.57)	Courtiers and Boatswain argue
58–68	Sebastian, Antonio and Gonzalo and mariners	Sebastian, Antonio, ?mariners (l.64) Gonzalo (l.68)	Confused noises as ship splits: Gonzalo's lament for dry land.

It is clear if we look at the shape of the scene that the Boatswain's physical movement on to and off stage (entering and exiting twice ll.1–27; 34–57) is equal to that of the courtiers (ll.9–33; 38–64 / 7). These literal passages across stage create a sense of urgency, adding rushed physical movement to the textual messages, orders and arguments. The Boatswain is on stage and engaged in debate and action for 50 lines; Antonio and Sebastian for 50 lines; Gonzalo for 53; the mariners for the whole scene; and Alonso for only 24 lines. The representation of characters within the scene does not echo the social structure of the boat's passengers: Alonso as king has hardly any physical stage presence. Whilst the courtiers share the stage equally with the Boatswain, much of the dialogue is an argument about who should be on deck.

A boatswain managed the mariners, the equipment and the supplies for the effective running of a ship. Here he has a key role in bringing to life the tempest's damaging impact on ship and people. The Master's peremptory 'Boatswain!' and his response 'Here, master. What cheer?' establish his serving status, and the question of service and work dominates the scene. The Master asks the Boatswain to manage and give orders to the mariners: the hierarchy of professional knowledge and work is verbally and visually performed in these first 14 lines. The Boatswain even repeats the Master's 'yarely' in his orders to the mariners ('Cheerly, cheerly my hearts! Yare, yare!', ll.5–6). This archaic nautical term both lends authenticity and underlines the hierarchical orders. The Boatswain's order to the mariners are friendly ('cheerly my hearts') trying to get the best out of his men and guide the ship to safety. Although he gives a set of short orders, his tone is less peremptory than the Master's, as he prefaces his orders with diminutive endearments. His repetition of the word 'cheer' to both the Master and the mariners suggests an ebullient confident character, engaging effectively with both his superior and inferiors. His pattern of speech is lively, including a rhetorical question as greeting; four exclamatory statements, and two short declarative sentences in the first two speeches. Each of those grammatical forms act as implicit stage directions: the boatswain is the man on stage directing the action (and the ship). When he apostrophises the tempest ('Blow, till thou burst thy wind, if room enough!' ll.7–8) he is shouting at the elements, a confidence-boosting performance of leadership to the mariners. This larger-than-life character comes into direct conflict with the new characters.

Alonso's opening statement ('Good boatswain, have care. Where's the master?', l.9) is a rebuke to the Boatswain's raging at the elements, and an insistence that one man of authority should speak only directly to another in authority. Throughout the subsequent argumentative encounter the Boatswain is insistent upon three key things: looking after the ship, helping his mariners, and the need for the courtiers to get below deck. Why does Shakespeare not reintroduce the Master to the action? All we know of him is the Boatswain's 'do you not hear him?' (l.13), implying that he is shouting orders from another part of the ship. The conflict Shakespeare wants to dramatise is therefore that between the Boatswain and the courtiers, within the framed setting of a terrible tempest. The Boatswain's language to the courtiers is peremptory (Antonio describes him as 'a wide-chopped rascal', or mouthy, l.56). 'You mar our labour. Keep your cabins – you do assist the storm' (ll.13–14), and Gonzalo's response ('Nay good be patient') signals the level of his anger at the courtier's demands in the midst of a life-threatening storm. The Boatswain's short, and occasionally incomplete, sentences suggest a breathless brusqueness: short responses whilst he is the midst of managing the ships' deck.

It is in this context that he shouts 'What cares these roarers for the name of king?' (l.17). He angrily voices the view that in the face of destructive nature all men are the same: differences of class and status are niceties which prevent salvation. Only those with professional knowledge can save the boat and the lives of those on board. Gonzalo's gentle reminder that he is speaking to a king prompts a more measured response: but he still insists on the primary authority of his crew over the courtiers: 'if you can command these elements to silence... we will not hand a rope more—use your authority' (ll.21–3). By invoking the word 'authority' with such irony, the Boatswain simultaneously implicitly asserts his own authority and asks questions about Alonso's political authority. This raises broader philosophical questions: under what circumstances is a leader's (or monarch's) authority invalid? What gives a leader authority: is it birth, circumstances or knowledge? These are questions implicitly asked through the combination of setting, situation and character. Even as he attempts to justify his potentially treasonous remarks, the Boatswain has to interrupt the disquisition to address the mariners to their work ('cheerly good hearts! – Out of our way I say'). His mind is on his job. The Boatswain speaks on ten separate occasions, and for two-thirds of the scene he speaks alternately with someone else. In most of his speeches he addresses multiple audiences at different points: first the mariners, then the storm; the courtiers; then the courtiers, then the mariners; then the mariners, then the courtiers. The switches of audience within a single speech (indicated partly by entrances, partly by tone and content), help produce a hectic delivery and performance to echo the crisis, as well as reinforcing the Boatswain's centrality.

The Boatswain's final words respond to the wet mariners' fatalistic cry ('All lost!'l.51), 'What, must our mouths be cold?' A cold mouth proverbially described death, but the vehicle to describe death invokes our senses of taste: his usage echoes his characterisation as a down-to-earth man with a liking for food and drink (Antonio claims he is a drunkard). Imagery of food is used in the play as a way of testing and teasing characters in need, so the phrase echoes on throughout subsequent scenes, creating a mournful chorus to those lost on the island.

The courtiers' characterisation is remarkably insouciant throughout this crisis: they alone seem unaware of impending doom and death. Gonzalo makes jokes about the Boatswain's appearance and treasonous comments ('he has no drowning mark upon him – his complexion is perfect gallows' l.29), and Sebastian and Antonio roundly wish him hanged with curses used to impugn the lower classes ('dog' and 'cur', ll.41,43) and a wish that he drowns (l.55). Their lines mainly talk about the Boatswain. The Boatswain's final interjection to the courtiers, 'work you then!' (l.42) is spoken as a counter-curse. Although a short exclamatory it complexly expresses the Boatswain's views: the only hope for salvation is through working to save the ship, and yet the courtiers (as aristocrats) do not work. The audience clearly sees two different groups of men. One is the mariners led by the Boatswain desperately labouring to save ship and lives from breaking up on the rocks in a storm, and the second is a group of useless courtiers, literally getting in the way, ignoring instructions, and cursing the workmen.

The technical vocabulary used by Master and Boatswain renders the situation and characterisation credible. The orders successively shouted to the mariners would stop a ship drifting onto shore with an on-shore wind: 'take in the top sail', prevents the ship drifting leeward; 'down with the top mast!' (l.34) lightens the overhead weight; and 'bring her to try with main-course' (l.35) would sail close to the wind using only the main sail. 'Lay her a-hold, a-hold! Set her two courses off to sea again' (ll.49–50) is an instruction to sail the ship close to the wind with two sails, attempting to move the ship away from shore and out to sea. Of course, these desperate instructions fail to save the ship, but the sailors are authentically trying every possible action to save ship, crew and passengers. The verisimilitude established by the technical accuracy helps lend the disaster emotional and dramatic depth.

The voices and presence of the mariners is textually marginal and yet central to the whole action in this scene. Although the mariners only speak directly once (l.51), this line marks the scene's key turning point, as it announces the ship's knell. We have seen the mariners labouring throughout the scene (on the boatswain's instructions), and their speech marks the end of their labouring. The anonymous cries that come from off-stage are from both the mariners and the passengers, and are indistinguishable. As the ship goes down, all men are the same. So the scene's action replicates the Boatswain's implicit social and political insight: when the labourers stop working, the world literally falls apart.

In such an action-packed scene there are few metaphors: both Gonzalo and the Boatswain personify the storm and the sea. By shouting at the storm, and naming the waves 'roarers', the Boatswain expresses a personal relationship with the elements and paradoxically tames and elevates their power. Gonzalo similarly animates the water ('He'll be hanged yet, / Though every drop of water swear against it'), and suggests an equivalent combination of familiarity and awe.

Gonzalo is the one character whose words seem to stand apart from the situation: he neither curses nor commands. His perspective on the situation is philosophical: riffing on the boatswain's gallows complexion as the storm worsens. He, the mariners, and the Boatswain are the only ones to invoke God. His imagery, like the jokes, displaces his perspective from the disaster. His image of the ship as 'no stronger than a nutshell, and as leaky as an unstanched wench' (ll.45–6) successively uses a metaphor and a simile. By hypothetically comparing the boat to an empty nut and a menstruating woman, he uses vehicles which are visually compelling, and both ridiculous and discomforting. However, the tenor of his images, is that even if the ship were these things, the Boatswain will not drown. Similarly, his substitution of the hypothetical rope which will hang the boatswain for the ships' cable (l.31), wittily tropes the boatswain's supposed destiny as the cable which will carry them all to safety. Of course, the black humour lying beneath this wit acknowledges that the ship's ropes may actually be the death of them all.

The scene ends on Gonazalo's dream of a dry acre of barren ground: no fantasy or utopia, simply solid ground. We do not know the fate of any of the characters as the ship breaks up. The scene is the quintessential cliffhanger, leaving us with a series of both practical and philosophical questions: not only, what happens next? But also, who has the right to rule?

Conclusions

It is always exciting to realise how much we can learn from a close analysis of the opening of a text, and how many of the possibilities and perspectives which the whole play opens up, are given to us in microcosm at the opening. We can make significant conclusions about how Shakespeare's stagecraft, plotting and language construct the play world and our engagement in it from the beginning.

1. Shakespeare uses a variety of openings in these plays, none of which are conventionally comic (the articulation of a generational or tribal conflict which the plot resolves). In *The Winter's Tale* the opening is deceptively oblique, an apparently desultory conversation between two courtiers marking time, which nevertheless presages uncertainties and a sense of time being out of joint. In *The Tempest* we are plunged *in medias res* into the heart of a pure storm, which displaces audience and characters from all

they know. *The Winter's Tale* and *Cymbeline* are overtly political in setting, content and the implied generic link to tragedy and conflict from the beginning. *Pericles* and *The Tempest* displace us, one in time and one in place, to different worlds, evoking strangeness, othering the audience from our accustomed ideas and experiences.

2. Shakespeare's opening scenes obliquely raise general questions essential to the play's philosophical debates. In *The Winter's Tale* political and philosophical questions are raised about the future state of Sicilia, albeit introduced under a cloak of banter. In *The Tempest* questions of leadership and status arise: who can or should lead in a crisis? What role does status play in our attitudes to and trust of others? In *Cymbeline* and *Pericles* questions about the rights of women to both inherit power and to choose their husbands are explicitly raised. The question of whether leadership should be determined by gender and birth are key open-ended interrogatives from the openings of all four plays.

3. In all the plays, the opening is hosted by characters not subsequently featuring as 'main' characters. This oblique window into the world of the play establishes and legitimises an 'outsider' perspective both on the action that is to come, but also as a general philosophical stance. Of course, by using marginal or marginalised characters, Shakespeare ensures that we do not miss the key action when the main characters do finally enter. But these beginnings are more than accidental. This outsider perspective invites a sceptical and enquiring audience, always aware that it is outside the action even when it becomes most intense. This perspective may be challenged by subsequent action and narrative

4. Shakespeare uses any opening scene as a door into a new world: a metaphor made explicit in the action of *The Tempest*, which literally plunges characters into water via a shipwreck that we see and hear. We do not know what will happen afterwards, only that a new situation must follow. In *The Winter's Tale* the opening scene is a metaphoric and literal ante-chamber to the subsequent public political meeting in the royal Sicilian palace, an entry-way into it for the courtiers and for us. The opening scene is both literally and metaphorically a space through and across which we

traverse *into* the heart of the play. In *The Tempest* we cross the ocean through the experience of the scene, in *The Winter's Tale* we amble through an ante-chamber and enter a different world. *The Tempest's* opening scene exemplifies self-consciously and meta-theatrically this sense of how an opening scene works, framing and constructing a crisis situation in a closed environment which literally explodes, opening out new possibilities of action and character.

5. Characters who hold power within the state represented within the story rarely appear in opening scenes. The exception to this is *Cymbeline*, where the Queen appears at line 70 and the King (Cymbeline) at line 125 of the first scene. Although Alonso (King of Naples) appears in the opening scene of *The Tempest*, he does not rule on the island or actively initiate any action in the story. Shakespeare's opening displacement technique may suggest Alonso's power is literally questioned by his structural placement in the play's opening.

6. Intense, private or discrete worlds open the plays: the scene's relationship to the rest of the play is metaphoric and narrational. Each scene plunges us into one aspect of the play's world which has significant verbal, thematic and dialectical relationships with key questions and ideas raised by the whole play. Each opening functions as a clear visual image as well as a story: the intense private conversation adjacent to the corridors of power; the violent and frightening storm which assaults all our senses; the aged lone seer standing on stage inviting us into a fireside story. The visual and verbal intensity of the openings scenes are integral to our subsequent experience and understanding of the play. They are also all uniquely theatrical in their concise combination of a condensed visual experience with the horizontal experience of a forward-moving narrative plot.

7. Each scene grabs our attention in different ways: but all paradoxically condense and bring together the action, the visuals and perspectives on that action.

8. Indirectly, the conflict which will precipitate each play's potentially tragic crisis is discernible: the threat of death to a son; war with Rome; a tempest which threatens lives; the problem of

having a daughter as an heir. Potential solutions are opaque, and outcomes are uncertain, even potentially tragic.
9. Themes of succession, parenthood and authority feature in each opening scenes, combining the political and the personal in relation to class, gender and race.
10. The two scenes we read in detail were either wholly or mainly in prose, and relatively free of imagery: this plain-spoken effect enables an opening scene to usher us gently into the new world, but also signals the marginal status of the opening's protagonists.
11. Setting, place and time of day are all invoked by imagery, action and dialogue: the atmospherics of the opening help suggest mood and emotion for the whole play. The language in each extract is fast-paced and in prose, marking a different social and experiential representation from subsequent scenes.

Methods of Analysis

We have used a variety of analytical methods in our discussion of the plays. It is helpful to delineate these as we go forward:

1. **The text as drama.** When you first read a play, imagine how it plays and looks on stage. What effect might the words or actions have on the audience? Where are characters placed on stage, and how do they move about? Which part of the stage do they appear on and why? Are there sounds effects, either explicit or implicit in the dialogue? Who speaks the most and when and where? It can be helpful to draw up a table (as we did for *The Tempest*) to map out the different significances of both structure and character within a scene.
2. **Visuals.** What do we literally *see*? What effect does this have on us, and on the characters on stage? Does costume affect our interpretation?
3. **Language.** Are there any key words or phrases? Is it in prose or verse? If verse, what does its metrical arrangement tell us? If there are metrical or rhyming irregularities, what effect does this create?

If prose, what effect does this have? Do individual characters have distinctive registers or words?
4. **Imagery.** Who uses imagery and why? Is its meaning clear to you? Is it meant to be clear or deliberately obscure? Do the images have anything in common, are there recurrent patterns?
5. **Scenic Structure.** Look at the way the scene is divided up into performing parts, structured by the entrances and exits of different characters, as well as thematically. What is the effect of division and juxtaposition?
6. **Sentences.** Look closely at sentences for meaning and delivery. Are they long or short, broken up, exclamatory, or declamatory? How does this close analysis illuminate character?
7. **Subject matter.** Don't forget to remember to comment on what actually happens and is said. How does the scene as a whole fit into the plot?
8. **Stage directions.** These are rarely explicit in Shakespeare's plays, but appear throughout the dialogue via interrogatives, declaratives, and prepositions (this, that, there, where, behind, below, behind, beneath, between, over, etc.). By reading the text carefully we can discover and recreate a sense of how an actor uses the language to direct the body through the scene.
9. We introduced some **new terms**, noticeably '*in medias res*' and 'vehicle' and 'tenor'. These are useful terms for analysing Shakespeare's writing, and will reoccur as we progress through the book. Definitions of these analytical terms can be found in the Introduction.

Suggested Work

The Tempest

Look at the remainder of Act 1. How is 1.2 given functional and emotional meaning by its contrast to the opening scene (think about character, atmosphere, setting and sound)? Comment on its long and complicated structure. What audience positions are set up by its action and by its link to 1.1?

The Winter's Tale

Think about the relationship between the two opening scenes in this play, using the same approach. How do our new insights and observations build on or contradict our conclusions about the opening scene itself? How has our 'outsider' position changed or been compromised? Does Shakespeare use a second scene to interrogate the first scene?

Pericles and *Cymbeline*

Using the methods trialled in this chapter, analyse the opening scenes of these two late plays. How does the prologue relate to the opening scene in *Pericles*? Are our conclusions borne out by your own analysis of the plays? Can you add any further conclusions yourself? *Cymbeline* begins in almost exactly the same way as *The Winter's Tale*, although its conversation between gentlemen segues seamlessly into the formal confrontation between queen and Innogen, which looks and feels like the beginning of *King Lear* and suggests a tragic plot. Its opening act is a complex political dance: draw a diagram of how it works. What do you notice? How is Innogen figured in the opening?

Your own analyses of these opening acts and scenes will further illuminate and extend your insights and conclusions into the plays' openings. You should now be finding it easier to visualise the scene as if it were on stage: sometimes it helps this visualisation to read it aloud as you go along.

2

Turning Points: Tragedy and Comedy

Successful plays work towards and away from a turning point, in which characters, setting and plot coalesce, conflict and combust, and then move onwards towards a resolution. Turning points are both ends and new beginnings, and these late plays make a particular virtue of playing with such fulcrums, forcing audience, characters and plot into asking questions and moving in new directions. Turning points occur roughly in the middle of each of our plays.

Analysis: *The Winter's Tale*, 3.2.1–147

Enter Leontes, Lords, and Officers

LEONTES This sessions, to our great grief pronounce,
Even pushes 'gainst our heart. The party tried
The daughter of a king, our wife, and one
Of us too much beloved. Let us be cleared
Of being tyrannous, since we so openly 5
Proceed in justice, which shall have due course
Even to the guilt or the purgation.
Produce the prisoner.

OFFICER It is his highness' pleasure that the Queen
Appear in person here in court.

[Enter Hermione as to her trial, Paulina and Ladies]

	Silence!	10
LEONTES	Read the indictment.	
OFFICER	Hermione, Queen to the worthy Leontes, King of Sicilia, thou art here accused and arraigned of high treason in committing adultery with Polixenes, King of Bohemia, and conspiring with Camillo to take away the life of our sovereign lord the King, thy royal husband; the pretence whereof being by circumstances partly laid open, thou, Hermione, contrary to the faith and allegiance of a true subject, didst counsel and aid them for their better safety to fly away by night.	15 20
HERMIONE	Since what I am to say must be but that Which contradicts my accusation, and The testimony on my part no other But what comes from myself, it shall scarce boot me To say 'not guilty'; mine integrity, Being counted falsehood, shall, as I express it, Be so received. But thus: if powers divine Behold our human actions, as they do, I doubt not then but innocence shall make False accusation blush and tyranny Tremble at patience. You, my lord, best know, Whom least will seem to do so, my past life Hath been as continent, as chaste, as true As I am now unhappy; which is more Than history can pattern, though devised And played to take spectators. For behold me A fellow of the royal bed, which owe A moiety of the throne; a great king's daughter, The mother to a hopeful prince, here standing To prate and talk for life and honour fore Who please to come and hear. For life, I prize it As I weigh grief, which I would spare; for honour, 'Tis a derivative from me to mine, And only that I stand for. I appeal To your own conscience, sir, before Polixenes Came to your court, how I was in your grace, How merited to be so; since he came, With what encounter so uncurrent I	25 30 35 40 45

	Have strained t' appear thus—if one jot beyond	
	The bound of honour, or in act or will	50
	That way inclining, hardened be the hearts	
	Of all that hear me, and my near'st of kin	
	Cry 'fie' upon my grave.	
LEONTES	I ne'er heard yet	
	That any of these bolder vices wanted	
	Less impudence to gainsay what they did	55
	Than to perform it first.	
HERMIONE	That's true enough,	
	Though 'tis a saying, sir, not due to me.	
LEONTES	You will not own it.	
HERMIONE	More than mistress of	
	Which comes to me in name of fault I must not	
	At all acknowledge. For Polixenes,	60
	With whom I am accused, I do confess	
	I loved him, as in honour he required;	
	With such a kind of love as might become	
	A lady like me; with a love even such,	
	So, and no other, as yourself commanded;	65
	Which not to have done I think had been in me	
	Both disobedience and ingratitude	
	To you and toward your friend, whose love had spoke	
	Even since it could speak, from an infant, freely,	
	That it was yours. Now, for conspiracy,	70
	I know not how it tastes, though it be dished	
	For me to try how. All I know of it	
	Is that Camillo was an honest man,	
	And why he left your court the gods themselves,	
	Wotting no more than I, are ignorant.	75
LEONTES	You knew of his departure, as you know	
	What you have underta'en to do in's absence.	
HERMIONE	Sir,	
	You speak a language that I understand not.	
	My life stands in the level of your dreams,	
	Which I'll lay down.	
LEONTES	Your actions are my dreams.	80
	You had a bastard by Polixenes,	

	And I but dreamed it. As you were past all shame—	
	Those of your fact are so—so past all truth;	
	Which to deny concerns more than avails; for as	
	Thy brat hath been cast out, like to itself,	85
	No father owning it—which is, indeed,	
	More criminal in thee than it—so thou	
	Shalt feel our justice, in whose easiest passage	
	Look for no less than death.	
HERMIONE	Sir, spare your threats.	
	The bug which you would fright me with I seek.	90
	To me can life be no commodity;	
	The crown and comfort of my life, your favour,	
	I do give lost, for I do feel it gone,	
	But know not how it went. My second joy,	
	And first-fruits of my body, from his presence	95
	I am barred, like one infectious. My third comfort	
	Starred most unluckily, is from my breast,	
	The innocent milk in its most innocent mouth,	
	Haled out to murder; myself on every post	
	Proclaimed a strumpet; with immodest hatred	100
	The child-bed privilege denied, which 'longs	
	To women of all fashion; lastly, hurried	
	Here to this place, i' th' open air, before	
	I have got strength of limit. Now, my liege,	
	Tell me what blessings I have here alive,	105
	That I should fear to die! Therefore proceed.	
	But yet, hear this—mistake me not: no life,	
	I prize it not a straw, but for mine honour,	
	Which I would free—if I shall be condemned	
	Upon surmises, all proofs sleeping else	110
	But what your jealousies awake, I tell you	
	'Tis rigor and not law. Your honours all,	
	I do refer me to the oracle:	
	Apollo be my judge.	
LORD	This your request	
	Is altogether just; therefore bring forth,	115
	And in Apollo's name, his oracle.	
	[*Exeunt certain Officers*]	

HERMIONE	The Emperor of Russia was my father.
	O that he were alive, and here beholding
	His daughter's trial! That he did but see
	The flatness of my misery, yet with eyes 120
	Of pity, not revenge!
	[Re-enter Officers, with Cleomenes and Dion]
OFFICER	You here shall swear upon this sword of justice,
	That you, Cleomenes and Dion, have
	Been both at Delphos, and from thence have brought
	The sealed-up oracle, by the hand delivered 125
	Of great Apollo's priest; and that since then,
	You have not dared to break the holy seal,
	Nor read the secrets in't.
CLEOMENES *and* DION	All this we swear.
LEONTES	Break up the seals and read.
OFFICER	(*reads*) 'Hermione is chaste, Polixenes blameless, 130
	Camillo a true subject, Leontes a jealous tyrant, his
	innocent babe truly begotten, and the King shall
	live without an heir, if that which is lost be not
	found.'
LORDS	Now blessed be the great Apollo!
HERMIONE	Praised! 135
LEONTES	Hast thou read truth?
OFFICER	Ay, my lord; even so
	As it is here set down.
LEONTES	There is no truth at all i' th' oracle.
	The sessions shall proceed; this is mere falsehood.

[Enter a Servant]

SERVANT	My lord, the King, the King!
LEONTES	What is the business? 140
SERVANT	O sir, I shall be hated to report it.
	The prince, your son, with mere conceit and fear
	Of the Queen's speed, is gone.
LEONTES	How? Gone?
SERVANT	Is dead.
LEONTES	Apollo's angry, and the heavens themselves

		Do strike at my injustice.	
		[Hermione falls to the ground]	
		How now there!	145
	PAULINA	This news is mortal to the Queen—look down	
		And see what death is doing.	

This scene is one of Shakespeare's great set pieces: a public trial of a queen for adultery, initiated by the king her husband. It is the climax of the narrative trajectory begun with Leontes' accusation of Hermione. We know the oracle's judgement is to come, so to some extent mark time in the first part of the trial. The situation echoes the public trial of Henry VIII's wife Anne Boleyn, accused and convicted of adultery and treason 80 years earlier. The Tudor back-story to Elizabeth I's reign was obliquely figured in Shakespeare's history plays, including *Henry VIII*, written two years after *The Winter's Tale*. However, Shakespeare avoids the contentious political and sexual debates surrounding Anne Boleyn, Henry VIII's motivations, and Elizabeth Tudor's conception, disinheritance and subsequent rehabilitation. Hermione and Leontes do not explicitly figure Anne and Henry, but their situations are remarkably parallel. The historical events render the play's characters' attitudes and responses more comprehensible. They are simultaneously public figures and private individuals, and the clash between these two identities and their associated languages is played out in a superb dramatic moment. The play offers a 'what if...' scenario to the historical and political conundrum of patriarchal prerogative: if a man who is also king decides a woman is unfaithful what kinds of redress does that woman have?

Visually this scene is formal and sumptuous. The initial entrance is a hierarchical march of king, lords and officers, the initial stage direction denoting a public and formal occasion. In most productions this is a solemn parade towards a throned bench, on which Leontes sits as judge. The court officer's announcement for the queen to 'appear' cues her entrance. Hermione has recently given birth, her baby removed and she has been imprisoned. What does she look like? Productions differ: some dress her regally, suggesting wealthy nurturing even whilst imprisoned; others show her meanly dressed, distraught and physically vulnerable. What is certain is that there is a staged contrast between the men and women: lords and officers with Leontes, Paulina and ladies with Hermione. The visual juxtaposition between court and accused, and between men and women is emphasised by the scene's opening structure. It looks as if gender is on trial.

What else do we see? Leontes must be formally attired, and he acts and sits as both monarch and judge. Hermione as the accused may be visually lower than him, and self-confessedly both weaker than usual ('before I have got strength of limit', l.104), and miserable ('the flatness of my misery', l.120). The trial does not call any witnesses, except the oracle's report, and so despite the crowded stage, the trial becomes a conflict between two protagonists. Of the 147 lines here, Hermione and Leontes speak 113: verbally and visually this is a conflict between two people. Dramatic organisation shows Leontes turns a legal process into a personal vendetta. Despite the formal setting and trappings of a legal trial, visual and verbal cues reduce this to the personal. When the judge also becomes chief witness for the prosecution he further undermines the validity of the legal process: does Leontes stay in his judge's seat when he engages in dispute, or does he move? Does Leontes snatch the paper with Apollo's judgment from the officer? ('as it is *here* set down' '*this* is mere falsehood!', l.139) And rattle it dismissively? We note the formal attire and bearing of the court officers, and Cleomenes and Dion, who have arrived hot-foot from the oracle but speak only to swear they have not tampered with the sealed judgment. Finally, we watch the members of the court respond to the switch-back succession of news and reaction in the last fifteen lines: first Hermione is announced chaste; second Leontes rejects the oracle; third, Mamillius's death is announced; and finally Hermione falls to her apparent death ('look *down* / And see what death is doing', l.147). In contrast to the first 130 lines, which are relatively static and very formal, the scene is now in disarray: background noises and physical movement in the court's response to the three tragedies echo our shock. Paulina's plea ('look down') suggests people surround Hermione, centre stage. Visually the literally fallen, broken, female body focuses our lines of sight and understanding: Leontes' obsession about his wife's body has ended in her death.

The whole scene falls naturally into four parts: the formal indictment and Hermione's initial defence statement (ll.1–53); the ensuing to-and-fro dialogue between Leontes and Hermione (ll.53–121); the arrival and delivery of the oracle's judgment (ll.122–138); and finally, the news of Mamillius's death and Hermione's apparent one. Scenic structure accelerates and intensifies the visual sense of moving from formal legal processes into more chaotic ones: the legal ones fail to produce Leontes' desired result, and so are rejected. The longest part of the scene is the intense argument between Hermione and Leontes, making their personal relationship central to the play's conflict and turning point.

A closer textual analysis will flesh out the dynamics and mechanics of the legal and personal confrontation. Leontes speaks far fewer words than Hermione (30 lines to her 83), although he speaks nearly twice as often (12 times, to her seven). The frequency of his interjections suggests his asserted political control of situation and location. The volume of Hermione's words testifies to her legal and moral entitlement to bear witness. In two earlier scenes women voice views significantly divergent from those of men: one at the prison (2.2) where Paulina and Emilia dispute the imprisonment of the queen and one at the court when Paulina tries to get the king to acknowledge the baby as his (2.3). These two scenes immediately precede this one, interrupted only by 3.1 as Cleomenes and Dion wait to see the oracle. The trial therefore culminates a sequence of scenes which focus on women speaking in public to men, but also of them being ignored or displaced. Here, that theme is crystallised and formalised in a trial, where both plaintiff and accused have speaking rights. One place where a woman had a legal right to public speech in early modern England was in a court of law.

Hermione speaks within the context of both the judge's initial opening words and the formal accusation. Leontes' opening statement is framed in formal legal language: the King refers to himself in the third person, a royal 'we' ('*our* great grief', 'of *us*' and 'let *us* be cleared' '*we* so openly'). This invokes his royal political identity not his personal relationship with Hermione, although his 'let us be cleared of being tyrannous' (ll.4–5) implicates his personal desire with the language of state. His sentences' grammatical structure is archaic. In the opening sentence ('This sessions, to our great grief, we pronounce...') the object comes first, and the subject and verb last, a pattern repeated in 'the party tried the daughter of a king' (ll.2–3). This Latinate structure has two effects: it establishes the formal atmosphere of a court trial, but it is also obfuscatory. Grammatical structure trips up sense: Leontes' case seems consequently less credible. The metrical delivery is regular iambic pentameters with the exception of lines 5 and 8. Line 5 ('of being tyrannous, since we so openly') has 12 beats, and disturbs the smooth delivery of the court's formal opening in regular rhythms. The line connotes personal involvement: the coincidence of a slippage of grammar with a slippage of metre shows Leontes falling from objectivity. His final line of only six beats ('produce the prisoner', l.8) leaves a metrical gap to enable the stage business of Hermione's entrance.

The formal 'indictment' of one long sentence in lucid plain prose, charges Hermione with treason on the dual grounds that her adultery threatens the King's body, and that she plotted with Camillo to kill the king. The simple blunt language strikes a simultaneous verbal blow on audience and Hermione.

It is in this context that Hermione first speaks. She has four long speeches (ll.21–53; 58–75; 89–114; 117–121), and three interjections or responses. All her speeches present a flowing logical argument based on the witty initial premise that since the court's accusation is that she is false, she will by definition not be believed. Her opening defence responds to the initial indictment, and at 31 lines is her longest speech. There are only six sentences, but the argument remains lucid, enhancing the effect of a highly-wrought rhetorical defence. She indirectly proclaims her pursuit of an offensive defence, commenting on her impossible situation: 'Since what I am to say must be but that / Which contradicts my accusation... it shall scarce boot me / To say not guilty' (ll.21–27). Hermione accuses the court of partiality from the beginning. Her second sentence moves from the present temporal powers to 'divine' ones who will 'make false accusation blush': contrasting the current partisan legal trial with absolute notions of theological truth and knowledge. Her third sentence moves to address Leontes and his direct knowledge of her chastity. Her fourth sentence ('For behold me', l.36) is an exclamatory stage direction addressed to the whole court ("fore / Who please to come and hear', l.40–41). Her fifth sentence, the shortest, is ruminative and reflective, yet personal ('for life, I prize it as I weigh grief... / For honour / 'Tis a derivative from me to mine / And only that I stand for', ll.41–4). Her sixth sentence is the longest (nine lines) and addressed initially to Leontes ('I appeal to your own conscience, sir'), but broadened by swearing an oath to court, audience and family. Her argument's trajectory moves from an opening gambit of questioning the validity of the court and its assumptions and to an appeal to higher judgment, to the specificities of Leontes' accusation and knowledge of her. The middle of the speech focuses on herself and her physical appearance ('behold me'), and the climax of the speech repeatedly focuses on a combination of her own familial history of honour with that of Leontes' own personal and historical knowledge of her actions. She thus calls upon four kinds of evidence: theological, familial and genealogical traditions, personal testament, and third-party evidence. The climax and crux of her argument, as the convoluted last sentence effectively acknowledges, is also the weakest part: Leontes knows her character, but it is he that is her accuser. This paradox exemplifies the problematic of the cuckolded male: how does or can a husband know that his wife's child is his? Hermione's spirited argument tries to answer this through evocation of her own character, family history, and divine judgment: but finally it resides in trust.

Hermione uses the first person pronoun, as subject, object or adjectival descriptor a remarkable 21 times in 31 lines ('I' eleven, 'my' five, 'me' three, and 'myself' and 'mine' once). This linguistic focus on her identity and body (*'behold me'*) underlines her explicit claim for autonomy and agency, despite Leontes' assumption and emphasis that her sole identity is as his dependent queen. Her autonomy is precisely what has worried Leontes: her grammatical strategy betrays her desire for autonomy (which Leontes reads as sexual), even as she uses 'I's to defend her sexual honour. Grammar exhibits the paradox of her opening sentence: if she speaks, she is damned, since she is already labelled a liar and adulterer.

Hermione's metrical delivery throughout the extract is in regular iambic pentameters, with a few notable exceptions. For example, line 35 has 11 syllables, in which the three-syllable 'behold me' forms the last metrical foot. This must be delivered either as a dactyl (one stress and two unstressed syllables) or the line must have a sixth stress ('me'). The line's semantic meaning suggests the latter works for sense, rhythm echoing Hermione's literally disruptive autonomy. Other

11-syllable lines (ll.38, 39, 41, 49) all use feminine endings, with an obvious dactyl ending the line. The one exception is line 45, ('To your own conscience sir, before Polixenes') with 12 syllables and six stresses. The break in regularity on this line, where the extra syllables speak the name of the man with whom she is accused of adultery, forces the actor to stumble over its delivery. Shakespeare's metre acts as stage directions enabling the expression of distress, anger, disbelief, or guilt.

The second part of the dialogue between Hermione and Leontes, (ll.53–121) sounds increasingly like a squabbling couple: their responses to each other complete a verse line, creating fast-moving and interrupting dialogue. Leontes' responses are either direct contradictions of what Hermione has said (ll.53–6 and 58), or direct accusations (ll.76–7 and 80–88). Hermione defends herself against the contradictions, but to his two direct accusations, her responses swerve into a new reflective direction. So, for example, her response to Leontes' claim that she knew of Camillo's departure, is both a personal attack and a philosophical observation ('You speak a language that I understand not', l.78) neatly encapsulating the fact that Leontes' words and discourse are completely alien to hers. Her response to his second accusation ('you had a bastard by Polixenes', l.81) is her most personal reflection: she again uses the first person pronoun in a variety of forms (25 times in 24 lines). She delineates the impact of Leontes' attitudes, accusations and defamations, in a simultaneously heart-rending description of her devastation, and a last-ditch appeal to the court ('your honours all / I do refer me to the oracle / Apollo be my judge', ll.112–14). The intimate details of her losses, withheld to date, overflow here and denote her dislocation: she has lost Leontes' love, her boy has been taken from her, and her new baby sent to be murdered. All physical connections and familial love have been snatched away ('the child-bed privilege denied', l.101). This is particularly powerful because despite her visible physical state, she has been reticent until now. She addresses Leontes directly as her intimate but superior interlocutor ('Sir' and 'your favour', 'my liege') retaining a deferential form of address, despite his attacks. However, she remains forthright ('The bug which you would fright me with I seek', l.90) and indifferent to Leontes' threats: having lost his love and her children, life means nothing to her. The speech's rhetorical climax returns to her opening critical assertion, creating a cyclical symmetry to the argument, 'condemned upon / Surmises, all proofs sleeping else' (l.109–10). This very personal speech silences Leontes for the first time: it is the officer who responds to her demand for the oracle. Hermione's final speech has a whimsical tone to it ('The Emperor of Russia was my father', ll.117), expressing a quieter sorrow. It is her only evocation of a male protective figure, albeit a dead one: simultaneously suggesting both her vulnerability within the absolutist world of the male prerogative and her own royal heritage and power.

In the extract's final section all characters, following the oracle's words, speak rapidly and in short interjections. Hermione's monosyllabic exclamation ('praised!') expresses through a combination of silence and a single word, her relief at her exoneration. She does not respond verbally to Leontes' denial nor to the news of Mamillius's death: this one word echoes as her response to the oracle, ironically echoing into the swift move towards tragedy. Her silence contrasts her earlier verbosity: positing a realistic state of shock, ending in her faint and apparent death. Leontes' conversion ('the heavens... do strike at my injustice', ll.144–5) comes too late. The succession of events (and Leontes' own judgement) dramatically connects his mistrust of his wife to his tragic losses. Man's tragedy is not cuckoldry but its opposite, a failure to conserve and love connubially, a breakdown of trust.

The language here is dense, although the overall meaning is always clear. Some of the complexity is grammatical, some metaphoric, and some simply opaque. For example, the grammatical inversion of Hermione's 'with what encounter so uncurrent I / Have strained to appear thus' (ll.48–9) has puzzled editors and critics, meaning 'what behaviour has been so unacceptable that I should be tested with this trial?' Her emplacing preposition ('thus') tells us she is gesturing to the court, and internal stage directions can help locate meaning even when semantics are less clear. Her characteristic ending of a line with an 'I', leads into a run-on line because of the sense, but focuses our hearing emphatically on her person: meaning is generated by aurality, gesture and verbal placing as much as conventional grammar.

The patterns of imagery and connotations of key words echo and coalesce ideas and themes. Both Hermione and Leontes make claims about the importance of appearance: Leontes wants the trial to show he is not tyrannous (l.5) and claims Hermione's actions with Polixenes 'mean' adultery. Hermione argues that her reputation stands for itself (l.36), and that her actions were conventional courtesy. Divergent interpretations of the same events are central to the matter of the trial itself. Leontes describes Hermione's actions as 'perform'ed (l.56), and Hermione describes her unhappiness as so deep that it cannot be turned into a play (ll.35–6). Theatricality and performance suggest guile and deceptiveness to Leontes but not to Hermione. Hermione argues that language and representation are partial and relative ('you speak a language I understand not', 'shall, as I express it', l.27), but Leontes refuses to see viewpoints and language as subjective. This antagonistic stand-off lasts until dissolved by the announcement of Mamillius's death.

Hermione's personal humiliation is visible in her language, appearance and action: 'Here standing / To prate and talk for life and honour 'fore / Who please to come and hear' (ll.39–41), 'myself on every post / proclaimed a strumpet' (ll.99–100). Her appearance and argument ask us to consider the appropriate boundaries between private life and public knowledge. Should private matters become matters of state? Is this justified? Her reiteration of the word 'honour' (ll.40, 42, 50, 62, 108) and 'honest' (l.73, referring to Camillo) acts simultaneously as a proactive defence and an attack on Leontes' strategy of insinuating adultery. The reiterated choral effect reminds audiences that her 'honour' comes from chastity, family, and royal reputation: but also asks how far these are guarantors of honesty.

Motherhood, maternity and children are implicitly and explicitly figured emotively throughout: Hermione looks like a woman who has recently given birth in prison. The source of Leontes' agony and the trial is his uncertainty about paternity. Hermione's emotive imagery about her children ('first-fruits of my body', 'the innocent milk in its most innocent mouth', ll.95, 98), in her personal speech is a turning point of emotional engagement for audience and Leontes. The announcement of Mamillius's death decisively turns the plot to tragedy.

Few formal figures of speech are used: despite the grammatical complexity, the language is not over-patterned. Hermione alone uses explicit imagery (the performance metaphor, ll.35–6); a simile to describe her exile from her child ('barred, like one infectious', l.96); a number of personifications (innocence, tyranny); and a reflective metaphorical comment on 'conspiracy / I know not how it tastes; though it be dished / For me to try' (ll.71–2). The images slow the delivery, creating a visual and visceral image of Hermione's emotions about three key imputations: her chastity, the loss of her child, and the accusation of conspiracy. Sparse imagery has a greater impact because used only by the accused and applied once to each of her emotional accusations. The scene's and speeches' rhetorical and linguistic structuring are calibrated to engage the audience's emotions moment by moment, but also to create a dynamic plot accelerating towards the turning point promised by the oracle's pronouncement. The predominantly non-metaphorical language enables this, but the passionate engagement of the characters in the trial and a situation where Hermione's life is at stake ensure we hang on every word of their confrontation.

Analysis: *The Tempest*, 3.3.1–110

Enter Alonso, Sebastian, Antonio, Gonzalo, Adrian, Francisco

GONZALO By'r lakin, I can go no further, sir,
My old bones aches. Here's a maze trod indeed
Through forth-rights and meanders! By your patience,
I needs must rest me.
ALONSO   Old lord, I cannot blame thee,
Who am myself attached with weariness,   5
To th' dulling of my spirits. Sit down, and rest.
Even here I will put off my hope, and keep it
No longer for my flatterer. He is drowned
Whom thus we stray to find, and the sea mocks
Our frustrate search on land. Well, let him go.   10
ANTONIO [*aside to Sebastian*] I am right glad that he's so out of hope.
Do not for one repulse forgo the purpose
That you resolved t' effect.
SEBASTIAN [*aside to Antonio*] The next advantage
Will we take throughly.

ANTONIO [*aside to Sebastian*] Let it be to-night;
For, now they are oppressed with travail, they   15
Will not nor cannot use such vigilance
As when they are fresh.
SEBASTIAN   [*aside to Antonio*] I say tonight. No more.
    Solemn and strange music, and Prospero on the top, invisible
ALONSO   What harmony is this? My good friends, hark!
GONZALO   Marvellous sweet music!

Enter several strange shapes, bringing in a banquet, and dance about it with gentle actions of salutations; and inviting the King, etc., to eat, they depart

ALONSO   Give us kind keepers, heavens! What were these?   20
SEBASTIAN   A living drollery. Now I will believe
That there are unicorns; that in Arabia
There is one tree, the phoenix' throne, one phoenix
At this hour reigning there.
ANTONIO   I'll believe both;
And what does else want credit, come to me,   25
And I'll be sworn 'tis true. Travellers ne'er did lie,
Though fools at home condemn 'em.
GONZALO   If in Naples
I should report this now, would they believe me?
If I should say I saw such islanders—
For certes these are people of the island—   30
Who though they are of monstrous shape, yet note,
Their manners are more gentle-kind than of
Our human generation you shall find
Many, nay almost any.
PROSPERO [*aside*]   Honest lord,
Thou hast said well; for some of you there present   35
Are worse than devils.
ALONSO   I cannot too much muse
Such shapes, such gesture and such sound expressing,
Although they want the use of tongue, a kind
Of excellent dumb discourse.
PROSPERO [*aside*]   Praise in departing.
FRANCISCO   They vanished strangely.

SEBASTIAN	No matter, since	40

They have left their viands behind; for we have stomachs.
Will't please you taste of what is here?

ALONSO   Not I.
GONZALO   Faith, sir, you need not fear. When we were boys,
         Who would believe that there were mountaineers
         Dewlapped like bulls, whose throats had hanging at 'em   45
         Wallets of flesh?—or that there were such men
         Whose heads stood in their breasts?—which now we find
         Each putter-out of five for one will bring us
         Good warrant of.
ALONSO   I will stand to and feed,
         Although my last—no matter, since I feel   50
         The best is past. Brother, my lord the Duke,
         Stand to and do as we.
                  Thunder and lightning.

         Enter Ariel, like a harpy, claps his wings upon the
         table, and with a quaint device the banquet vanishes

ARIEL   You are three men of sin, whom Destiny,
         That hath to instrument this lower world
         And what is in't, the never-surfeited sea   55
         Hath caused to belch up you, and on this island
         Where man doth not inhabit—you 'mongst men
         Being most unfit to live. I have made you mad;
         And even with such-like valour men hang and drown
         Their proper selves.
                  Alonso, Sebastian etc. draw their swords
                  You fools! I and my fellows   60
         Are ministers of Fate—the elements,
         Of whom your swords are tempered may as well
         Wound the loud winds, or with bemocked-at stabs
         Kill the still-closing waters, as diminish
         One dowl that's in my plume. My fellow ministers   65
         Are like invulnerable. If you could hurt,
         Your swords are now too massy for your strengths
         And will not be uplifted. But remember—
         For that's my business to you—that you three

| | From Milan did supplant good Prospero, 70
| | Exposed unto the sea, which hath requit it,
| | Him and his innocent child; for which foul deed,
| | The powers delaying, not forgetting, have
| | Incensed the seas and shores, yea all the creatures,
| | Against your peace. Thee of thy son, Alonso, 75
| | They have bereft; and do pronounce by me
| | Ling'ring perdition, worse than any death
| | Can be at once, shall step by step attend
| | You and your ways; whose wraths to guard you from,
| | Which here, in this most desolate isle, else falls 80
| | Upon your heads, is nothing but heart's sorrow,
| | And a clear life ensuing.
| | *He vanishes in thunder. Then, to soft music, enter the*
| | *shapes again, and dance with mocks and mows, and*
| | *carrying out the table* [*they depart*]
PROSPERO | Bravely the figure of this harpy hast thou
| | Performed, my Ariel; a grace it had, devouring.
| | Of my instruction hast thou nothing bated 85
| | In what thou hadst to say; so, with good life
| | And observation strange, my meaner ministers
| | Their several kinds have done. My high charms work
| | And these, mine enemies, are all knit up
| | In their distractions. They now are in my power; 90
| | And in these fits I leave them, while I visit
| | Young Ferdinand, whom they suppose is drowned,
| | And his and mine loved darling.   *Exit above*
GONZALO | I' th' name of something holy, sir, why stand you
| | In this strange stare?
ALONSO | O, it is monstrous, monstrous! 95
| | Methought the billows spoke and told me of it,
| | The winds did sing it to me; and the thunder,
| | That deep and dreadful organ-pipe, pronounced
| | The name of Prosper: it did bass my trespass.
| | Therefore my son i' th' ooze is bedded; and 100
| | I'll seek him deeper than e'er plummet sounded,
| | And with him there lie mudded.
SEBASTIAN | But one fiend at a time,
| | I'll fight their legions o'er.

ANTONIO	I'll be thy second.	
	Exeunt Sebastian and Antonio	
GONZALO	All three of them are desperate: their great guilt,	105
	Like poison given to work a great time after,	
	Now 'gins to bite the spirits. I do beseech you	
	That are of suppler joints, follow them swiftly,	
	And hinder them from what this ecstasy	
	May now provoke them to.	
ADRIAN	Follow, I pray you.	110
	[All exeunt]	

This scene follows those of Ferdinand and Miranda hauling logs and confessing their mutual love (3.1), and Caliban, Trinculo and Stephano plotting Prospero's overthrow (3.2). The play carefully intersperses the different experiences of those lost on the island after the shipwreck, juxtaposing divergent experiences of assimilation, appropriation and engagement with the 'natives'. In successive scenes, each group (Ferdinand / Stephano and Trinculo / the elder statesmen) reach a definitive crisis point in their experiences. This scene falls naturally into four parts: the lost men's journey (ll.1–17); the arrival of the banquet (ll.18–53); the harpy's appearance and the banquet's removal (ll.54–93); and the Europeans' varied response to the crisis (ll.94–110). This structural organisation creates a tight and dynamic dramatic set piece: weary and lost travellers who desire warmth, comfort and food are suddenly confronted with an astonishing banquet. The magical effect evokes medieval romances or fairy stories where the tired warrior is offered suspiciously sumptuous hostelry (implicit in Sebastian's unicorns and phoenixes, ll.22–3). The audience's sense of the false hope offered by the illusion is underlined by Prospero's oversight of and commentary on progressing action. As in fairy-tales and romances, once the protagonists attempt to taste the food, it metamorphoses: here a winged Harpy whisks the food away, and they are lectured about past sins. Alonso alone repents, and his final discordant, crazed and guilty departure contrasts Antonio and Sebastian's continued cynical and military response to any confrontation. The scene is a microcosm of a number of the play's narratives: western encounters with 'others'; the recognition and resolution of old feuds; and the quest. Its structure and motifs are drawn from classical and medieval quest stories (both Virgil's *Aeneid* and Malory's *Morte d'Arthur*), deliberately invoking magic, displacement and a moral lesson. The structure enables Shakespeare to use this crisis encounter as a moral test for Alonso, Sebastian and Antonio: Alonso passes, the others fail.

Stage directions create spatial, visual, material and aural experiences: they enumerate physical stage properties and the dancers' movements. The opening list of characters 'and others' visually evokes the weary travellers' straggling line. The directions for the banquet detail key character's positioning and choreography: '*Prospero on the top, invisible*' (l.18); '*several strange shapes bringing in a banquet, and dance about it with gentle actions of salutations; and inviting the King, etc., to eat*' (l.19); '*Ariel, like a Harpy, claps his wings upon the table*', (l.52); '*vanishes in thunder. Then, to soft music, enter the shapes again, and dance with mocks and mows, and carrying out the table*', (l.82). This explicit blocking reiterates the physical contrast between the weary men and the controlled dancing creatures and magical feast, and between them and Prospero, both on the physical stage (literally 'above') and metaphorically. The creatures' visual appearance is stage-directed: '*strange shapes*'; '*Ariel, like a Harpy... his wings*' emphasising their alien effects. These are the first island 'people' these Europeans have met. Music is stage directed, underlining the magical other-worldly representation of the banquet, given its appearance in the midst of a barren landscape. The '*gentle*' (l.19) actions and salutations contrast the men's previous experiences of an alien and unwelcoming place.

The scene's opening conversation emphasises the men's hard physical and emotional experiences: of exhaustion ('my old bones ache' l.2; 'attached with weariness to the dulling of my spirits' ll.5–6); of the spatial experience of walking a barren island lost ('a maze trod... through forth-rights and meanders', ll.2–3; 'this most desolate isle', l.80); and of emotional grief for the loss of a son. In contrast, Sebastian and Antonio continue to plot political usurpation and seem unaffected by the physical and emotional deprivation. They must speak apart rather than congregated with the group of survivors: the necessity of their speech being private literally blocks them at a different part of the stage.

The music announces a shift in the action, wondrously observed by Alonso and Gonzalo ('harmony' and 'marvellous sweet music', ll.18–19). Their ambivalent response is voiced in their imprecations to God against the 'strange shapes' to ward off evil ('give us kind keepers, heavens!', l.20). Both Gonzalo's 'If in Naples / I should report this now, would they believe me?'(ll.27–8) and Antonio and Sebastian's initial comparisons to unicorns and phoenixes, invoke the doubled wonder and disbelief of all early-modern traveller narratives about the new world. Antonio and Sebastian use creatures of myth and fantasy, distancing and 'othering' what they see from their European frame of reference. Gonzalo, by contrast, describes literally what he sees and gives the shapes autonomous identity: 'certes, these are people of the island—/ Who, though they are of monstrous shape, yet note/ their manners are more gentle-kind than of / Our human generation' (ll.29–32). He uses empirical language ('monstrous shape') combined with comparative judgement ('more gentle kind') which elevates them above Europeans. Gonzalo displays a more open, enquiring and unselfish personality than do Antonio and Sebastian, a judgement echoed by Prospero's comment (ll.34–6). Antonio and Sebastian's initial response is the only time in the play where their wonder overwhelms their cynicism: unlike their encounter with Caliban at the end of the play, they do not suggest marketing the shapes, although their language ('a living drollery' l.21) objectifies and mythologises (the unicorns). Alonso's reluctance to eat ('not I') is countered by Gonzalo's argument about how we accept new experiences: previous generations' disbeliefs (about dew-lapped men or those whose heads grew from their chests) are now discredited, since travel writers give 'good warrant' (l.49). Gonzalo's humanistic attitude marks him apart intellectually (he can conceive of new experiences with an open mind) and also socially, as he tries to reassure Alonso and encourage him to eat.

The scene's turning-point is triggered as Alonso encourages the courtiers to 'stand to' (eat): and 'thunder and lightning' dramatically interrupts them. A feast symbolises communal celebration and friendship, a social gathering and social values, health and security: so stopping a feast intimates the destruction of these. The men are weary, lost and hungry and the vision of the feast tantalising, so its disappearance is both poignant and dramatically signals potentially tragedy. Many recent productions use a freeze-frame effect here to emphasise the visual and emotional shock of the interruption of a feast and the disappearance of the food ('*with a quaint device the banquet vanishes*', l.52). Ariel's speech of 30 lines is his longest in the play, intoned in character 'like a harpy', a mythological creature from Virgil's *The Aeneid* and Dante's *Inferno*, half bird, half woman, who vengefully stole and fouled food and feasts. By using this character, winged, monstrous and visually frightening and disgusting, Prospero terrifies and subjugates the courtiers and augurs divine judgement. Ariel's speech echoes this function of judgemental revenge: claiming that Ferdinand's death is punishment for these past sins.

Ariel's speech, at the play's centre, is the first time the courtiers are told how their past lives have now coincided with the present. The audience has been waiting for this crisis to come to a head: although here it does so obliquely since they do not come face-to-face with Prospero, only his agent. By using Ariel as a proxy, Prospero both postpones resolution, and make their sins appear to be judged by objective outsiders. Ariel's language has a legal weight, emphasised by rhythm and content: the first line is a sonorous regular iambic pentameter, the stress falling equally and regularly on alternate syllables ('You are three men of sin, whom Destiny...', l.53), and much of the speech as a whole continues this toll-like effect. Even where a line looks like 12 syllables (for example ll.58–9 and 65) elisions and the dominating beat enable the actor to deliver it as five alternate stresses. Ariel personifies both destiny and the sea, indirectly linking the sea to divinity and fate. The sea, winds, and nature lie beyond the control of men: for example, his rebuke to the courtiers for drawing their swords: 'You fools! I and my fellows / Are ministers of Fate: the elements, / Of whom your swords are tempered, may as well / Wound the loud winds' (ll.60–64), and his claim that 'the powers...have / incensed the seas and shores, yea all the creatures / Against your peace' (ll.33–6). Wild nature is larger than individual humans: a perspective threading throughout the play from the opening scene. Ariel's speech addresses the men collectively and individually: and many of the vocative addresses are effective stage directions. In telling them not to draw their swords, he implies an attempt to do so; and 'your swords are now too massy for your strengths / And will not be uplifted' (ll.167–8), implies the courtiers attempt to lift their swords.

Ariel's directorial injunctions demonstrate his (and Prospero's) physical power over elements and men, one complemented by his intellectual power. It is this prescience which seems to terrify his listeners even more than his magical physical control over their bodies and weapons. He singles out Alonso as the direct addressee of the final part of the speech using the language of a formal judgement and sentencing: 'pronouncing' him to 'lingering perdition' (ll.76–7). Yet the judgment, and his subsequent advice (aim for 'heart-sorrow and a clear life', l.81) has a spiritual, theological tinge. By situating himself as judge and priest, Ariel (and Prospero) promise both justice and potential salvation. Alonso is moved and altered by the speech, literally driven mad as Gonzalo suggests, by the images of his son and the recollection of, and judgement on, his past sins. Ariel (and Prospero)'s double function as controlling judge and forgiving priest foreshadows Prospero's role towards Caliban, Alonso and Antonio in the final act.

The physical actions of the 'shapes' when they appear to carry out the table ('*dance with mocks and mows*') and Sebastian's judgement of it ('a drollery', l.21) suggest an exaggerated dance, emphasising their over-theatrical performance. Although we know it is a fiction (because we can see Prospero directing above), the courtiers see it first as an encounter with strange island inhabitants, and then as one with 'fiends' (l.103). The exaggerated gestures serve both to emphasise to the courtiers the other-worldly nature of the performance, and to us its meta-theatrical nature.

Prospero's commentary on Ariel's actions (ll.83–92) punctuates his control of the action. It marks an end point of his current plans ('these, mine enemies, are all knit up... they now are in my power' ll.89–90), and a look towards the future as he purposes to visit Ferdinand and 'mine loved darling' (l.93). Paradoxically at this moment of triumph and power, as Prospero looks towards the future, the play asks what happens now?

The scene's finale leaves all the courtiers on stage alone, although only Gonzalo, Alonso and Adrian speak. Antonio and Sebastian remain silent: prefiguring their silence at the play's closure, refusing now and later to be moved by pleas for justice and repentance. Alonso's emotional response to the judgement ('monstrous, monstrous', l.95) and his perception that all the natural forces of the island have been personified into vengeful agents ('it did bass my trespass', l.99), has driven him to a melancholic frenzy ('ecstasy', l.109).

The language is predominantly straightforward in its referents, with some key legal metaphors and terms threading the scene, bolstering its function as a physical and pseudo-legal trial. Gonzalo's description of their journey's route uses legalese ('forth-rights' l.3) and Ariel 'pronounce(s)... perdition ll.76–7'. Metaphors of eating recur in Ariel and Prospero's language (the sea 'belched' (l.56) up the men; Ariel's 'grace... devouring' ll.84). These vehicles reinforce the banquet's tantalising appearance and disappearance, and the material fake-presence and absence of food for the lost men. Nature and natural forces are personified: Ariel claims the sea 'belches' and 'requits' and Alonso that the 'billows spoke', 'the winds did sing' and 'the thunder...did bass my trespass' (ll.96–99). Neither Prospero nor Gonzalo personify or anthropomorphise nature in this way: in Ariel's case it suggests his affinity with forces of nature, in Alonso's his 'great guilt' (l.105), as he patterns the external world to his inward imaginings. Alonso sees strange natural phenomena: we are privileged to see these are engineered by Prospero. This aids his characterisation as all-powerful magus ('they now are in my power', l.90), and Alonso's madness is produced to his direction. However, the idea that nature is larger and more destructive than the mere human is one that dominates the play, forcing us to ask deeper philosophical questions about the world, both spiritual and material. Alonso's grief may have been manipulated by Prospero: but the play's overall effect is to suggest human agency is finally powerless in the face of natural and divine forces.

Alonso's final despairing and suicidal cry of loss 'my son i'th'ooze is *bedded*' (ll.100–101) envisages Ferdinand's body planted in the sea bed. But for the audience the word 'bedded' resonates punningly: we have seen his son alive and thinking of a much warmer 'bed'. Tragic loss is combined with comic potential, through language and situation.

Conclusions

1. Shakespeare coalesces dramatic meaning in key 'set pieces', which occur at crisis points in the plot. In each case the mid-point of the play is a scene which is self-consciously very public and formal (a trial scene, a banquet), involving key characters and fusing

two separate conflicting narrative strands in a confrontation (Hermione / Women vs Leontes / patriarchalism; Prospero vs Alonso / Antonio). The scene culminates the conflict established in the opening act: but the conflict's 'resolution' does not end the play, but sends the narrative in a different and new direction. It is a turning-point for character as well as plot: Leontes and Alonso confess to their wrongdoing: what will happen with that knowledge now?
2. These set pieces tilt the action and denouement in the direction of tragedy: what has appeared to be a comedy suddenly and definitively turns to the typical modes of tragedies: death, insane jealousy, banishment, melancholic self-destruction. The scenes' endings leave us bereft and lost: where can the narrative go now? In each subsequent scene comedy dominates (the shepherd's discovery of Perdita, the preparations for Miranda and Ferdinand's wedding). This is not 'comic relief' following intense tragic scenes: Shakespeare suggests redemption follows repentance. Dramatic scenic structure echoes a psychological and spiritual journey.
3. Family conflict is central to the public trials. Conventional family conflict (brother vs. brother, husband vs. wife) is intensified by making it simultaneously a political and legal one. Political conflict is given an emotional violence and passion, suggesting that the personal is political.
4. The action is slowed down for the full emotional and dramatic effect to be realised performatively. This pacing comes through necessary stage business scripted in the stage directions and dialogue, making the scenes more spectacular and sonorous. These scenes are simultaneously packed with action yet condensed experiences of a gamut of human emotions. Past grievances clash with present circumstances at a symbolic occasion: a trial, a banquet. Formal occasions quickly become private and personal: a trial an extended personal battle between husband and wife; a banquet a battle between brothers. The long speeches are surprisingly spellbinding because the situation itself is mesmeric.
5. Extraordinary stage effects enhance the dramatic moment: art and illusion are literally affective. The banquet in *The Tempest* is visually astonishing and timely: it speaks exactly to the men's

physical and emotional needs. However, the audience sees it within a broader context as well, that of the romance-inflected temptation to men in the wilderness. Illusion is demonised. The 'illusion' of Hermione's death is shockingly affective: neither the characters nor the audience are prepared in any way for it. When she reappears at the end of Act 5, we look back on Paulina's righteous anger at her 'death' with scepticism: why did illusions lead us astray? Perhaps this is part of Shakespeare's enterprise: built into his spectacular dramatic illusionism is the warning that illusions are dangerous.

6. New characters appear to initiate a shift in direction, and suggest a world in which fate has a place to play. Cleomenes and Dion bring the word of Apollo's oracle, affecting the tenor, nature and outcome of the set piece trial. Ariel as Harpy acts as a direct agent of 'fate' and 'destiny': wrong-doers' punishment belongs to an external moral power (allied to the divine). A turning-point scene's outcome is tragic but forces truth into the open: the cost of truth is death or madness.

7. Language, imagery and action are intertwined and tightly significant: language and metaphors echo and embed key scenic conflicts. Imagery, metre and rhythm establish and direct characters emotions, and act as proxy indicators and intensifiers for the audience of the physical experience of character, action and emotion.

8. Key binary oppositions are articulated, crystallised and visualised: oppressor vs. victim; masculinity vs. femininity; betrayal vs. loyalty; appearance vs. reality; comic vs. tragic; youth vs. age; old world vs. new world. The crucial turning point from tragedy to comedy balances between oppositions, and the shift from one to another tilts the narrative trajectory towards resolution, where the 'old world' is marked as morally corrupt.

Methods of Analysis

This chapter builds on our methods of analysis delineated in the opening chapter. In addition we have introduced and applied an understanding of dramatic structure and staging to help analyse the text.

1. We have identified key scenes which coalesce the play's central narrative conflicts. This involves thinking about the play as a structural whole and looking for scenes which change the direction of the plot.
2. We have considered how setting and stage directions (internal and external) intensify a theatrical experience, and contribute to our reading of character and conflict.
3. We have looked at **Poetry** for the first time, and considered:
   - metre (syllables per line), looking for both regular and irregular verse;
   - metaphors and similes, their meaning and effect;
   - rhetorical repetition, and its effects;
   - assonance or deliberate dissonance, and its effects;
   - line endings and the significance of the last word in a line;
   - rhymes when they occur;
   - different 'registers' of different characters – asking how and why it varies?
4. We have implicitly used ideas of 'genre' and the ways in which audience response can be manipulated and anticipated using generic motifs.
5. We have introduced additional terms of theatrical analysis (blocking, scenic juxtaposition, stage props, choreography) and considered how these integrate with the broader theatrical dynamic of text and performance.

Suggested Work

Before considering turning-point scenes in the other late plays, there are some additional questions to pursue. Think about how previous and subsequent scenes to those here have affected our interpretation. Are the characters changed subsequently? How does the turning-point scene's language and imagery inform the rest of the play? Are there additional 'spectacular' or / and turning-point scenes? How do they ensure we look back at this one? How do the binary oppositions play out in the remainder of the action?

Now look at *Cymbeline* (4.2) and *Pericles* (scenes 18 and 19), and consider the following questions: how do these scenes coalesce and exemplify the play's key conflicts and themes? In what ways do personal mythic conflicts (e.g. stepmother vs. daughter etc.) reinforce wider political conflicts? How are spectacle and stage properties used to enhance the dramatic experience and position the audience? Look at character blocking, scenic structure, scenic juxtapositioning and language. Think carefully about what happens after the turning point: how and where are characters positioned? Is tragedy inevitable?

3

Endings

A play's ending should be memorable: shocking or satisfying; emotionally fulfilling or traumatising. It resolves the plot's narrative strands, possibly leaving some open questions for the audience to consider. Effective endings coalesce and distil emotions and experiences which have dominated the play's action: and great performances enable images and experiences to stay in our imaginations and minds. The nature of the ending (who is married, who is silent, who dies, who is left out) tells us about the play's dramatic intent. Does the ending resolve conflict or perpetuate it? Is the ending idealistic or pessimistic? Does it answer questions raised by the play's action and opening? Have the characters been changed by their experiences and learned anything? Let us now turn to the endings of these plays, and first the finale of *The Winter's Tale*.

Analysis: *The Winter's Tale*, 5.3.8–155

LEONTES   O Paulina,
　　We honour you with trouble; but we came
　　To see the statue of our Queen. Your gallery   10
　　Have we passed through, not without much content
　　In many singularities, but we saw not
　　That which my daughter came to look upon,
　　The statue of her mother.
PAULINA   As she lived peerless,

	So her dead likeness I do well believe	15
	Excels whatever yet you looked upon,
	Or hand of man hath done; therefore I keep it
	Lonely, apart. But here it is—prepare
	To see the life as lively mocked as ever
	Still sleep mocked death:
	[*Paulina draws a curtain, and reveals*
	Hermione standing like a statue]
	Behold, and say 'tis well.	20
	I like your silence; it the more shows off
	Your wonder. But yet speak—first you, my liege.
	Comes it not something near?
LEONTES	Her natural posture.
	Chide me, dear stone, that I may say indeed
	Thou art Hermione—or rather, thou art she	25
	In thy not chiding; for she was as tender
	As infancy and grace. But yet, Paulina,
	Hermione was not so much wrinkled, nothing
	So aged as this seems.
POLIXENES	O, not by much.
PAULINA	So much the more our carver's excellence,	30
	Which lets go by some sixteen years, and makes her
	As she lived now.
LEONTES	As now she might have done,
	So much to my good comfort as it is
	Now piercing to my soul. O, thus she stood,
	Even with such life of majesty—warm life,	35
	As now it coldly stands—when first I wooed her.
	I am ashamed. Does not the stone rebuke me
	For being more stone than it? O royal piece!
	There's magic in thy majesty, which has
	My evils conjured to remembrance, and	40
	From thy admiring daughter took the spirits,
	Standing like stone with thee.
PERDITA	And give me leave,
	And do not say 'tis superstition, that
	I kneel and then implore her blessing. Lady,
	Dear Queen, that ended when I but began,	45
	Give me that hand of yours to kiss.

PAULINA	O, patience!
	The statue is but newly fixed; the colour's
	Not dry.
CAMILLO	My lord, your sorrow was too sore laid on,
	Which sixteen winters cannot blow away, 50
	So many summers dry. Scarce any joy
	Did ever so long live; no sorrow
	But killed itself much sooner.
POLIXENES	Dear my brother,
	Let him that was the cause of this have power
	To take off so much grief from you as he 55
	Will piece up in himself.
PAULINA	Indeed, my lord,
	If I had thought the sight of my poor image
	Would thus have wrought you—for the stone is mine—
	I'd not have showed it.
LEONTES	Do not draw the curtain.
PAULINA	No longer shall you gaze on't, lest your fancy 60
	May think anon it moves.
LEONTES	Let be, let be.
	Would I were dead, but that methinks already—
	What was he that did make it?—See, my lord,
	Would you not deem it breathed, and that those veins
	Did verily bear blood?
POLIXENES	Masterly done! 65
	The very life seems warm upon her lip.
LEONTES	The fixture of her eye has motion in't,
	As we are mocked with art.
PAULINA	I'll draw the curtain.
	My lord's almost so far transported that
	He'll think anon it lives.
LEONTES	O sweet Paulina, 70
	Make me to think so twenty years together!
	No settled senses of the world can match
	The pleasure of that madness. Let 't alone.
PAULINA	I am sorry, sir, I have thus far stirred you, but
	I could afflict you farther.
LEONTES	Do, Paulina, 75
	For this affliction has a taste as sweet

| | As any cordial comfort. Still methinks,
| | There is an air comes from her. What fine chisel
| | Could ever yet cut breath? Let no man mock me,
| | For I will kiss her.
| PAULINA | Good my lord, forbear: 80
| | The ruddiness upon her lip is wet;
| | You'll mar it if you kiss it, stain your own
| | With oily painting. Shall I draw the curtain?
| LEONTES | No, not these twenty years.
| PERDITA | So long could I
| | Stand by, a looker-on.
| PAULINA | Either forbear,   85
| | Quit presently the chapel, or resolve you
| | For more amazement. If you can behold it,
| | I'll make the statue move indeed, descend
| | And take you by the hand—but then you'll think,
| | Which I protest against, I am assisted   90
| | By wicked powers.
| LEONTES | What you can make her do
| | I am content to look on, what to speak,
| | I am content to hear; for 'tis as easy
| | To make her speak as move.
| PAULINA | It is required
| | You do awake your faith. Then all stand still—   95
| | Or those that think it is unlawful business
| | I am about, let them depart.
| LEONTES | Proceed.
| | No foot shall stir.
| PAULINA | Music; awake her—strike!
| | [*Music*]
| | [*To Hermione*] 'Tis time; descend; be stone no more;
| | approach;
| | Strike all that look upon with marvel—come,   100
| | I'll fill your grave up. Stir—nay, come away,
| | Bequeath to Death your numbness, for from him
| | Dear life redeems you. [*To Leontes*] You perceive she stirs.
| | [*Hermione descends*]
| | Start not; her actions shall be holy as
| | You hear my spell is lawful. Do not shun her   105

	Until you see her die again, for then	
	You kill her double. Nay, present your hand.	
	When she was young you wooed her; now in age	
	Is she become the suitor?	
LEONTES	O, she's warm!	
	If this be magic, let it be an art	110
	Lawful as eating.	
POLIXENES	She embraces him.	
CAMILLO	She hangs about his neck—	
	If she pertain to life let her speak too!	
POLIXENES	Ay, and make it manifest where she has lived,	
	Or how stol'n from the dead.	
PAULINA	That she is living,	115
	Were it but told you, should be hooted at	
	Like an old tale; but it appears she lives,	
	Though yet she speak not. Mark a little while.	
	[*To Perdita*] Please you to interpose, fair madam; kneel	
	And pray your mother's blessing. Turn good lady;	120
	[*To Hermione*]	
	Our Perdita is found.	
HERMIONE	You gods, look down,	
	And from your sacred vials pour your graces	
	Upon my daughter's head! Tell me, mine own,	
	Where hast thou been preserved, where lived, how found	
	Thy father's court? For thou shalt hear that I,	125
	Knowing by Paulina that the oracle	
	Gave hope thou wast in being, have preserved	
	Myself to see the issue.	
PAULINA	There's time enough for that,	
	Lest they desire upon this push to trouble	
	Your joys with like relation. Go together,	130
	You precious winners all; your exultation	
	Partake to everyone. I, an old turtle,	
	Will wing me to some withered bough, and there	
	My mate, that's never to be found again,	
	Lament till I am lost.	
LEONTES	O, peace, Paulina.	135
	Thou shouldst a husband take by my consent,	
	As I by thine a wife. This is a match,	
	And made between's by vows. Thou hast found mine—	

> But how is to be questioned, for I saw her,
> As I thought, dead, and have in vain said many   140
> A prayer upon her grave. I'll not seek far—
> For him, I partly know his mind—to find thee
> An honourable husband. Come, Camillo,
> And take her by the hand, whose worth and honesty
> Is richly noted, and here justified   145
> By us, a pair of kings. Let's from this place.
> (*To Hermione*) What! Look upon my brother. Both your pardons,
> That e'er I put between your holy looks
> My ill suspicion. This your son-in-law,
> And son unto the King, whom heavens directing,   150
> Is troth-plight to your daughter. Good Paulina,
> Lead us from hence, where we may leisurely
> Each one demand an answer to his part
> Performed in this wide gap of time since first
> We were dissevered. Hastily lead away.   *Exeunt*   155

This final scene is an extraordinary reversal of plot and events: echoing the astonishing revival of a dead Claudia in *Much Ado About Nothing*, and Innogen in *Cymbeline*. However, in *The Winter's Tale* the audience has been actively deceived: we saw Hermione die, and there has been no hint that this was an illusion. Audience and characters are alike in the dark, enhancing the magical effect, and demanding a greater suspension of disbelief. The scene's action moves gradually from a low-key visit to a private gallery to a luminous, magical, even supernatural, experience in which a statue appears to metamorphose into a live woman.

The scene's slowly evolving pace gradually heightens tension. Leontes talks about walking through the gallery (ll.10–11): the physical positioning of characters emphasising the centrality and immobility of the revealed statue. At the walk's end lies a discovery which promises a closure to their grieving. However, the usual closure of marking a death with a monument, and therein moving onto another stage in life, here becomes literally a new life.

The choreography of the revelation involves characters' and audience's sight converging on a single figure. The stage direction ('*reveals Hermione standing like a statue*', l.20) intimates she is standing behind the 'discovery' space at up-stage centre, and that the characters crowd around (Perdita kneels and wants to kiss her hand). This reverential, nigh-religious ecstatic response to an inanimate object invokes an atmosphere of spirituality and strangeness, acknowledged by Paulina's 'do not say 'tis superstition', l.43. Her fussy protection of the statue suggests her movement around it. Leontes' imprecations ('do not draw the curtain', 'Let be, let be!', ll.59–61) act as impatient stage directions to prevent Paulina hiding the statue away, and suggest both his physical approaches to the statue and its mesmerising qualities. Paulina's management of the people and space around the statue increases tension and emphasises her directorial role ('good my lord, forbear!', l.80; 'Either forbear... or resolve you for more amazement', ll.85–7). She speaks nearly as many lines as the King (54 to 64), illustrating her pivotal role in managing the situation. The final act's closures and stage directions are literally in the hands of a woman servant.

Paulina's dramatic promise that she can make a statue move and speak implies a dark magic, which she simultaneously acknowledges and protests (ll.89–91, and again at ll.104–6), although she transposes this to the realm of faith ('It is required / you do awake your faith' (ll.94–5)). Magic, faith, spiritual belief and power intersect, in contrast to the *realpolitik* of the play's first half. Equally, that power is explicitly dramatic and spectacular: the power to entrance an audience, make characters come alive, direct music, words and action all belong to Paulina (and analogously, Shakespeare). This is Shakespeare's only play in which such power is explicitly figured as female. Paulina directs the action, characters and magic of a statue becoming a flesh-and-blood woman ('music awake her—strike!', l.98): she has also nurtured Hermione's 16-year retreat. Leontes' submission to a woman and one of lower status ('I am content to look on, what to speak I am content to hear', ll.92–3) marks a radical social and gender transformation, in direct contrast to the play's opening half.

Paulina's teasing relationship with Leontes is framed through the language of combat ('I could afflict you further', l.75), command ('It is required / ... all stand still', l.92) and belittling sarcasm ('My Lord's almost so far transported that / he'll think anon it lives' (ll.68–9), which Leontes meekly accepts. Their power relationship has been inverted since the trial scene. When Hermione descends from the plinth Paulina implies she is changing time and nature ('I'll fill your grave up... / Bequeath to death your numbness'), accruing to herself divine or magical powers in her ability to wake the dead. The Ovidian myth of Pygmalion, the man who made his ideal wife from a statue, is implicitly invoked: however, the statue here is both 'created' and given life by a woman. Paulina continues to direct the action when Hermione moves, telling Leontes to take her hand, and asking Perdita to interpose and kneel, and Hermione herself to 'turn... / Our Perdita is found' (ll.120–21). Hermione's only speech in the scene is to Perdita directly, addressing no other characters. Female dialogue and communication brings her voice alive, and the relationship between mother and daughter is central to this. Although Paulina has kept Hermione secretly alive, she only comes alive publicly when her daughter is recovered. Familial reunions, reconciliations and new life are staple comic endings: here Shakespeare has stretched our suspension of disbelief by showing death and rebirth. However, the slowly choreographed revelation of Hermione's revival enables the audience to see it as simultaneously fantasy and truth: life and future are possible through forgiveness and change configured through women. The scene is a self-conscious fantasy: old age, sin, and loss can be simultaneously forgotten and remembered.

Hermione's continued silence slows down time, eerily forcing us to focus on her movements. Leontes' wondrous exclamation ('O she's warm! / If this be magic, let it be an art / Lawful as eating', ll.109–11), and Camillo's and Polixenes' descriptions of Hermione's embrace of Leontes enable us to both watch and hear about the action, partially distancing and framing it. Although the courtiers demand an explanation of the missing years, Paulina's indirect refusal ('Were it but told you, should be hooted at / Like an old tale', ll.116–17) sustains the mystery of both past and present. The simile once again self-consciously invokes the play's fairy-tale fictionality. Silence creates suspense: what will happen? Is it real? The extension of time is part of the magic of the scene.

Hermione's first words are to "you gods" (l.121), and her explanation restricted to saying that she continued hoping the oracle's words meant that Perdita would be found. She says nothing to or about Leontes. How do we see this on stage? Although she has embraced him (the courtiers describe this), her focus is on Perdita. The awkwardness of the husband / wife reunion is viewed by us, experienced by Hermione, but not perceived by either courtiers or Leontes. Leontes' final closing speech borders on the triumphalist: he rediscovers his monarchical dominance. His speech patterns are assertive: ordering Paulina and Camillo to marry. Although he acknowledges Paulina's agency ('thou hast found mine', l.138), such agency is placed in the past tense and denies her both voice and choice. He tries to direct actions and responses on stage, through imperatives ('let's from this place' 'What! Look upon my brother' ll.147). He introduces Florizel to Hermione through his status and relationships ('son unto the king / ...troth plight to your daughter', ll.150–51). Thus his former sense of power and status are reasserted. His final words focus on dynastic power and his state's future: Hermione's future concentrates on her daughter. For both, resolution of past jealousy is magically transformed through sexual congress in the next generation. The ending is both conventionally conservative (political succession through arranged marriages and an emphasis on masculine power) and critically radical (women are the agents of change).

Leontes' sketchy apology contrasts with his earlier humble approach to the statue. His last words ('*Hastily* lead away' l.155) provide necessary dramatic closure, but simultaneously reassert his impulsive character. Hermione's silence and Leontes' triumphal sweep from the stage allow different productions to suggest that despite Leontes' promises, this ending still poses questions about his character and the perpetuation of controlling masculinity. Is Paulina an agent of masculine desire, facilitating Leontes as a proxy-Pygmalion, whose wife is restored to him despite his older murderous and jealous actions? Or do Paulina, Perdita and Hermione's powers constitute a more feminised ending? Productions can emphasise the magical, romantic quality of a family reunion and its message of a hopeful future, or question such ideals by emphasising Hermione's failure to speak to Leontes, her connection to her daughter, and Leontes' return to domineering patriarch.

The final scene's theatrical spectacle shares themes and motifs with the trial scene and the sheep-shearing festival (4.4). Characters are publicly tested in situations where they are literally on view to characters on stage and to the audience: Hermione as accused, Leontes as judge; Perdita as hostess, Florizel as son and potential king; Hermione as statue and living woman, Leontes as king and man. Public occasions explicitly require performances from characters in their public, not private, identities. Moments of theatricality and performance are used explicitly to figure forth key ideas about identity: when can we be private? When is it right to speak out? Are we ever not on show? The play's finale shows theatre is literally magic, can literally make the dead speak again, and create in an audience a belief in success, future, and rebirth ('as we are mocked with art', l.68). Humour, emphasised by the courtiers' comments on the statue's wrinkles and Paulina's warnings not to touch the wet paint, helps displace the audience from Leontes' sorrowful intense abjection. The repetition of 'mocked' ('the life as lively mocked as ever / Still sleep mocked death', ll.19–20) hints subliminally that we are all being teased.

Textual metaphors and similes echo the dominant material one of the statue coming to life. Leontes uses it as vehicle for his metaphor on his emotions (as cold as its stone for 16 years, ll.36–8); and its literal revivification is used as a metaphoric vehicle to denote magic (the statue conjures up Leontes' past). Grammar and semantics are lucid and flowing. Leontes' speech (beginning 'let be, let be!' l.61) is one exception, refusing to let the statue be recurtained, and obsessively cataloguing its appearance. The choppy grammar and the broken off 'methinks already –' (l.62), demonstrate emotional turmoil and confusion, and enables the actor to deliver this through language and body. Leontes' final metaphor acknowledges theatricalised identities ('each one demand an answer to his part / Performed in this wide gap of time', ll.153–4), but although he suggests we all play social parts, his own lack of self-consciousness remains his central flaw.

Finally, this scene crystallises through a concrete stage-property and stage business, the human psychological balance between eros and thanatos (love and death), between the terror of loss and the joy of reunion, inverting life's trajectory towards death. Here, life follows death, and death is represented as literally conquered, albeit with some tongue-in-cheek sleight-of-hand. Love and youth are superseded by the experiences of middle age: wrinkles, the bearing of children, the loss of friends. Lost memories are literally re / membered (limbs come to life: 'conjured to remembrance', l.40), and old mistakes rectified and forgiven. This promise echoes the Christian faith in forgiveness and new life. Hermione does not explicitly forgive Leontes, but the theatrical management of her revival makes us believe she will, although simultaneously we note the reassertion of Leontes' natural character.

Nevertheless, the numinous effect of a wife slowly coming alive after 16 years believed dead, the husband's awe and sorrow at his past sins, and their physical reunion is choreographed to illuminate middle-aged reunion as redemptive. In contradistinction to conventional comic endings which focus on the hopes of a younger generation through their marriage, this ending displaces the youngsters and their resonance from the dramatic closure, imaging futurity instead through a mother–daughter reunion.

Let us look briefly at a short extract from the ending of *Pericles*.

Analysis: *Pericles*, Scene 22, ll.21–65

PERICLES	Hail, Dian. To perform thy just command	
	I here confess myself the King of Tyre,	
	Who, frighted from my country, did espouse	
	The fair Thaisa (*Thaisa starts*) at Pentapolis.	
	At sea in childbed died she, but brought forth	25
	A maid-child called Marina, who, O goddess,	
	Wears yet thy silver livery. She at Tarsus	
	Was nursed with Cleon, who at fourteen years	
	He sought to murder, but her better stars	
	Brought her to Mytilene, 'gainst whose shore riding	30
	Her fortunes brought the maid aboard our barque,	
	Where, by her own most clear remembrance, she	
	Made known herself my daughter.	
THAISA	Voice and favour—	
	You are, you are—O royal Pericles!	
	She falls	
PERICLES	What means the nun? She dies! Help, gentlemen!	35
CERIMON	Noble sir,	
	If you have told Diana's altar true,	
	This is your wife.	
PERICLES	Reverend appearer, no.	
	I threw her overboard with these same arms.	

CERIMON	Upon this coast, I warrant you.	
PERICLES	'Tis most certain.	40
CERIMON	Look to the lady. O, she's but o'erjoyed.	
	Early one blustering morn this lady	
	Was thrown upon this shore. I oped the coffin,	
	Found there rich jewels, recovered her, and placed her	
	Here in Diana's temple.	
PERICLES	May we see them?	45
CERIMON	Great sir, they shall be brought you to my house,	
	Whither I invite you. Look, Thaisa is	
	Recoverèd.	
THAISA	O let me look upon him!	
	If he be none of mine, my sanctity	
	Will to my sense bend no licentious ear,	50
	But curb it, spite of seeing. O my lord,	
	Are you not Pericles? Like him you spake,	
	Like him you are. Did you not name a tempest,	
	A birth and death?	
PERICLES	The voice of dead Thaisa!	55
THAISA	That Thaisa	
	Am I, supposèd dead and drowned.	
PERICLES	[*taking Thaisa's hand*] Immortal Dian!	
THAISA	Now I know you better.	
	When we with tears parted Pentapolis,	
	The King my father gave you such a ring.	60
PERICLES	This, this! No more, you gods. Your present kindness	
	Makes my past miseries sports; you shall do well,	
	That on the touching of her lips I may	
	Melt, and no more be seen.—O come, be buried	
	A second time within these arms.	

Pericles shares two similarities with the endings of *The Winter's Tale* and *The Tempest*: a husband–wife–daughter reunion, and an epilogue. Its epilogue (not shown here) is spoken by the master-of-ceremonies of the play, Gower, and is a rather flat plot summary. This extract (ll.21–69) is the moment in the Temple of Diana when Pericles and Thaisa are reunited after 16 years. The story's magic, represented deliberately as a self-consciously archaic 'mouldy tale' narrated by the medieval poet Gower, enables the reunion's mythical nature to be credibly represented. The play demands successive suspensions of disbelief: so tales of a wife mistakenly believed dead and coffined in the sea, only to magically reappear in the very temple where her daughter is being married, are part of that suspension. The reunion between daughter and father, as in *The Winter's Tale,* occurs prior to that of husband and wife. In *Pericles* the emotional intensity of the father–daughter meeting condenses and releases the trauma of the father's loss: recognition resolves tragedy. In *The Winter's Tale,* the father–daughter reunion is narrated by courtiers and occurs off-stage. The final recognition (husband of wife) therefore plays differently: in *The Winter's Tale* all the emotional intensity is focussed on the husband–wife reunion, which is played out on stage. In *Pericles* the husband–wife reconciliation repeats what has already been seen and felt in the father–daughter reconciliation. Thaisa speaks the recognition, and her fainting emphasises her emotionally vulnerable response. Her first words focus on Pericles ('You are, you are—O royal Pericles!', l.34; 'O, let me look Upon him! / If he be...', ll.48–9), and not her daughter. Marina's desire for her mother ('My heart / leaps to be gone into my mother's bosom', l.65–6) is hierarchically put after that of husband / wife. Unlike in *The Winter's Tale* the reunion is not drawn out, nor the wife's response so ambiguously represented. Although dynastic rule is reasserted and confirmed (ll.93–6) Pericles does not revert to the language and identity of power Leontes rediscovers. This is far more low-key than the theatricality of *The Winter's Tale* final revelation or the earlier reunion between Pericles and Marina, where music, vision, rebirth and near-death usher in a personal transformation. Although this scene is in the temple of Diana, accruing both aural and visual solemnity, sound and setting seem external to the revelation of events. The cathartic focus in *Pericles* is earlier than this finale, and absents the mother: it is his daughter's reappearance that assures his emotional and political future. This is true of *The Winter's Tale,* but it is not central to the play's emotional climax: there dynastic and political joy is seen on stage only when a mother reappears: maternal connections are central to Bohemian futures. Of course, these plays are completely different stories, about different characters, so we should not expect them to deliver the same ending. However, by comparing their endings, it is easier to appreciate *The Winter's Tale*'s numinous and radical closure.

Let us now turn to the epilogue of *The Tempest*.

Analysis: *The Tempest*, 5.1.319–338

Epilogue *spoken by Prospero*
Now my charms are all o'erthrown,
And what strength I have's mine own, 320
Which is most faint. Now, 'tis true,
I must be here confined by you,
Or sent to Naples. Let me not,
Since I have my dukedom got,
And pardoned the deceiver, dwell
In this bare island by your spell,
But release me from my bands
With the help of your good hands.
Gentle breath of yours my sails
Must fill, or else my project fails, 330
Which was to please. Now I want
Spirits to enforce, art to enchant,
And my ending is despair
Unless I be relieved by prayer,
Which pierces so that it assaults
Mercy itself, and frees all faults.
As you from crimes would pardoned be,
Let your indulgence set me free.

The epilogue follows *The Tempest's* final scene: many plays in performance had a prologue and epilogue, usually written specifically for a particular performance and place. Plays published with an epilogue or prologue are rare, because their transitory origins means many have been lost. Prospero's epilogue has been interpreted as Shakespeare's personal statement about the theatre and faith. However, through analysing the text and its meaning in conjunction with the play it ends, a deeper understanding of its meanings will emerge. We can then come to our own conclusions about its significance and resonances.

In the final scene all the characters converge at Prospero's cell, where, following mutual recognition and explanation, Alonso's desire to see his son again is granted as we watch Miranda and Ferdinand play chess. Prospero's rebuke to (and forgiveness of) his brother remains unanswered by Antonio. Caliban jettisons his infatuation with Stephano and Trinculo and promises to be 'wise hereafter'. Prospero frees Ariel and invites everyone back on to the boat: hoping to celebrate the wedding in Naples and his retirement in Milan. Most narrative threads are concluded: the two significant exceptions are Antonio and Caliban. Antonio's refusal to be included in reconciliatory forgiveness leaves his ambitions and discontent unanchored. Caliban is not invited back to Europe, and is implicitly left as king of the island.

The epilogue's opening ('now...') draws the audience into the ambience of the present and the space of the speaker on stage. The second word ('my') focuses on Prospero as character and on the actor who has played him: playing on the doubleness of his status as actor in the world and character in the play-world. Meta-theatrical self-consciousness characterises the whole play: from Prospero's watching over the initial tempest, through his manipulation of the tribulations of Alonso, the wooing of Ferdinand and Miranda, to the more conventionally dramatic marriage masque, the audience have both experienced the drama and been made to see stage action as physically directed, worked and produced. Shakespeare has also ensured that we have noticed how action can exceed Prospero's directorial control: Caliban's rebellion and its near success; Miranda carrying wood for Ferdinand and actively wooing him; Antonio's failure to be moved and repent. Meta-theatricality is used to create multiple points of view: we can be both involved and critical. Conversely, Prospero's character is demonstrated to be both over-controlling and only partly successful: he cannot dictate and direct all the final events. The humbled apology of these first few lines ('what strength I have's mine own / which is most faint', l.320) recognises this.

The jokey self-deprecation (' 'tis true / I must here be confined by you / Or sent to Naples' ll.321–2) conflates the actor's identity into that of the character and demands to be set free of it, spoken in a voice unlike Prospero's characteristic certainty. The audience and actor are always aware of this doubleness: Prospero wants to go to Naples, but the actor does not, and the final clapping will separate actor from character, enabling them to go their separate ways, one to Naples, one to Bankside. Prospero echoes his decision to abjure magic (5.1.57) and graciously places the idea of magic into the power of the audience ('dwell / In this bare island by *your* spell', ll.325–6). Magic is redefined here as the magic of the theatre, in which the audience is a key participant. This trope is continued throughout the next eight lines: the audience's breath as they shout or roar approval for the play will magically fill the sails of their ships as they set for Naples. Prospero's apparently mournful elegy for his magic ('Now I want / Spirits… / And my ending is despair / Unless I be relieved by prayer', ll.331–4) is often interpreted as Shakespeare's advocacy of spiritual retreat. However, this part of Prospero's direct address is to the audience on *their* powers ('let *your* indulgence', l.338). It is the breath of the audience (for blowing sails, praying, and roaring approval) which is essential to theatrical power: the power to approve and acknowledge an ending. The religious language of prayer and mercy places salvation in the audience's hands. In many ways this is a radical and liberating idea: the audience is the judge not only politically but spiritually as well.

Prospero's powers (political, philosophical, magical, spiritual) are dependent upon the contract of performance which writer, actor and audience share. This invocation of an artistic and social contract reflects back on the play. Prospero's political powers on the island intersect with his theatrical and magical ones: such as his theatrical powers are, so his political ones are equally subject to a social contract. When he returns to Milan Prospero cannot rule successfully as an absolute ruler: he has learned this on the island, a knowledge explicit in the parallel linking of powers of theatricality and rulership, and their mutual dependence on an engaged audience.

Prospero's final couplet ends with the word 'free', and, attuned to the intersection between theatrical and political meanings, this reverberates forwards through the theatre, and backwards through our interpretation of the play. Freedom and liberty were passionately argued about and fought for by Ariel, Ferdinand and Caliban. The play debates ideas about political responsibility, status, and the position of the individual, in which ideas of freedom are both implicit and explicit. At the most literal level, Prospero is merely asking the audience to release his actor's 'bands' (both costume and his work contract, l.327) that tie him to the present stage. The final word places 'freedom' (for the actor) in the audience's hands. But in the context of the epilogue's dialogue with the audience, Prospero and Shakespeare suggest it is up to the audience, the people, to give meaning to the word 'free', whether in the context of the play or any broader political debate initiated by the play.

The metre of these 20 lines is a four-stressed line, sometimes of seven syllables, sometimes eight, in rhyming couplets. Both rhythm and rhyme invoke a song's metre, demonstrated in Ariel's 'Where a bee sucks, there suck I', and 'Full fathom five thy father lies' (1.2.397), and those in the wedding masque. The rhythmic echo of the play's previous songs creates a slightly mournful retrospective sense of what is lost now the play is ending. The quick-step and song-like rhythm of the delivery ensure the words make their mark on us, an effect reinforced by the rhyming couplets. The rhymes are the words which stay in our minds, since they create links between lines and a forward-moving effect as we look forward to the next rhyme. The coupled rhymes here create an imagistic pattern: o'erthrown / own; true / you; not / got; dwell / spell; bands / hands; sails / fails; want / enchant; despair / prayer; assaults / faults; and be / free. Each rhyme in miniature covertly creates a paradoxical commentary, evoking the intersection of politics, audience, theatre and actors.

Let us now consider *Cymbeline*'s ending.

Analysis: *Cymbeline*, 5.4.436–486

SOOTHSAYER *reads [the tablet]* 'Whenas a lion's whelp shall,
to himself unknown, without seeking find, and be
embraced by a piece of tender air; and when from a
stately cedar shall be lopped branches, which being
dead many years, shall after revive, be jointed to the   440
old stock, and freshly grow, then shall Posthumus end
his miseries, Britain be fortunate and flourish in peace
and plenty.'
Thou, Leonatus, art the lion's whelp;
The fit and apt construction of thy name,   445

	Being *leo natus*, doth import so much. [*To Cymbeline*]	
	The piece of tender air thy virtuous daughter,	
	Which we call '*mollis aer*'; and '*mollis aer*'	
	We term it '*mulier*', [*to Posthumus*] which '*mulier*' I divine	
	Is this most constant wife, who even now,	450
	Answering the letter of the oracle,	
	Unknown to you, unsought, were clipped about	
	With this most tender air.	
CYMBELINE	This hath some seeming.	
SOOTHSAYER	The lofty cedar, royal Cymbeline,	
	Personates thee, and thy lopped branches point	455
	Thy two sons forth, who by Belarius stol'n,	
	For many years thought dead, are now revived,	
	To the majestic cedar joined, whose issue	
	Promises Britain peace and plenty.	
CYMBELINE	Well,	
	My peace we will begin; and Caius Lucius,	460
	Although the victor, we submit to Caesar	
	And to the Roman empire, promising	
	To pay our wonted tribute, from the which	
	We were dissuaded by our wicked queen,	
	Whom heavens in justice both on her and hers	465
	Have laid most heavy hand.	
SOOTHSAYER	The fingers of the powers above do tune	
	The harmony of this peace. The vision,	
	Which I made known to Lucius, ere the stroke	
	Of this yet scarce-cold battle, at this instant	470
	Is full accomplished. For the Roman eagle,	
	From south to west on wing soaring aloft,	
	Lessened herself, and in the beams o' th' sun	
	So vanished; which foreshowed our princely eagle,	
	Th'imperial Caesar, should again unite	475
	His favour with the radiant Cymbeline,	
	Which shines here in the west.	
CYMBELINE	Laud we the gods,	
	And let our crookèd smokes climb to their nostrils	
	From our blest altars. Publish we this peace	
	To all our subjects. Set we forward. Let	480

> A Roman and a British ensign wave
> Friendly together: so through Lud's town march,
> And in the temple of great Jupiter
> Our peace we'll ratify, seal it with feasts.
> Set on there. Never was a war did cease,   485
> Ere bloody hands were washed with such a peace.
>
> [*Flourish*] *Exeunt*

This finale promises a combination of revelation, recognition and conflict resolution in familial and political arenas. The final scene is long drawn-out, with different familial betrayals and abandonments resolved: Cymbeline has already been reunited with his daughter and his lost sons, and Posthumus with his lost wife Innogen. The stepmother's death is reported, and Cymbeline figures himself as birthgiver on his regaining of his children ('O what am I, / A mother to the birth of three?', ll.369–70). The emotional and psychological intensity of trauma lanced and cured by discovery. This is the final part of that resolution, a move towards explanation and political peace. Posthumus has asked for the prophecy to be read and explained. The prophecy's imagery successively uses metaphors of lions as monarchs, the tree as nobility, and horticultural breeding as generation. The soothsayer explicates the images' vehicle and tenor. Posthumus is the only one named and linked directly to the flourishing of Britain (not Cymbeline or his sons).

Cymbeline is not rocked or damaged by the trauma of past events: he takes charge of the negotiations and the emotions. His army has just defeated the Roman imperial army. Cymbeline's acquiescence to Rome despite the victory is a clever political decision: he blames Britain's rebellion on 'our wicked queen', whose machinations caused both the loss of his children and the descent into war. The wicked stepmother becomes the narrative motif for familial and political chaos, whilst a naturalised masculine royalty the symbol of continuity and peace. Maternal femininity is demonised and patriarchal masculinity associated with order and pragmatic nationalism. This closing symbolism is softened a little by Innogen's characterisation (although she remains silent): as the daughter of Cymbeline, and loyal wife of Posthumus, her position as one of the future dynastic rulers of Britain is secured.

The prophetic discourse creates an atmosphere of inevitability: the future is ordained by forces external to individuals. Providential order, linked to the plot resolution of royal reconciliation, fuses divinity, royalty and narrative resolution. This conservative political dynamic suggests order can only be established when royal and patriarchal rights are recognised. Cymbeline's final speech humbly echoes this political prognosis: 'Laud we the gods / And let our crooked smokes climb to their nostrils' (ll.476–7). Although pagan gods are invoked (explicitly Jupiter), a Jacobean audience might infer this to parallel James I's defence of his royal prerogative which made direct links between his rule, that of God's, and fathers in their households. Cymbeline's final word ('peace') echoes James I's political renowned reputation as an advocate of political peace with Spain and France, through treaties and his children's arranged marriages. The ending thus reinforces Jacobean political messages which argued that masculine patriarchal power analogously flowed from God, to monarch, to father.

Conclusions

1. Shakespeare's late plays all end in a conventional comic frame: the resolutions involve a marriage, reconciliations, and festivities. The personal and familial confusions, arguments and mistakes are resolved and explained.
2. However, these conventional comic closures are countered in two ways: first an additional scene of transformation (for example in *The Winter's Tale*), or an extra-dramatic commentary (the epilogue to *The Tempest* and *Pericles*); and second, some characters are excluded from the reconciliation. The social and personal sense of rebirth and renewal that conventional festive comedy brings is darkened and queried by the closures (as it is in the so-called 'problem comedies'). The acknowledged costs of generational conflict mute the celebration. Human nature and social and political systems are acknowledged as flawed. The endings admit individual and political change is only possible at a personal and political price, and that political idealism (in the form of marriage or national unity) is a

temporary icon of an impossible ideal. Pragmatic political realism is acknowledged in these darkened moments: the ideal union of Milan and Naples will be always overshadowed by the dark plotting of an Antonio and Sebastian.

3. The narrative emphasis is on maturity reconciled to youth, and new beginnings. This plays a riff on the conventional comic closure which reconciles youth to maturity: where young people rebel against older ways, people or conventions, and gradually woo the older to their new outlook (celebrated through marriage). In contrast these plays' resolutions emphasise how the younger generation are brought into the fold of the older generation: the narrative and emotional trajectory is backwards, a socially conservative model.

4. The endings' focus on new political worlds, as well as new familial ones, suggests questions of authority, individual greed for power, responsibility, and political autonomy can all be seriously debated via a tragic-comic framework.

5. Romance elements (magical endings) are used to generate happy endings: the unlikely meeting; the statue that comes alive; the parent or child that returns from the dead; the stolen child returned. However, the *deus ex machina* narrative device is self-consciously acknowledged as a choreographed ending. Meta-theatrical self-consciousness enables the audience a simultaneous response of redemptive inclusion *and* suspension of disbelief. This is crystallised in *The Winter's Tale*, and made concrete in the doubled language of Prospero's epilogue.

6. The *deus-ex-machina* effect in the finale is achieved without a literal *deus*: 'providence' is invoked as the divine force which has managed the magical narrative happy reconciliation. Providential belief structures narrative closures.

7. Each play includes an earlier false ending, when political and personal conflicts clash and produce disaster or death. These scenes act as turning points on the action: a terrible loss or trauma tears apart a family, an individual and a state, brought on by individual blindness or familial conflict. In Shakespeare's tragedies this moment would mark the irresolvable ending. In the late plays we watch what happens afterwards, moving on to different times and

a different ending. By including both tragic and comic closures, Shakespeare encompasses both death and rebirth as narrative and emotional experiences. By ordering it in this way (death and then rebirth) he suggests a Christian and spiritual subtext to the narrative journey.

8. Recognition (of a father for his daughter, a husband of his wife, a mother for her child) is linked to new beginnings, discoveries and understandings. By using both turning–point scenes and endings to pinpoint dramatic points of cognition and re-cognition Shakespeare reflects on such moments as psychologically and humanly defining. Recognition crystallises emotion, forces us to pause, think and ask questions. Shakespeare's sense of the semantics of 're-cognition' (a reknowing) is intertwined in the plot, asking us: what rescues us from tragedy? Fate, magic, children, mothers, fathers, magicians, God?

9. Self-conscious theatricality creates a meta-theatrical awareness about our theatrical experience. The unveiled statue in the gallery, the soothsayer's prophecy, and Prospero's final speech as he divests himself of his robes, all slow down time and crystallise the plays' thematic ideas. These moments acknowledge the fictionality of the dramatic world, enable magical spectacle, and engage the audience. However, the moments are simultaneously critical commentators on the action preceding the finale. Self-conscious theatricality introduces 'authorial' and 'actors' voices onto stage, creating a direct relationship between audience and fiction.

10. Women's voices are muted in the endings. However, in *Pericles* and *The Winter's Tale* mothers are given a visual centrality to the emotional and psychological resolution. In *The Winter's Tale*, the jealous demands of masculine uncertainty are closed off by the physical union of the supposed adulterers' children, and by the revivification of the dead wife. The text emphasises a female-to-female voice, as Hermione speaks only to Perdita. However, the Pygmalion motif echoes uncannily: as Leontes speaks again as authoritative father, husband and ruler, he sees the enlivened statue as his creation, speaking to his script. There is a radical discontinuity in the spoken perceptions of husband and wife.

Methods of Analysis

In these first chapters we have used both textual and theatrical modes of reading and analysing the plays. In particular we have:

1. thought about how the final moments are played out on stage and how this is integrated with character, language and plot;
2. explicitly considered how the endings may be conventionally comic, and how far they answer, or leave open, problems and conflicts raised in the play's action and plot: a methodological and an analytic approach (endings leaving questions or issues unresolved, or characters excluded, force the audience to think);
3. seen how a tragic-comic mode can enable debate about social and psychological issues: by focussing on moments of recognition and change the plays force us to think both about personal change and insight, and social and political change;
4. introduced further new terms (*deus ex machina, peripeteia, recognition*), and used these to explain structural narrative effects which have theatrical validity and emotional resonance.

Suggested Work

For a deeper and more sensitive analysis you should look at the whole scene and succession of scenes leading up to the finale. Map out the whole of the final act, using a table and a grid to show which characters appear and where, how individual scenes relate to each other, and any particular iconic moments and stage properties. Why are the endings so drawn out? Does the pace of the scene or act contrast with previous ones? Do you find a turning point within each end?

The Tempest

Why are Miranda and Ferdinand displayed as a visual icon to the on-stage audience? Why are they playing chess? Why do they not speak to the rest of the characters but only to each other? What do we think of Caliban's contrition? What happens to Caliban at the end of the play? What do we think of Antonio's silent response to Prospero's knowledge of their treachery? Why does he remain silent? When he does speak, what is significant about it, for him and the play?

How do different productions stage the endings: do they emphasise the inclusionary or exclusionary? Is the magic theatrically wondrous, or is it used tongue-in-cheek? The directorial perspective on an ending tells you how a director interprets character and narrative. We are beginning to see how a dramatist manipulates and inter-relates scenes, openings and endings, linguistic images and visual icons to create a complex narrative of moving pictures and words.

4
Fathers, Sons and Husbands

Family relationships, between parents and children, husbands and wives, and particularly fathers and daughters, are central to the plays' crises and resolutions. Fathers are the source of tragic potential, but also the fulcrum of the final reconciliation scenes. Each play shares a double focus on familial and political patriarchy, a perspective articulated by James I's political theory. Shakespeare's late plays typically feature fathers or husbands whose tyrannical or obsessive characters and actions result in tragic familial conflict, finally only averted through a combination of the passage of time and personal epiphany. How credible is the shift in characterisation from tyrant to kindly patriarch? How and why are the familial and political interlinked? Lets us begin with *Cymbeline*.

Analysis: *Cymbeline*, 1.1.110–54

INNOGEN	Nay, stay a little.	110
	Were you but riding forth to air yourself	
	Such parting were too petty. Look here, love,	
	This diamond was my mother's. Take it, heart,	
	[*She gives him a ring*]	
	But keep it till you woo another wife,	
	When Innogen is dead.	
POSTHUMUS	How, how? Another?	115
	You gentle gods, give me but this I have,	

	And cere up my embracements from a next	
	With bonds of death! Remain, remain thou here	
	[*He puts on the ring*]	
	While sense can keep it on; and sweetest, fairest,	
	As I my poor self did exchange for you,	120
	To your so infinite loss, so in our trifles	
	I still win of you. For my sake wear this.	
	[*He gives her a bracelet*]	
	It is a manacle of love; I'll place it	
	Upon this fairest prisoner.	
INNOGEN	O the gods!	
	When shall we see again?	

Enter Cymbeline and Lords

POSTHUMUS	Alack, the King!	125
CYMBELINE	Thou basest thing, avoid hence, from my sight!	
	If after this command thou freight the court	
	With thy unworthiness, thou diest. Away,	
	Thou'rt poison to my blood.	
POSTHUMUS	The gods protect you,	
	And bless the good remainders of the court!	130
	I am gone.	*Exit*
INNOGEN	There cannot be a pinch in death	
	More sharp than this is.	
CYMBELINE	O disloyal thing,	
	That shouldst repair my youth, thou heap'st	
	A year's age on me.	
INNOGEN	I beseech you, sir,	
	Harm not yourself with your vexation.	135
	I am senseless of your wrath; a touch more rare	
	Subdues all pangs, all fears.	
CYMBELINE	Past grace, obedience?	
INNOGEN	Past hope and in despair; that way, past grace.	
CYMBELINE	That mightst have had the sole son of my queen!	
INNOGEN	O blest that I might not! I chose an eagle,	140
	And did avoid a puttock.	
CYMBELINE	Thou took'st a beggar; wouldst have made my throne	
	A seat for baseness.	

INNOGEN	No, I rather added
	A lustre to it.
CYMBELINE	O thou vile one!
INNOGEN	Sir,
	It is your fault that I have loved Posthumus. 145
	You bred him as my playfellow, and he is
	A man worth any woman, overbuys me
	Almost the sum he pays.
CYMBELINE	What, art thou mad?
INNOGEN	Almost sir, heaven restore me! Would I were
	A neatherd's daughter, and my Leonatus 150
	Our neighbour shepherd's son!

Enter the Queen

CYMBELINE	Thou foolish thing.
	[*To the Queen*] They were again together; you have done
	Not after our command. Away with her,
	And pen her up. 154

This extract illustrates the fracturing of Cymbeline's political and familial world in a mere 40 lines, in three parts: the lovers' exchange; the conflict between father and daughter; and the final attack on the queen. This is an archetypal comic opening: two young people pledge their love in adverse circumstances, against the opposition of an authority figure. The audience is immediately drawn into the young lovers' world: Posthumus has been exiled but has not yet departed, so the situation is tense. Their solemn exchange of pledges through gifts is concretised through the prepositions ('look *here*', 'remain thou *here*', 'wear *this* ... / Upon *this* fairest prisoner'), showing the lovers placing rings and bracelets on each other's fingers and arms. Physical contact visually connects man and woman, but is literally torn apart as Cymbeline enters. Posthumus's curt despairing, 'Alack, the King!' (l.125), speaks his panic and a warning to Innogen. Cymbeline as foster-parent to Posthumus, father to Innogen and King of Britain, figures various forms of paternal power: a status congruent with James I who styled himself *parens patriae*, parent of the country.

Modern viewers see Cymbeline's angry response as irrational extremism. However, parental opposition to a child's choice of lover is common, and arranged marriages are successful in many cultures. Cymbeline feels betrayed both by his daughter and by the man he treated as a son. He denigrates Posthumus's social status ('thou basest thing', 'thy unworthiness', 'thou'rt poison to my blood' ll.126, 128, 129) to belittle him, suggesting his marriage to Innogen would taint the royal family's blood. His prejudice, linked with the dramatic convention of an old authority figure who blocks change, positions Cymbeline's racism as feudal and out-of-date. Posthumus's mien to Cymbeline remains respectful and fearful in their short exchange ('The gods protect you, / ... / I am gone', ll.129–31). Whatever autonomy he displays elsewhere in the play, here he is the obedient subject: his political loyalty supersedes his emotional and sexual desires.

Cymbeline's attack on Innogen begins more gently: 'O *disloyal* thing / That shouldst repair my youth, thou heapst / A year's age on me' (ll.132–3), but suggests deeper betrayals: 'Past grace, obedience?' (l.137). Within this short statement there are three key issues about the parent–child relationship, which resonate through both this extract and the whole play. First, the words 'disloyal' and 'obedience' imply both familial and political rebellion: Innogen's personal desires are contested by Cymbeline's ideology of the necessary intersection of the familial and political. As the daughter of the king, Innogen was socially and politically subject to public duties, including the provision of a stable political succession: personal choices are subordinate to public interest. Cymbeline wants her to marry Cloten (the new queen's son, l.139). How does, or can, a public figure have a private life or private desires? This problem can be metaphorically represented through the conventional comic plot-line when one of the young lovers also has wider public responsibilities conflicting with their private desires, and is doubled when the authority figure preventing the marriage also represents the political public world. Cymbeline's debate with Innogen makes his political objections explicit: 'thou tookst a beggar, wouldst have made my throne / A seat for baseness' (ll.142–3). Innogen's argument radically suggests that worth is more important than birth and status (ll.145–7 and 149–52), whilst Cymbeline's 'What, art thou mad?' (l.148) suggests they have completely different frames of reference. He asserts the absolute supremacy of the political status quo and the social hierarchy. Narrative trajectories tend to link us with young lovers, but the play's title asks us to focus on Cymbeline, maintaining a doubled perspective of rebelling child and angry parent.

The second resonating issue is that through suggesting Innogen's actions are against God ('past grace'), Cymbeline implies a child's obedience to both king and father and the social and political hierarchies of blood and status cohere with God's ordering of the world. The intersection of God, king and father implies patriarchal authority is natural and God-given. This particular political and gendered philosophy is one explicitly articulated by James I in his *The True Law of Free Monarchies* (published in 1598, and reissued on his ascent to the throne in 1603). The third issue is Cymbeline's belief that his children 'repair' his old age: a reverse nurturing. Children provide hope and continuity to old age, a sense that the future is promising. A parent's involvement in a child's marriage (to early modern sensibilities) was economically, politically and emotionally crucial: and even in the twenty-first century our children's future is central to our emotional and spiritual well-being. Children and their futures bring us a sense of hope: the loss of children makes us old. Here Cymbeline loses a natural daughter and an adopted son in one moment.

Cymbeline's attack on his wife ('thou foolish thing / ... You have done / Not after our command', ll.151–3), in the final part of this extract, balances and contrasts the loving exchange between Posthumus and Innogen. This reinforces both the opposition between generations, and Cymbeline's characterisation as irascible, authoritarian and patriarchal. Wife, daughter, stepson, adopted son are all expected to submit to his political will.

Language rhythms echo emotions. In the second part of the extract, they are quite irregular: several short lines of five beats, and a few with six beats. The patchy beat gives the encounter an emotional intensity, suggesting broken words, tears and anger. The most regular iambic pentameters are in the initial exchange between Posthumus and Innogen, giving their pledges solemnity and fluidity compared to the jumpiness of the angry exchanges. The dialogue that follows the king's entrance is very fast-moving: of fifteen speeches, only three commence at the beginning of a line, the first of which is Cymbeline's opening. Most speeches here are immediate and engaged responses to the previous one, as the rhythm of the line demands the actor completes the line begun by the previous speaker. Rhythm acts as an internal stage direction to the actor about fast-flowing and angry emotions: characters are so wound up they jump in on another's speech: rhythm punctuates the scene's emotional energies.

Let us now look at *The Winter's Tale*.

Analysis: *The Winter's Tale*, 1.2.152–209

LEONTES	Looking on the lines
	Of my boy's face, methoughts I did recoil
	Twenty-three years, and saw myself unbreeched,
	In my green velvet coat, my dagger muzzled 155
	Lest it should bite its master and so prove,
	As ornaments oft do, too dangerous.
	How like, methought, I then was to this kernel,
	This squash, this gentleman. Mine honest friend,
	Will you take eggs for money?
MAMILLIUS	No, my lord, I'll fight. 160
LEONTES	You will? Why, happy man be's dole! My brother,
	Are you so fond of your young prince as we
	Do seem to be of ours?
POLIXENES	If at home, sir,
	He's all my exercise, my mirth, my matter;
	Now my sworn friend and then mine enemy; 165
	My parasite, my soldier, statesman, all.
	He makes a July's day short as December,
	And with his varying childness cures in me
	Thoughts that would thick my blood.
LEONTES	So stands this squire
	Officed with me. We two will walk, my lord, 170
	And leave you to your graver steps. Hermione,
	How thou lov'st us, show in our brother's welcome;
	Let what is dear in Sicily be cheap—
	Next to thyself and my young rover, he's
	Apparent to my heart.

HERMIONE	If you would seek us,	175

HERMIONE We are yours i' th' garden—shall's attend you there?
LEONTES To your own bents dispose you: you'll be found
Be you beneath the sky. [*Aside*] I am angling now,
Though you perceive me not how I give line.
Go to, go to! 180
How she holds up the neb, the bill to him!
And arms her with the boldness of a wife
To her allowing husband!
Exeunt Polixenes and Hermione
Gone already!
Inch-thick, knee-deep, o'er head and ears a forked one!
[*To Mamillius*]
Go, play, boy, play—thy mother plays, and I 185
Play too, but so disgraced a part, whose issue
Will hiss me to my grave; contempt and clamour
Will be my knell. Go, play, boy, play. There have been,
Or I am much deceived, cuckolds ere now,
And many a man there is, even at this present, 190
Now, while I speak this, holds his wife by th' arm,
That little thinks she has been sluiced in's absence
And his pond fished by his next neighbour, by
Sir Smile, his neighbour—nay, there's comfort in't
Whiles other men have gates, and those gates opened, 195
As mine, against their will. Should all despair
That have revolted wives, the tenth of mankind
Would hang themselves. Physic for't there's none;
It is a bawdy planet, that will strike
Where 'tis predominant; and 'tis powerful, think it, 200
From east, west, north and south; be it concluded,
No barricado for a belly. Know't;
It will let in and out the enemy
With bag and baggage—many thousand on's
Have the disease, and feel't not. [*To Mamillius*] How now, boy?
205
MAMILLIUS I am like you, they say.
LEONTES   Why, that's some comfort.
What, Camillo there?
CAMILLO   Ay, my good lord.
LEONTES Go play, Mamillius; thou'rt an honest man.   *Exit Mamillius*

This is from the play's second scene, which begins in social and political harmony and ends in chaos. As Hermione departs for the garden with Polixenes, Leontes has his first opportunity to openly articulate his jealousy, albeit in his young son's presence. The extract falls into two halves: the first where Leontes, Hermione and Polixenes are debating courteously; and the second, once Hermione and Polixenes leave, where Leontes gives free verbal reign to his thoughts. Leontes and Polixenes, paralleled from the play's opening, continue to be so in their expressed emotions towards their sons. Both voice commonplace parental attitudes to children: Leontes sees his younger self in his child; Polixenes feels that children shorten our sense of time ('makes a July's day short as December', l.167) and make us forget age and public responsibilities ('thoughts that would thick my blood', l.169). Their dialogue is ostensibly celebratory of mutually indulgent and loving fatherhood. However, Leontes' vocabulary betrays his emotions: implying Mamillius is a mirror for his own youth, he uses the word 'recoil' (l.153), instead of 'recollect' or 'remember', a semantic swerve betraying both self-disgust and distaste for a son whose mother he suspects of sexual betrayal. Similarly, he sees his youthful self in Mamillius 'unbreeched', with 'dagger muzzled' (ll.154–5): but the semantic sexualised connotations imply his feared castration and disempowerment. In giving these linguistic slippages to Leontes, Shakespeare characterises the gap between Leontes' perceptions and emotions, and what Polixenes and Hermione see and hear.

Leontes only intermittently addresses Mamillius directly. The fake-jollity of his direct addresses ('Mine honest friend / Will you take eggs for money?', ll.158–9) implicitly asks if outward shows of innocence deceive? Leontes' dialogue, even to Mamillius, all carries this doubleness, making it both emotionally and dramatically compelling. Though we think his jealousy is unfounded and extreme, we are still repelled and fascinated by his descent into fanatical obsession.

Mamillius's presence on stage is dramatically crucial. Visually, it suggests a tangible innocence, evoked through his playful encounters with the women servants, and echoed in Hermione's visible pregnancy. Young children and families thread their way through the scene: Mamillius, Polixenes and Hermione all emphasise children as social and political health and wealth, and the retreat into the garden by Hermione and Polixenes reinforces a sense of pastoral innocence. However, to Leontes, Mamillius represents the political future of his kingdom. As he was once a boy, so Mamillius will one day be king: the authority of a political succession is authorised by a combination of political and sexual stability. If he cannot be sure that his children are his, if his wife is an adulterer, both his personal and political worlds fall apart. Mamillius's presence is therefore at once a promise and a threat.

Leontes' long speech (ll.177–205) acts as a soliloquy. This mode does not feel contrived, because Leontes oversteps the conventions of polite society: his terrible suspicions are so overwhelming he cannot help speaking. The shifts of address (from son to self) betray his disjointed mind and remind us he is failing as a father to listen to his child. The reiteration of 'go play, boy, play' (ll.185, 188, 209) acts as a constant reminder of Mamillius's desire to be with his father, and of Leontes' dismissal of him. Semantics dominate and betray Leontes' emotions. In dismissing Mamillius with a conventional 'go play', the literal meaning slips into pun as Leontes' language betrays his jealousy ('Thy mother plays and I / Play too' (ll.185–6). 'Play' could mean sexual sport, and Leontes' obsessions re-read all language and signs as sexualised. He self-consciously shifts the metaphor to his self-perceived theatricalised status in Hermione and Polixenes' 'play', where Hermione is active and he the passive victimised husband, played upon (a subtextual fourth connotation). Leontes describes his own actions using a game metaphor from fishing ('I am angling now / Though you perceive me not how I give line', ll.178–9), implying his own public behaviour and policy is theatrical. However, he does not apply this to Hermione's behaviour. Her warm welcome of Polixenes, an ambassadorial role taken on at Leontes' request, is read by Leontes only as representative of sexual betrayal ('arms... with the boldness of a wife', l.182).

Leontes uses a succession of metaphors, eliding into each other, to connote his suspicions about Hermione: metaphoric vehicles of fishing, property, politics, war and illness (ll.192–205). The first imagines other men 'that little think she has been sluiced in's absence / And his pond fished by his next neighbour' (ll.192–3). This metaphor's vehicle evokes the cleaning and fishing of a pond: the tenor posits women as ornamental lakes, owned and objectified by men, 'sluiced' echoing nastily, reflecting Leontes' disgust at Hermione's body and reducing sex to the exchange of bodily fluids. The second metaphor's tenor ('other men have gates, and those gates opened / As mine', l.195), implies wives are land and property owned by men. This elides into the third metaphor ('all despair that have *revolted* wives', ll.196–7), where sexual infidelity is equated to political rebellion. The tenor of the fourth metaphor ('No barricado for a belly; know't / It will let in and out the enemy / With bag and baggage', ll.202–4), viscerally and visually imagines women's bodies as territory to be fought over and as physically vulnerable to foreign invasion. The fifth metaphor, in the long sentence beginning 'Physic for't' (l.198) and ending on 'many thousands on's / Have the disease' (ll.204–5), is an extended medicinal vehicle, the tenor implying wives and sexuality are diseases to which all humanity is subject. The cumulative effects of these five intersecting metaphors is to represent women as objects owned by men, subject to male political power in a masculinised world where competition for women is the primary motivator of politics, war and games. Women are characterised as all body and impulse, completely sexualised: a harsh and unlovely world, and Leontes knows it, for it sends him mad. Fundamental to his despair is the age-old conundrum: how does a father know a child is his? A mother always knows, for a child develops inside her body: but a father can only have faith in a woman to 'really' know. This conundrum, this terror of not knowing or trusting, is a very human one: and in that sense the audience can sympathise with Leontes' pathological jealousy.

The speech's linguistic features enable the intensity of emotion and situation to be expressed and felt. The rhythm is relatively consistently iambic, with most lines having five stresses, although there are many with eleven syllables, requiring elision of syllables or lines in delivery. The shorter and longer lines are significantly points at which emotion overflows, tripping up the actor. The line 'Go to, go to!' contains only four monosyllables, and two beats, creating a rhythmic pause of three or so seconds, leaving time for the exit of Hermione and Polixenes, and for Leontes' choking emotion to be expressed physically. The longest line ('And many a man there is, even at this present', l.190) contains thirteen syllables and at least six stresses. It is the central point of Leontes' fears and justifications: are all men betrayed thus? Do all men feel this? The stresses are often irregular: 'inch-thick, knee-deep, o'er head and ears a forked one' (l.184) forms a strong and unusual beat of four stresses in the opening four syllables. This uneven and unique beat intensifies and pronounces his emotions.

The rapidity of shifts between metaphors is echoed by the large number of run-on lines: 18 of the 28 lines are run-on. This creates a rapidly forward-moving argument, the actor is always rushing into the next line and the next thought, tripping over himself to spill out his thoughts and feelings. Leontes launches himself into the main part of the speech with five exclamatory statements in the four lines after Hermione has left the stage (ll.180–84): ratcheting up his anger and emotion, voice and hysteria. Assonance and occasional alliteration further an atmosphere of obsession and jealousy. The sibilants of '*s*o di*s*graced a part, who*s*e i*ss*ue / Will hi*ss* me', suggest obsessive whispering. The plosives of '*C*ontempt and *c*lamour' spit out anger. Language through metaphor, rhythm, stresses and sounds enable the actor to find the emotions and actions to deliver a credible portrayal of nigh-crazed jealousy that both repels and attracts the audience: we watch and hear, we recognise and sympathise, but we don't want to be in that position ourselves.

Let us look very briefly at another scene in *The Winter's Tale* where paternal rather than husbandly control is figured.

Analysis: *The Winter's Tale*, 4.4.378–438

OLD SHEPHERD	Take hands, a bargain;	
	And friends unknown, you shall bear witness to 't—	
	I give my daughter to him, and will make	380
	Her portion equal his.	
FLORIZEL	O, that must be	
	I' th' virtue of your daughter. One being dead,	
	I shall have more than you can dream of yet;	
	Enough then for your wonder. But come on,	
	Contract us fore these witnesses.	
OLD SHEPHERD	Come, your hand,	385
	And daughter, yours.	

POLIXENES	Soft, swain, awhile, beseech you.
	Have you a father?
FLORIZEL	I have, but what of him?
POLIXENES	Knows he of this?
FLORIZEL	He neither does nor shall. 390
POLIXENES	Methinks a father
	Is at the nuptial of his son a guest
	That best becomes the table. Pray you once more,
	Is not your father grown incapable
	Of reasonable affairs? Is he not stupid 395
	With age and alt'ring rheums? Can he speak, hear?
	Know man from man? Dispute his own estate?
	Lies he not bedrid, and again does nothing
	But what he did being childish?
FLORIZEL	No, good sir;
	He has his health, and ampler strength indeed 400
	Than most have of his age.
POLIXENES	By my white beard,
	You offer him, if this be so, a wrong
	Something unfilial. Reason my son
	Should choose himself a wife, but as good reason
	The father, all whose joy is nothing else 405
	But fair posterity, should hold some counsel
	In such a business.
FLORIZEL	I yield all this,
	But for some other reasons, my grave sir,
	Which 'tis not fit you know, I not acquaint
	My father of this business.
POLIXENES	Let him know't. 410
FLORIZEL	He shall not.
POLIXENES	Prithee, let him.
FLORIZEL	No, he must not.
OLD SHEPHERD	Let him, my son; he shall not need to grieve
	At knowing of thy choice.
FLORIZEL	Come, come, he must not.
	Mark our contract.
POLIXENES	[*removing his disguise*] Mark your divorce, young sir,
	Whom son I dare not call—thou art too base 415
	To be acknowledged, thou a sceptre's heir,

	That thus affects a sheep-hook! Thou, old traitor,
	I am sorry that by hanging thee I can
	But shorten thy life one week. And thou, fresh piece
	Of excellent witchcraft, whom of force must know 420
	The royal fool thou cop'st with,—
OLD SHEPHERD	O, my heart!
POLIXENES	I'll have thy beauty scratched with briars and made
	More homely than thy state. [*To Florizel*] For thee, fond boy,
	If I may ever know thou dost but sigh
	That thou no more shalt see this knack—as never 425
	I mean thou shalt—we'll bar thee from succession,
	Not hold thee of our blood, no, not our kin,
	Far than Deucalion off. Mark thou my words;
	Follow us to the court. [*To the Old Shepherd*] Thou, churl, for this time,
	Though full of our displeasure, yet we free thee 430
	From the dead blow of it. [*To Perdita*] And you, enchantment,
	Worthy enough a herdsman— yea, him too
	That makes himself, but for our honour therein,
	Unworthy thee—if ever henceforth thou
	These rural latches to his entrance open, 435
	Or hoop his body more with thy embraces,
	I will devise a death as cruel for thee
	As thou art tender to't. *Exit*

Comedy often features young lovers resisting parental obstacles, and this encounter signals the play's turn to comic conflict. The audience know Polixenes is present, and that both son and father are in disguise, and present under false pretences. As with any disguised or hidden characters, this creates anticipatory tension, and gives a comic if clumsy irony to Polixenes' 'soft swain awhile, beseech you / Have you a father?' (ll.386–7) and 'Methinks a father / Is at the nuptials of his son a guest...' (ll.391–2). This heavy-handedness (pursued for 30 lines) increases the audience's sympathy for Florizel. Why does Polixenes need to test him with the succession of rhetorical questions? It raises dramatic tension and increases Florizel's anxiety. Whilst he is ignorant of the guest's identity, he wants the marriage finalised and his father kept in ignorance both for political reasons (the shepherds would reject him because he is a prince) and because his father would forbid it.

Polixenes' eight rhetorical questions in five lines (ll.394–99) imply by their nature that the listeners agree, and cumulatively suggest his points are reasonable: that a father should be involved in a son's marriage. He argues Florizel's resistance is 'unfilial' (l.403) and reasonably puts the case of patriarchal authority: 'reason my son / Should choose himself a wife, *but as good reason* / The father all whose joy is nothing else / But fair posterity, should hold some counsel / In such a business' (ll.403–7). Polixenes believes both child and father have some say in choosing a wife.

Florizel presents as a naive young man here: his stubborn reiterations ('He shall not' 'No he must not' 'come come he must not', ll.411–13), sound petulant. The flow of the happy pastoral celebration which was culminating in this marriage has suddenly been interrupted by this stranger insisting on parental authority and presence, and Florizel's impatience is also ours. However, Florizel's denials are also those of someone who knows they are in the wrong: and the suddenness of his peremptory 'mark our contract' suggests panicked desperation, a panic fulfilled in Polixenes' repetition of his grammatical imperative and completion of his line with the revelatory '*Mark* your divorce young sir' (l.414), as he whips off his disguise.

We meet Polixenes here as if for the first time: his repudiation of his son ('whom son I dare not call' l.415), like Leontes' of his wife, is for a perceived besmirching of his family. The feudal mind-set which demands that social equals marry and that the purity of aristocratic blood must not be tainted by 'churls' (l.429) is given full expression. His attack on Perdita, accusing her of witchcraft (as Leontes does Paulina) because she has attracted his son, exemplifies his attitude to women. The threatened and implied violence display a character very different from his previous appearances: 'I'll have thy beauty scratched with briars, and made / More homely than thy state' (ll.422–3). He ignores the shepherd's possible heart attack, and he threatens Perdita with execution if she ever embraces Florizel again. In the play's first half Leontes and Polixenes' behaved very differently: but Polixenes had not been personally tested. Once tested, he also aggressively and violently defends aristocratic and patriarchal concepts of family honour.

Florizel is speechless in the wake of Polixenes' words. He literally plays catch-up at each point to Polixenes' assertions, completing his father's lines. He says nothing at all once Polixenes has revealed himself: literally subservient and impotent in his father's physical presence. The debate between Florizel and Polixenes connotes an opposition between personal desire and familial duty and obedience, between autonomy and fatherly authority. The narrative conflict is initially avoided by Camillo's offer to take the young couple to Sicilia. But the play's ending magically resolves the conundrum by revealing that Perdita is royally born, Polixenes' objections disappear, and no social or political revolution is threatened.

Let us now turn to Ferdinand, Alonso and Prospero in *The Tempest*.

Analysis: *The Tempest*, 1.2.388–422

FERDINAND	Where should this music be?—I' th' air or th' earth?	
	It sounds no more; and sure, it waits upon	
	Some god o' th' island. Sitting on a bank,	390
	Weeping again the king my father's wreck,	
	This music crept by me upon the waters,	
	Allaying both their fury and my passion	
	With its sweet air. Thence I have followed it,	
	Or it hath drawn me rather; but 'tis gone.	395
	No, it begins again.	
ARIEL *(sings)*		
	Full fathom five thy father lies,	
	Of his bones are coral made;	
	Those are pearls that were his eyes;	
	Nothing of him that doth fade,	400
	But doth suffer a sea-change	
	Into something rich and strange.	
	Sea-nymphs hourly ring his knell	
	(Burden) Ding-dong	
	Hark! now I hear them, ding-dong, bell.	405
FERDINAND	The ditty does remember my drowned father.	
	This is no mortal business, nor no sound	
	That the earth owes—I hear it now above me.	
PROSPERO	*(To Miranda)* The fringed curtains of thine eye advance,	
	And say what thou seest yond.	

MIRANDA	What is't? —a spirit?	410

                Lord, how it looks about! Believe me, sir,
                It carries a brave form. But 'tis a spirit.
PROSPERO   No, wench, it eats and sleeps, and hath such senses
                As we have—such. This gallant which thou seest
                Was in the wreck; and but he's something stained   415
                With grief—that's beauty's canker—thou mightst call him
                A goodly person. He hath lost his fellows
                And strays about to find 'em.
MIRANDA   I might call him
                A thing divine, for nothing natural
                I ever saw so noble.
PROSPERO (*aside*)   It goes on, I see,   420
                As my soul prompts it. [*To Ariel*] Spirit, fine spirit! I'll free thee
                Within two days for this.

This extract illustrates the relationship of Ferdinand and Miranda to their fathers. We meet Ferdinand here for the first time, only moments before Miranda does. Ariel (seen by the audience but not by Ferdinand) leads him on stage with his song 'Come unto these yellow sands', and his first words respond to this song. Music surrounds him: Ariel's second song 'Full fathom five thy father lies' echoing through Ferdinand's emotions and senses as he meets Prospero and Miranda. The first two things we know about Ferdinand are his curiosity ('Where should this music be? – i'th' air? Or th' earth?' l.388) and his grief for his father ('weeping again the King my father's wrack' l.391). Despite his filial grief, the island and its magical music fascinate him. We discuss Ariel's song in detail in Chapter 9.

    The counter-tenor voice adds to the eerie experience Ferdinand describes ('its sweet air... hath drawn me', ll.394–5). The words sound strangely beautiful but their content is horrific to a young man who has just seen his father's ship sink. The detailed and gruesome imagining of what has happened to his body in the sea is given a gothic edge in the conversion of body parts into sea jewels. 'The rich and strange' (l.402) conversions suggest visually gorgeous images, yet are terrible points of grief for Ferdinand because they simultaneously emphasise his father's death. As he realises the disjunction between music and sense Ferdinand decides 'this is no mortal business' (l.407): his anger and grief unite. He does not voice his thoughts and feeling until he speaks to Miranda (after this extract), but many actors show him breaking down in grief, or angrily trying to find the source of the taunting song.

Dramatically this is very the point when Shakespeare shows us Prospero is deliberately controlling the action: Prospero and Miranda must be standing to the side of the stage (since they speak to Ferdinand in a moment). Prospero leads Miranda up to view Ferdinand from afar ('say what thou seest', ll.409–10) and we are made to see this is an arranged encounter. Paternal involvement in the sexual affairs of their children is literally played out here: Prospero engineered Ferdinand's grief, and now he engineers both Miranda's and Ferdinand's sight of each other. Miranda's naivety about other humans ('What is't—a spirit? / Lord how it looks about!', l.410) is comical: despite her education by her father she is a complete innocent. Miranda, like Caliban, has been brought up in isolation on an island a long way from 'civilisation'. Her father and a lack of society have kept her innocent: she is the only woman on the island and free of European constructions of femininity. Ferdinand's wondered response to her ('if you be maid or no? l.428) spells out her unique character and appearance, as well as Ferdinand's confusion about his island encounters. Prospero's comments ('It goes on, I see, / As my soul prompts it', ll.420–21), made as asides, remind us of his controlling involvement. The young people's apparently spontaneous love is simultaneously moving, comical and slightly tense, because of Miranda's naivety and Prospero's invisible oversight.

The dramatic juxtaposition of Ferdinand's grief with meeting Miranda allegorises the journey for a young man as he moves from home and parental influence into adulthood and marriage. By showing this as engineered by the woman's father, Shakespeare involves the audience in the journey. Ferdinand's grief and the music make us emotionally ready for a cathartic change. However, by using magic Shakespeare emphasises the controlling nature of this patriarchal engineering, asking questions about paternal controls and arranged marriage, which we shall consider further in the next chapter.

Let us now turn to Alonso.

Analysis: *The Tempest*, 2.1.100–133

GONZALO	Is not, sir, my doublet as fresh as the first day I	100
	wore it? I mean, in a sort.	
ANTONIO	That sort was well fished for.	
GONZALO	When I wore it at your daughter's marriage.	
ALONSO	You cram these words into mine ears against	
	The stomach of my sense. Would I had never	105
	Married my daughter there, for coming thence	
	My son is lost and, in my rate, she too,	
	Who is so far from Italy removed	
	I ne'er again shall see her. O thou mine heir	
	Of Naples and of Milan, what strange fish	110
	Hath made his meal on thee?	
FRANCISCO	Sir, he may live:	
	I saw him beat the surges under him,	
	And ride upon their backs; he trod the water,	
	Whose enmity he flung aside, and breasted	
	The surge most swoll'n that met him; his bold head	115
	'Bove the contentious waves he kept, and oared	
	Himself with his good arms in lusty stroke	
	To th' shore, that o'er his wave-worn basis bowed,	
	As stooping to relieve him: I not doubt	
	He came alive to land.	
ALONSO	No, no, he's gone.	120
SEBASTIAN	Sir, you may thank yourself for this great loss,	
	That would not bless our Europe with your daughter,	
	But rather lose her to an African,	
	Where she, at least, is banished from your eye,	
	Who hath cause to wet the grief on't.	125
ALONSO	Prithee, peace.	
SEBASTIAN	You were kneeled to and importuned otherwise	
	By all of us, and the fair soul herself	
	Weighed between loathness and obedience at	
	Which end o' th' beam should bow. We have lost your son,	
	I fear, for ever. Milan and Naples have	130
	More widows in them of this business' making	
	Than we bring men to comfort them.	

ALONSO	The fault's your own. So is the dear'st o' the loss.

Gonzalo's evocation of Alonso's daughter's marriage re-triggers Alonso's explosive anger and grief. He voices his terrible losses: a daughter to marriage, and a son to the sea. His articulation of grief ('O thou mine heir / Of Naples and of Milan, what strange fish / Hath made his meal on thee?', ll.109–11) is equally about his lack of an heir as about his son. After this burst of anger, his responses become monosyllabic ('No, no he's gone', 'Prithee peace', ll120, 125), completing lines which others feed to him.

Sebastian's gives us the back-story of Claribel's marriage: courtiers implored Alonso not to marry his daughter to an African (ll.122–3), and to find a European. Claribel 'weighed between loathness and obedience' (l.128), submitted to her father. Sebastian uses this arranged marriage, and the contentious debates it invoked, to blame Alonso for bad political management: he risked the future stability of his dukedom by sailing with both children, and marrying away his daughter. More broadly, the back-story evokes Prospero's own plans for an arranged marriage for his daughter. Here courtiers debate such decisions and indirectly express muted female resistance to such arrangements. It also suggests the broad geographical reach of the political alliances forged by Italian states: uniting Naples and North Africa through marriage suggests a global conception of hybridised identities through arranged (as well as other) marriages. This diverse and cosmopolitan political and cultural world is one in which the new world of the island is included.

Fatherhood is therefore defined both emotionally ('I ne'er again shall see her' l.109) and politically, a combination implying political responsibility and echoing the debates of *The Winter's Tale*. Let us now look at our final extract.

Analysis: *The Tempest*, 4.1.13–33

PROSPERO	Then, as my gift and thine own acquisition Worthily purchased, take my daughter. But If thou dost break her virgin-knot before	15

>   All sanctimonious ceremonies may
>   With full and holy rite be ministered,
>   No sweet aspersion shall the heavens let fall
>   To make this contract grow; but barren hate,
>   Sour-eyed disdain, and discord shall bestrew   20
>   The union of your bed with weeds so loathly
>   That you shall hate it both. Therefore take heed,
>   As Hymen's lamps shall light you.
> FERDINAND   As I hope
>   For quiet days, fair issue, and long life,
>   With such love as 'tis now, the murkiest den,   25
>   The most opportune place, the strong'st suggestion.
>   Our worser genius can, shall never melt
>   Mine honour into lust, to take away
>   The edge of that day's celebration
>   When I shall think or Phoebus' steeds are foundered, 30
>   Or Night kept chained below.
> PROSPERO   Fairly spoke.
>   Sit then and talk with her, she is thine own.
>   What, Ariel! My industrious servant, Ariel!

Prospero 'gifts' his daughter to Ferdinand, and once Ferdinand has promised to obey his strictures, puts on a lavish wedding masque. This speech exemplifies Prospero's paternalistic concerns and preoccupations: Miranda is not named, described instead as a 'gift' from Prospero and an 'acquisition' for Ferdinand (l.13). The trading of women between men, implicit in the discussion of Claribel's marriage, is here explicit. This contextualises Prospero's emphasis on virginity: if Miranda loses her virginity, she loses her value as a precious political trading gift, because of the possibility that she might be carrying another man's child. The succession to Naples and Milan must be genealogically pure. In a political patriarchal system which sees marriage as an essential tool of diplomacy and women as subordinate to men, an insistence on the control and surveillance of women's bodies is necessary. Whether all Shakespeare's audience accepted this premise is debateable: at certain points we are asked to observe the over-authoritarianism of absolute patriarchalism. However, the play's ending includes a visual approbation and mutual acceptance of the dynastic success of this arranged marriage in the chess-match (analysed in the next chapter): so the play's messages are ambivalent. Prospero's invokes divine approval of his words: if Ferdinand disobeys, 'the heavens' will 'let fall' 'barren hate' and 'discord' (ll.18–20). The assertion of a direct link between God, father and husband-to-be explicitly and implicitly illustrates James I's patriarchal pronouncements on divine right, and posit Prospero as an equivalent father, ruler and god-like magician.

Ferdinand accepts Prospero's assumptions: that Miranda is in his 'gift', that virginity and sexual abstinence are essential to legal and religious marriage, and that he needs to negotiate with Prospero to win her. The end of the conversation 'she is thine own' (l.32) shows this strategy works: decisions and order flow through the accepted hierarchy in patriarchal worlds from older to younger men. Ferdinand uses the conventional Renaissance opposition between physical lust and rational 'honour', linking lust to 'our worser genius' (physical desire and Satan), and opposes immediate material sensation and pleasure to 'quiet days, fair issue, and long life' (l.24). The classical imagery (imagining the sun as Phoebus and night as a chained god) positions Ferdinand as a learned Renaissance man, eloquent and conversant in classical philosophy. Although this betrothal happens on a remote island somewhere in the Atlantic Ocean, it is between an educated European, and a woman from a new world, whose language eschews such references. This figures masculinity alongside patriarchy as a civilised European discourse in opposition to woman as 'other'.

Conclusions

1. Shakespeare uses certain stock figures from comedy (for example, the 'old man' and 'the young lovers') as a starting point for the character examination of masculinity at different life stages. In both *The Winter's Tale* and *Cymbeline* conflict between these generational figures is used as starting points for serious conflict at different stages in the narrative arc, conflict which results in both tragedy and reconciliation. By using the conventional model, but complicating and extending it through making these conflicts

political and gendered as well as generational, Shakespeare deepens the model and directly raises questions about both politics and gender.
2. The fathers of Shakespeare's late plays are presented as variously flawed individuals, embedded in solipsistic worlds, whose solipsism is tested and changed by the play's action. In *The Winter's Tale* and *Cymbeline* in particular, irascible fathers cause political chaos: the audience recognise their folly, both through the perspectives of other characters and through language. Prospero is a milder version, explaining his own solipsism as a thing of the past in his back-story. Although the play demonstrates his over-controlling practices, to daughters, sons-in-law and fostersons, he does not experience the terrible consequences of paternal extremism faced by Leontes and Cymbeline. The narrative focus on reconciliation and resolution allows the fathers personal and political redemption: but have they learned to be different kinds of fathers? Alonso's grief for Ferdinand, albeit expressed as both a personal and political loss, posits paternity as attentive and loving. Is he one model for a less authoritarian father? This question is left open-ended as young lovers look forward to the creation of their own dynastic line.
3. Husbands are seen to share this ideological and personal failing (except for Ferdinand in *The Tempest*), either from the beginning or during the play's action (for example Posthumus in *Cymbeline*). The persistent representation of flawed masculinity (from fathers and husbands) is partly embedded in the discursive and structural systems of patriarchy. The late plays can be read as dramatic interventions in the Jacobean debate about gender and familial identity.
4. Shakespeare's focus on fathers and sons in the late plays is unusual, and the endings generally swerve away from an emphasis on the reconciliation between fathers and sons. In *The Winter's Tale*, Leontes loses his son altogether; in *Cymbeline*, although lost sons return, the focus of reconciliation is on Innogen and Posthumus; in *The Tempest*, father and son are parted by an accident of nature, and their final meeting is mediated both through Prospero and in watching a chess game, where Ferdinand may be a pawn in a political game won by Prospero and Miranda.

5. Lost sons feature in many of the late plays, figuring allegorically an inverted Oedipal narrative trajectory: fathers rediscover lost sons in the finales of *Cymbeline* and *The Tempest*. The experience of losing children, and sons in particular echoes a social and psychic anxiety about aging and a changing economic world.
6. Paternal control and authority are shown as flawed, obsessive and eventually ineffective in all of the plays. Negotiation, love, and nurturing kindness prove to be more successful modes of parenting.
7. Although paternal intervention in marriage arrangements is different in each play, the closures share common inclusive messages. In *Cymbeline* parental intervention is represented as personally and politically dangerous, but the young people's choice is approved by both the oracle and the play's resolution. In *The Winter's Tale*, the play's romance resolution reveals Florizel's lover to be of royal birth: the caste-protection of parental objections is validated by the narrative and political resolution but it coincides with the desires of young love.
8. Self-knowledge and an awakening appreciation of 'others' convert all the main male protagonists who are fathers or husbands. Romance resolutions enable fathers and husbands to re-greet their past losses and rectify mistakes, and suggest personal change is possible. Such conversion is achieved through semi-magic or providential intervention.

Methods of Analysis

This chapter has continued to build on our earlier approaches, including thinking about setting, rhythm, metre and metaphor to analyse characterisation. The following questions are essential tools.

1. Examine the characteristics of an individual speech: how do shifts in metre and meaning indicate changes of mood and emotion? What do metaphors indicate about character both from vehicle and tenor? Is the character in charge of his language or vice-versa?
2. Always contextualise: who is s/he speaking to? Should s/he be listening? Is their response irrational or rational? What is actually

being said? How are the audience positioned by the character? How should we respond? Does our view change at any point?
3. How does this particular speech develop or change our view about this character? How does any change integrate with the play's action and narrative arc? Is the speech linked to others through language or content?
4. What is the reasoning and point of view behind a speech: are we asked to share or critique it? What do other characters think?

Suggested Work

You need to do further work to deepen and strengthen your analysis: identify other key speeches and moments in the plays, as well as characters not considered here.

Pericles

1. Look at the relationships between Antiochus and his daughter in Scene 1: how and why does this twisted parental relationship predicate Pericles' exile and what resonance does it have over the whole play?
2. Look at Scenes 6, 7 and 8, the negotiations between Simonides, Thaisa's father and Pericles, his potential son-in-law. Comment on these, including language, scenic positioning and characterisation.

Cymbeline

1. Consider the reconciliation between father and sons preceding the play's finale: how is this represented and how does it resonate?
2. Look at the encounter between Posthumus and Giacomo in Rome: why is competitive masculinity so important? How are the audience positioned? How does it resonate in the play? Why are these two characters paralleled and what effect does that have? Look closely at the characterisation of Giacomo.
3. Consider Posthumus's scenes. How does the idea of a 'foster-son' function in the story?

The Winter's Tale

1. Leontes is the central character of the first three acts: we have only looked at one speech through the explicit prism of characterisation. Look at all the scenes in which he appears and think about how his solipsism is represented, and audience positioning. How do other characters respond? Do we ever sympathise? Where and how? Comment on his grief over Mamillius and Hermione in 3.2. Do we find his change of character in Act 5 credible? How is this achieved?
2. Look at the account of his meeting with Perdita in 5.2: how is he seen by the courtiers? What is the effect of this as reportage?
3. In 5.1 we meet him again after 16 years: has he changed? How do his politics look? What kind of parental and political point of viewpoint does he display towards Florizel? Has his language retained the dense emotional intensity of the earlier acts? If not why not? Does that return?

The Tempest

1. Look closely at all of Prospero's dialogues with Miranda: what kind of parenting does he display? How are we positioned?
2. Prospero is father and ruler to Miranda, Caliban, Ariel and Ferdinand: does he behave differently to each, and does this affect our reading of his character? Why does Shakespeare represent rulership over a woman, a servant, a slave and a man?
3. How does Prospero's magic intersect with his role as father? Why?
4. Look closely at Ferdinand: how does his language position him? Look at the wooing of Miranda: much of the language is conventional. Does Miranda's unique perspective change this?

5

Mothers, Daughters and Wives

Shakespeare's women are memorable and resonant. The female characters from the late plays perform dramatically central functions more actively than the women of earlier plays. This chapter shows that heroines are central to dramatic meaning and action, even when they are partially erased by the action, endings and content. The heroines' heroic nature, their confinement by male relationships, the few women characters present, and the persistent absence of mothers create a polarised gender system. We have already seen how patriarchal ideologies intersect with familial structures and actions, and how masculinity is variably represented. In this chapter we will analyse both how women are placed within that ideology, and how they react to and resist it. This first extract occurs in the midst of the sheep-shearing rural summer festival in Bohemia: Perdita is welcoming the stranger-guests to the festival.

Analysis: *The Winter's Tale*, 4.4.97–135

POLIXENES	Then make your garden rich in gillyvors,
	And do not call them bastards.
PERDITA	I'll not put
	The dibble in earth to set one slip of them; 100
	No more than, were I painted, I would wish
	This youth should say 'twere well and only therefore
	Desire to breed by me. Here's flowers for you,

	Hot lavender, mints, savoury, marjoram,	
	The marigold that goes to bed wi' th' sun,	105
	And with him rises weeping—these are flowers	
	Of middle summer, and I think they are given	
	To men of middle age. You're very welcome.	
CAMILLO	I should leave grazing, were I of your flock,	
	And only live by gazing.	
PERDITA	Out, alas!	110
	You'd be so lean, that blasts of January	
	Would blow you through and through. [*To Florizel*]	
	Now, my fair'st friend,	
	I would I had some flowers o' th' spring, that might	
	Become your time of day; [*to the Shepherdesses*] and yours,	
	and yours,	
	That wear upon your virgin branches yet	115
	Your maidenheads growing—O Proserpina,	
	For the flowers now that frighted thou let'st fall	
	From Dis's waggon! Daffodils,	
	That come before the swallow dares, and take	
	The winds of March with beauty; violets dim,	120
	But sweeter than the lids of Juno's eyes	
	Or Cytherea's breath; pale primroses,	
	That die unmarried, ere they can behold	
	Bright Phoebus in his strength—a malady	
	Most incident to maids; bold oxlips and	125
	The crown imperial; lilies of all kinds,	
	The flower-de-luce being one—O, these I lack,	
	To make you garlands of, and my sweet friend,	
	To strew him o'er and o'er.	
FLORIZEL	What, like a corpse?	
PERDITA	No, like a bank for love to lie and play on,	130
	Not like a corpse; or if, not to be buried,	
	But quick, and in mine arms. Come, take your flowers;	
	Methinks I play as I have seen them do	
	In Whitsun pastorals—sure this robe of mine	
	Does change my disposition.	135

This is Perdita's longest speech and dialogue in the act: her role elsewhere is that of submissive daughter to her shepherd father, or lover to

Florizel. This encounter is one of the key moments where her character expresses distinctive qualities. Her conversation enacts her function as the lead shepherdess in the festival: her father has asked her to welcome and entertain the guests. The audience know that the guests are aristocratic invaders, here to prevent the young lovers' union and restore the social hierarchy of a natural aristocracy. The disguised aristocrat at a rural festival was a convention of renaissance pastoral.

Perdita's conversation with the guests is both homely and jokily flattering: she talks about the flowers she holds, but with increasingly erudite knowledge as she proceeds. Her gifts of flowers for the guests and performers are chosen as appropriate to their dispositions: either medicinally or symbolically. She gives the flowers out as she speaks ('*here's* flowers for you', '*these* are flowers of middle summer', ll.103, 106): prepositions are stage directions built into her dialogue. The physical act of distributing the flowers gives her control of the stage space and action: moving round and delivering gifts with their attendant explanatory meanings. The stage properties implicit in this are both the diversity of the flowers and something in which to carry them (perhaps a basket). Visually this enhances her ownership of the role of pastoral shepherdess. Her wide knowledge of the different properties of plants is extraordinary: from their popular meanings to their medicinal qualities, from the range of herbs and flowers available in summer, to their poetic symbolisms. This knowledge is worn lightly and wittily.

Her first spirited speech ends a debate with Polixenes about the role of 'art' in the cultivation of flowers. Perdita arraigns his defence of hybrid flowers such as the gillyvor, arguing instead that 'nature' should breed flowers and plants, not human intervention. The irony of this debate is not lost on the audience: Polixenes defends hybrid agricultural breeding, using the word 'bastards' approvingly for such breeding, but rails against his son's potential breeding with a shepherdess. Perdita argues the opposite: that artistry is deceit, paralleling the falsity of using cosmetics to attract a young man 'to breed by me' (l.103). Thus she portrays herself as defined by the natural and her local environment. Yet such self-characterisation is belied by two linguistic features: first her explicit acknowledgement of the parallels between the breeding of flowers and a sexual union of herself and Florizel; and second her erudite classical references. Whilst the role and knowledge of medicine woman is fully congruent with her shepherdess status, her linguistic references to Dis and Proserpina set her apart from the average rural peasant. After gifting the flowers to Polixenes and Camillo (ll.103ff), she laments to Florizel and the shepherdesses the lack of spring flowers to give them as suitable to their age and station in life (they are unmarried). However, the extended lament is a direct address to Proserpina, the Greek goddess of spring, who was stolen from the world by Dis, the lord of the underworld, whilst gathering spring flowers (ll.116–18). Each flower in her list of spring flowers has a classical referent. Violets which are 'sweeter than the lids of Juno's eyes' (l.121) or 'Cytherea's breath' (l.122), invoking the queen of gods and Venus; primroses hide from 'bright Phoebus' (l.124), the classical god of the sun. The invocation of Greek classical gods has a number of dramatic effects, signalling in particular to the audience that events and characters are more sophisticated than they seem. Additionally, the language distances Perdita from a direct connection to the natural world she defends and represents, and allies her implicitly with the courtly visitors and Florizel. Metaphorically, her invocation of Proserpina introduces a classical narrative about a lost daughter, although Perdita does not refer to that part of the story. By invoking Proserpina, the daughter of Ceres the goddess of fertility, Perdita reinforces her role as fertile shepherdess: but she also unknowingly suggests parallels to her own mother Hermione who lost a daughter and her father Leontes as a king who stole a daughter. After Dis had stolen Proserpina, Ceres descended to the underworld to rescue her, and gained a compromise that Proserpina should live with Dis in the winter but be allowed to return to her mother in spring and summer. This particular 'tale of winter' was used in the renaissance to figure natural rural cycles of harvest and planting, maternal and female power, and Christian resurrection. Through Perdita it promises a dramatic resolution the audience can feel coming: Perdita as Proserpina tropes a reconciliatory resolution. However, the paternal figure continues to be demonised as Dis.

The shift from blushing shepherdess to classically educated young woman is facilitated through the flowers as stage props and imagery, and these in turn are the physical means through which she embraces and sexualises her emotions for Florizel. The sexuality implicit in her floral language overflows into her descriptions of the shepherdesses as chaste but blossoming ('upon your virgin branches yet / Your maidenheads growing', ll.115–16), and vice versa in her attribution of virgins' 'green' sickness to primroses. The erosion of natural and human boundaries in her metaphors posits pastoral identities as literally conversant with nature, and her frank sexuality and fertility. Her representation of Florizel ('my gentle friend / To strew him o'er and o'er', ll.128–9) imagines his body lying down covered in spring flowers. He jokingly comments 'what like a corse?' (l.129), evoking the imagined physical abandonment, her literal physical superiority, and the static beauty of the young male body. Perdita's response is sexually playful and frank: his body imagistically merging with a verdant grassy bank, corpse-like only because he will be buried in her arms. The female body becomes an active wooer and giver of love. For Perdita this is achieved with, expressed through and played out in, nature.

Perdita's characterisation is complex: beginning as she does as an innocent, naive, young daughter of a plain shepherd, it quickly becomes clear that she has wit, playful leadership skills, (theoretical) sexual knowledge, and hidden political skills. Her performance is to a triple audience: us, the courtiers from Bohemia, and the rest of the festival participants. By using natural and floral imagery and stage properties, she speaks to each of these audiences differently, presenting herself successively yet simultaneously as shepherdess, lost daughter, lover and queen-to-be. Her self-confident sexuality is overt yet modest, her generosity to guests does not erase her own ideas and character, and her inclusion of everyone on stage through her gifts and verbal play is the agent which establishes a communal festive feel to the gathering.

Let us turn to another scene in this play, where another female character displays similarly independent characteristics.

Analysis: *The Winter's Tale*, 5.1.34–75

PAULINA	There is none worthy,	
	Respecting her that's gone. Besides, the gods	35
	Will have fulfilled their secret purposes;	
	For has not the divine Apollo said,	
	Is't not the tenor of his oracle,	

	That King Leontes shall not have an heir	
	Till his lost child be found? Which that it shall	40
	Is all as monstrous to our human reason	
	As my Antigonus to break his grave	
	And come again to me, who, on my life,	
	Did perish with the infant. 'Tis your counsel	
	My lord should to the heavens be contrary,	45
	Oppose against their wills. [*To Leontes*] Care not for issue;	
	The crown will find an heir. Great Alexander	
	Left his to th' worthiest; so his successor	
	Was like to be the best.	
LEONTES	Good Paulina,	
	Who hast the memory of Hermione,	50
	I know, in honour, O, that ever I	
	Had squared me to thy counsel! Then, even now,	
	I might have looked upon my Queen's full eyes,	
	Have taken treasure from her lips—	
PAULINA	And left them	
	More rich for what they yielded.	
LEONTES	Thou speak'st truth.	55
	No more such wives, therefore no wife. One worse,	
	And better used, would make her sainted spirit	
	Again possess her corpse, and on this stage,	
	Where we offenders now, appear, soul-vexed,	
	And begin, 'Why to me?'	
PAULINA	Had she such power,	60
	She had just cause.	
LEONTES	She had, and would incense me	
	To murder her I married.	
PAULINA	I should so.	
	Were I the ghost that walked, I'd bid you mark	
	Her eye, and tell me for what dull part in't	
	You chose her; then I'd shriek, that even your ears	65
	Should rift to hear me, and the words that followed	
	Should be 'Remember mine.'	
LEONTES	Stars, stars,	
	And all eyes else dead coals—fear thou no wife;	
	I'll have no wife, Paulina.	
PAULINA	Will you swear	

	Never to marry but by my free leave?	70
LEONTES	Never, Paulina, so be blest my spirit.	
PAULINA	Then, good my lords, bear witness to his oath.	
CLEOMENES	You tempt him over-much.	
PAULINA	Unless another, As like Hermione as is her picture, Affront his eye.	75

At the beginning of the final act, Paulina is represented as the power behind the throne. A latecomer arriving at the play at this point would find it hard to identify the relationship between Leontes and Paulina. Her language is didactic from the start, rebuffing the courtiers who have suggested Leontes might marry again. Paulina assertively defends Hermione, as though no time has passed. How do the audience respond? Do we side with the male courtiers who are urging Leontes to marry? Paulina has just thrown out the accusation that Leontes 'killed' (l.15) Hermione, and berates him throughout. Each sentence of her opening speech is argued as if from a position of power. She reiterates the words of the oracle through a rhetorical question ('has not the divine Apollo said...' l.37), and reinforces the impossibility of its fulfilment oracle through emotive language ('as monstrous to our human reason', l.41) to belittle those who think the oracle's prophecy could come true, and finally implies the lords' counsel (to marry again) is against God's will. Having aggressively argued against marriage, Paulina turns to directly address Leontes in a more personal and soothing manner: 'care not for issue: / The crown will find an heir; great Alexander / left his to the worthiest' (ll.46–8). She is more nurturing towards Leontes than to the courtiers.

The rest of this extract is an intimate rapid and intense debate between Leontes and Paulina, each interjecting or completing the other's comments, beginning their speeches in mid-line. Paulina's responses to Leontes are interruptions, contradictions or refinements of what he has said, never allowing him to stand unchallenged (ll.54–5, 60–61). When he evokes Hermione's ghost urging him to murder any new wife, Paulina strangely translates herself into the position of his wife's ghost ('were I the ghost that walked, I'd bid you mark...', l.63). Her enthusiastic rendering of the ghost shrieks ('Remember mine', ll.65–7) has a manic quality. She is meant to be enacting a joke, and the exaggerated histrionics are produced to make the courtiers and Leontes laugh. But the oracle's ambiguous prophecy, and the reappearance of Perdita, have attuned the audience to Hermione's possible reappearance. Paulina's comic ghost distracts Leontes from thinking about marriage again, and unconsciously betrays her own emotions towards him as they have evolved over the past 16 years. Paulina's implicit denials (verbal and performed) about the impossibility of Hermione reappearing are the words of a rational plain-spoken woman, but are potentially misleading and increasingly desperate strategies to keep Leontes unmarried and beholden to her.

Paulina's spirited, outspoken and slightly manic, bossy control of Leontes can be discomfiting: in enacting Hermione's ghost she is ambiguously figured as queen. Her melancholic imagining of her lost husband ('my Antigonus to break his grave / And come again to me', ll.42–3) may suggest she is still grieving, or signal she is ready to move on. The language and action are deliberately left ambiguous. An audience will make up their mind through a performance, and may well change it again when the finale brings Hermione back and Leontes offers various lords to Paulina to marry. Different productions show Paulina variously feeling she has been usurped by Hermione, surprising herself with that feeling; or, having carefully worked for 16 years to enable Hermione to come back to the court, as a nurturing and strategic operator. Her apparent unevenness here may merely be an 'act' to ensure Leontes remains single until Hermione can return. The dialogue and language support each of these interpretations, and actors and directors will decide depending on the directorial and production values of a particular performance.

Let us now look at two extracts where Miranda speaks in *The Tempest*.

Analysis: *The Tempest*, 3.1.48–91

MIRANDA   I do not know
            One of my sex, no woman's face remember,
            Save from my glass, mine own; nor have I seen   50
            More that I may call men than you, good friend,

	And my dear father. How features are abroad	
	I am skilless of; but, by my modesty,	
	The jewel in my dower, I would not wish	
	Any companion in the world but you;	55
	Nor can imagination form a shape,	
	Besides yourself to like of. But I prattle	
	Something too wildly, and my father's precepts	
	I therein do forget.	
FERDINAND	I am, in my condition,	
	A prince, Miranda; I do think, a king—	60
	I would, not so!—and would no more endure	
	This wooden slavery than to suffer	
	The flesh-fly blow my mouth. Hear my soul speak:	
	The very instant that I saw you did	
	My heart fly to your service, there resides,	65
	To make me slave to it, and for your sake	
	Am I this patient log-man.	
MIRANDA	Do you love me?	
FERDINAND	O heaven, O earth, bear witness to this sound,	
	And crown what I profess with kind event	
	If I speak true; if hollowly, invert	70
	What best is boded me to mischief: I,	
	Beyond all limit of what else i' th' world	
	Do love, prize, honour you.	
MIRANDA	I am a fool	
	To weep at what I am glad of.	
PROSPERO [aside]	Fair encounter	
	Of two most rare affections! Heavens rain grace	75
	On that which breeds between 'em!	
FERDINAND	Wherefore weep you?	
MIRANDA	At mine unworthiness, that dare not offer	
	What I desire to give, and much less take	
	What I shall die to want. But this is trifling,	
	And all the more it seeks to hide itself,	80
	The bigger bulk it shows. Hence, bashful cunning,	
	And prompt me, plain and holy innocence!	
	I am your wife if you will marry me;	
	If not, I'll die your maid. To be your fellow	
	You may deny me, but I'll be your servant	85

		Whether you will or no.
FERDINAND		My mistress, dearest,
		And I thus humble ever.

[*He kneels*]

MIRANDA	My husband, then?	
FERDINAND		Ay, with a heart as willing
	As bondage e'er of freedom. Here's my hand.	
MIRANDA	And mine, with my heart in't. And now farewell	90
	Till half an hour hence.	
FERDINAND		A thousand-thousand!

Exeunt [*Ferdinand and Miranda separately*]

This scene occurs roughly at the mid-point of the play: Ferdinand is alone on stage stacking logs, and Miranda comes to suggest he rests, since she believes her father is at study. During the conversation she presents as a fresh and innocent young woman: eagerly and frankly speaking to Ferdinand, but rebuking herself after she has told him her name ('O my father I have broke your hest to say so', ll.36–7). The conflict between her father's commands and her own desires is played through her words, which seem to flow without the intervention of any internal censoring device. All Miranda's words have this freshness, and present her as both innocent and uneducated in European social conventions. This linguistic freshness is explained in her description of isolation: 'I do not know / One of my sex, no woman's face remember, / Save from the glass mine own' (ll.48–50). Miranda's identity as a woman has only been forged by herself and her father (whom she mentions two lines later). Her childhood distinguishes Miranda as both of and not-of Europe, and the absence of a mother but presence of a God-like father mimics the creation of Eve. Prospero's presence throughout the conversation as he watches from above remains disturbing. It reminds us of his patriarchal influence over Miranda: what seems to be fresh, innocent desire is partly tainted by the sense that he might be controlling the action. To what extent do the words and character of Miranda here exceed Prospero's control and surveillance? To what extent does she discover and display an autonomous desire and identity?

Although describing herself as untutored in feminine arts, Miranda denotes a conventional female virtue ('my modesty, the jewel in my dower' ll.53–4), implying her father has taught her conventional codes of female behaviour. Tutored and untutored identities are equally present in her 'But I prattle / Something too wildly and my father's precepts / I therein do forget' (ll.57–9). In other characters these words would be an aside as internal thoughts, or conveyed through more oblique language. Miranda's speeches contain both direct addresses and commentaries to herself spoken alike out loud to the addressee. This mode of address in which all information and thoughts are delivered sequentially and spontaneously is typical of Miranda.

In the second long speech, the conflict between her father's precepts and her personal and sexual desires are expressed through physicality and language. Ferdinand's 'Wherefore weep you?' (l.76) acts as internal stage direction, denoting that Miranda is overwhelmed with emotion. Miranda voices the conflicting pressures via paradoxes: 'my unworthiness that dare not offer / What I desire to give' (ll.77–8) and 'much less take / What I shall die to want' (ll.78–9). These (in both form and content) show she has internalised some European constraints on female expression and yet speaks out. This typifies Miranda's character: she acknowledges the constraints on her, but decides, nonetheless, to voice her own feelings and desires. This makes her seem naive and honest, and provides young modern audiences with a sympathetic role model of a Renaissance woman who fights against early-modern gendered prejudices. Her invocation to herself ('Hence, bashful cunning, / And prompt me, plain and holy innocence!' ll.81–2) celebrates plainness as a positively chosen quality not merely natural to her situation and education. She associates her plain speech with 'holy innocence', confirming a link between language and character. Her subsequent 'I am your wife if you will marry me' (l.83) denies the trappings of older models of appropriate feminine conduct (bashful cunning, unworthiness), speaks her own desires and directs the action. Miranda's dedication of herself to Ferdinand is complete: if not a wife, then a maid; if not a fellow equal, then a servant. She, not her father, gives herself away. Ferdinand's mirrored acceptance of 'bondage' echoes her language of marriage as mutual service: there is no hierarchy of husband–wife.

Her frank and direct questions to Ferdinand are characteristic of her innocence and of the absence of a conventional female education: her modesty is important, but this does not mean she should not speak or ask questions. It is Miranda who asks questions ('Do you love me?' and 'My husband then?' ll.67, 88). This keeps the balance of power in the scene in her hands: Ferdinand is physically subordinate since he is enslaved by Prospero, engaged in unaccustomed labour hauling wood, a physical subjection echoed in him kneeling ('And I thus humble ever', l.87). This line is the one short line (only seven syllables), leaving a silence of three or four syllables for appropriate stage action: perhaps she raises Ferdinand, perhaps they embrace, or she takes his hands. The short line leaves performance time and space for physical expressions which are a part of Miranda's frank nature.

Let us now move on to the second example of Miranda's characterisation.

Analysis: *The Tempest*, 5.1.165–184

PROSPERO	Welcome, sir;	165
	This cell's my court. Here have I few attendants,	
	And subjects none abroad. Pray you look in.	
	My dukedom since you have given me again,	
	I will requite you with as good a thing,	
	At least bring forth a wonder to content ye	170
	As much as me my dukedom.	
	Here Prospero discovers Ferdinand and Miranda	
	playing at chess	
MIRANDA	Sweet lord, you play me false.	
FERDINAND	No, my dearest love,	
	I would not for the world.	
MIRANDA	Yes, for a score of kingdoms you should wrangle,	
	And I would call it fair play.	
ALONSO	If this prove	175
	A vision of the island, one dear son	
	Shall I twice lose.	
SEBASTIAN	A most high miracle!	
FERDINAND [*coming forward*]	Though the seas threaten, they are merciful.	

	I have cursed them without cause.	
	[He kneels before Alonso]	
ALONSO	Now all the blessings	
	Of a glad father compass thee about!	180
	Arise, and say how thou cam'st here.	
	[Ferdinand rises]	
MIRANDA	O wonder!	
	How many goodly creatures are there here!	
	How beauteous mankind is! O brave new world	
	That has such people in't!	
PROSPERO	'Tis new to thee.	184

Prospero has engineered the converging of the shipwrecked aristocrats and crew to his cell, and welcomed them back to comfort, food and the possibility of passage home to Europe. Gonzalo and Alonso are reconciled to him, although Antonio and Sebastian are not. Prospero narrates his past experiences and claims he has lost his daughter in the late tempest, prompting Alonso's expressed desire for a marriage between their lost children. Prospero's visual disclosure of the couple playing chess acts as a dramatic revelatory full-stop to Alonso's imagined desires, and a concluding image of Prospero's sought-for political union between Naples and Milan.

The image of the couple at the back of the stage playing chess on opposite sides of a table visually opposes man and woman, Naples and Milan, white and black. The game of chess invokes strategy, political intrigue, action, and implicit war: and yet the couple playing it have hitherto been represented to us as isolated from such a world, and very much in love. How does this new (and final) image of them affect our reading of Miranda in particular? It very obviously places her within the European political frame from which she has hitherto been exiled: it also invokes allegorical parallels between chess pieces and dramatic characters. Do Miranda and Ferdinand each represent one hostile army facing another? Or are they pawns subject to their fathers' political needs and desires? Various productions have used the visual and political symbolism to suggest these interpretations: and both are equally valid.

Is there anything in the short dialogue here which aids an answer? Miranda's flirtatious half-line 'my sweet Lord you play me false', is completed by Ferdinand's denial, and establishes the chess game as an erotic encounter. Miranda's second response ('for a score of kingdoms you should wrangle / And call it fair play', ll.174–5) transforms the erotic into the political, showing her consciousness of the political nature of their marriage and the political actions required of public figures. She implies they both should 'wrangle' for kingdoms, and that whatever political 'wrangling' Ferdinand performed, she would approve. This pragmatic political sensibility is far removed from her earlier innocent naivety. Has marriage matured her sexual, political and public understanding of her future and current role? Some of her original innocence recurs here when she gazes on Alonso with the same wonder with which she originally greeted Ferdinand. The sequence of cumulative exclamatory statements exposes the enthusiastic young girl beneath the flirtatious but politically acute young woman, reminding us that Miranda can be both of the new and old world, both outspoken and astonished, and acquiescent in the old world's political and marital arrangements. When she exclaims, 'O wonder! / How many goodly creatures are there here / How beauteous mankind is! O brave new world / That has such people in't' (ll.181–4), by inverting Europeans as her 'new world' she makes them anew in her own image. This radical re-viewing places a woman as an equal partner with her husband in erotic encounters, political machinations and the philosophical re-visioning of the relationship between old and new worlds. Miranda's characterisation, dramatic function and active role in the narrative position her as a new type of woman: active, vociferous, educated, outspoken, and confident. Although she here implies partial submission to her husband (she will call anything he does politically fair play), she has played a dominant and active part in their courtship and marriage, and in approving political machinations places herself firmly within the discourse and practice of public life.

Let us now move on to briefly consider our last extract from *Pericles*.

Analysis: *Pericles*, Scene 19 ll.47–150

[Enter Pander with Marina]

BAWD   Here comes that which grows to the stalk, never plucked yet, I can assure you. Is she not a fair creature?

LYSIMACHUS	Faith, she would serve after a long voyage at sea. Well, there's for you, leave us.	50
	[He pays the Bawd]	
BAWD	I beseech your honour, give me leave: a word, and I'll have done presently.	
LYSIMACHUS	I beseech you, do.	
BAWD	*[aside to Marina]* First, I would have you note, this is an honourable man.	55
MARINA	I desire to find him so, that I may honourably know him.	
BAWD	Next, he's the governor of this country, and a man whom I am bound to.	
MARINA	If he govern the country you are bound to him indeed, but how honourable he is in that, I know not.	60
BAWD	Pray you, without any more virginal fencing, will you use him kindly? He will line your apron with gold.	
MARINA	What he will do graciously I will thankfully receive.	65
LYSIMACHUS	*[to Bawd]* Ha' you done?	
BAWD	My lord, she's not paced yet. You must take some pains to work her to your manège. *[To Boult and Pander]* Come, we will leave his honour and hers together. Go thy ways. *[Exeunt Bawd, Pander, and Boult]*	70
LYSIMACHUS	Now pretty one, how long have you been at this trade?	
MARINA	What trade, sir?	
LYSIMACHUS	Why, I cannot name it but I shall offend.	
MARINA	I cannot be offended with my trade, please you to name it.	75
LYSIMACHUS	How long have you been of this profession?	
MARINA	E'er since I can remember.	
LYSIMACHUS	Did you go to 't so young? Were you a gamester at five, or at seven?	80
MARINA	Earlier too, sir, if now I be one.	
LYSIMACHUS	Why, the house you dwell in proclaims you to be a creature of sale.	
MARINA	Do you know this house to be a place of such resort, and will come into it? I hear say you're of honourable parts, and are the governor of this place.	85
LYSIMACHUS	Why, hath your principal made known unto	

	you who I am?	
MARINA	Who is my principal?	
LYSIMACHUS	Why, your herb-woman, she that sets seeds	90

and roots of shame and iniquity.
   [*Marina weeps*]
O, you've heard something of my power, and so
Stand off aloof for more serious wooing.
But pretty one, I do protest to thee
I am the governor, whose authority   95
Can wink at blemishes, or on faults look friendly,
Or my displeasure punish at my pleasure,
From which displeasure all thy beauty shall
Not privilege thee, nor my affection
Which hath drawn me to this place abate,   100
If thou with further lingering withstand me.
Come, bring me to some private place. Come, come.

MARINA My Lord, I entreat you but to hear me.
If as you say you are the governor,
Let not authority which teaches you   105
To govern others be the means
To make you misgovern much yourself.
If you were born to honour show it now;
If put upon you, make the judgment good
That thought you worthy of it.

LYSIMACHUS   How's this?   110
How's this? Some more, be sage.

MARINA   What reason's in
Your justice, who hath power over all,
To undo any? If you take from me
Mine honour, you are like him that makes
A gap into forbidden ground, whom after   115
Too many enter, and you are guilty
Of all their evils. My life is yet unspotted,
My chastity unstainèd even in thought.
Then if your violence deface this building,
The workmanship of heaven, made up for good,   120
And not for exercise of sin's intemperance,
You kill your honour, abuse your justice,
And impoverish me.

LYSIMACHUS	Why this house	
	Wherein thou liv'st is a receptacle	
	Of all men's sins, and nurse of wickedness.	125
	How canst thou then be otherwise than naught	
	That liv'st in it?	
MARINA	My yet good lord,	
	IF there be fire before me, must I fly	
	There straight and burn myself? Suppose this house—	
	Which too too many feel such houses are—	130
	Should be the doctor's patrimony and	
	The surgeon's feeding, follows it that I	
	Must needs infect myself to give them maintenance?	
	O my good lord, kill me but not deflower me,	
	Punish me how you please but spare my chastity,	135
	And since 'tis all the dowry the gods have given	
	And men have left me, do not take it from me.	
	Make me your servant, I willingly obey you,	
	Make me your bondmaid, I'll account it freedom.	
	Let me be the worst that is called vile;	140
	So I may still live honest, I am content.	
	Or if you think't too blest a happiness	
	To have me stay so, let me even now, [*she kneels*]	
	Now in this minute die, and I'll account	
	My death more happy far than was my birth.	145
LYSIMACHUS	[*lifting her up*]	
	Now surely this is virtue's image, nay,	
	Virtue herself sent down from heaven a while	
	To reign on earth and teach us what we should be!—	
	I did not think thou couldst have spoke so well;	
	Ne'er dreamt thou couldst.	150

The situation and setting resonates with the audience as a moment where the play could veer again into tragedy: Marina has been captured and sold into sexual slavery, and urged into a sexual meeting with the brothel's chief client and the governor of the city, Lysimachus. This extract is the presentation of Marina as virginal booty to Lysimachus, and falls into three parts: the first where the Bawd and the men talk of and about Marina (ll.46–70), the second where Lysimachus engages Marina in the foreplay of small talk (ll.70–102); and the final shift where Marina's rhetorical arguments force Lysimachus to see the error of his ways. In the first, the Bawd literally refuses to understand Marina's words, calling her questioning of meanings 'virginal fencing' (l.60). Semantics is at issue throughout their exchange: where the Bawd uses the term 'honourable' to describe Lysimachus, Marina does too, but the Bawd used 'honourable' to connote high status, whereas Marina implies it is a benchmark of virtue. The Bawd uses the term 'kindly' to suggest Marina should submit sexually, Marina's response ('what he will do *graciously* I will thankfully receive' l.63) deliberately misconstrues the Bawd's 'kind' (in her adverb 'graciously') to connote Lysimachus's status and moral behaviour. Marina's responses are therefore both witty and assertive: even if she has no physical power to resist the Bawd's coercion or Lysimachus's sexual advances, her language acts as a counterpoint and moral anchor against them.

Marina's wit and rhetorical facility are equally powerful in the first part of her debate with Lysimachus: each exchange is punctured by linguistic quibbling. Where Lysimachus engages in the pre-date dialogue of 'do you come here often?' type, Marina's ambivalent answers puncture the evasive nature of his semantics. Through direct questions she tries to force him to expose his equivocation and refusal to name his sin. Her 'what trade, Sir?' (l.73), and 'Who is my principal?' (l.89) have a tripartite effect: they perform her innocence; expose his prevarication and refusal to use plain language; and try to force Lysimachus to defend himself or acknowledge his actions. She uses rhetorical prevarication self-consciously: to his 'were you a gamester at five, or at seven?' she responds 'earlier too... if now I be one' (l.81). When he insists that she must know what kind of a house she is working in, she turns this knowledge against him, because he knowingly 'will come into't' (l.85). Marina's doubled language shows that her 'innocence' is not about what sex is or what men do when they visit brothels, but about her moral integrity: she has not bought and sold another human being, nor allowed herself to be bought and sold.

Lysimachus's initial response to her questioning and parrying techniques is to read her sophistication as an attempt to manipulate more money or status from him (you 'stand off aloof for more serious wooing', l.93), and this makes him roughen his language ('come, come', l.102). This roughness predicates Marina's much more forceful and direct language: moving from the linguistic parrying to fluent and extended argument. Throughout that argument she remains respectful of his status ('My lord' and 'My yet good lord', ll.103, 127), even though she uses imperatives ('*Let* not authority which teaches you...', l.105) to one of higher status. Marina's immoveable insistence on reminding him about concepts of honour (whether 'born' to it or 'put upon' him, l.97) proves she refuses to give up the intellectual battle when he is physically pressurising her to have sex.

She uses sophisticated rhetorical techniques: hypotheses ('if you take from me mine honour...', ll.113 14–; 'if there be fire before me', l.128; 'suppose...'); metaphors (body as forbidden territory, or heavenly building, ll.115, 119, 129); and sermon-like language ('exercise of sin's intemperance', l.121). Her final self-abasement (she will be his bondmaiden but not his sexual slave) comes as she fears her arguments have failed, reinforced through her physical kneeling. Lysimachus's conversion was prompted by her combined appearance, language and physical supplication. His 'I did not think thou couldst have spoke so well' (l.149) emphasises Marina's eloquence as central in identifying both her virtue and her status: rhetorical facility is a marker for female virtue in these late plays.

Conclusions

1. Shakespeare's interest in active female characters is evident in the focus on the vulnerability of women at different stages of their lives to the authority and demands of an explicitly patriarchal culture. A pregnant mother, an abandoned daughter, a lone young woman, a woman sold into sexual slavery, a middle-aged woman negotiating friendship: all are defined in relation to masculine culture, and visibly and narrationally trapped by male power.
2. The dramatic situations each woman character finds herself in relate to key moments in the early modern woman's life cycle: birth, first sexual experience, marriage, childbirth, and old age. Each of these key moments coincide with a dramatic narrative turn in the late plays, which examine early-modern women's experiences

through narrative and generic modelling. However, by using the play's crisis point to be *about* these moments, Shakespeare makes drama out of the domestic, and shows that these moments have resonance in political, social and sexual worlds. By showing that the victimisation of women because of their sex leads to political and social crisis, Shakespeare dramaturgically suggests a radical re-visioning of the role of women in social and political drama.

3. Female characters remain steadfast and their views and reputation are legitimated by the plays' closure. Although *The Tempest*, includes only one woman, and its resolution is predominantly that engineered by Prospero, Miranda's agency is both autonomous from but coincident with her father's. Rhetorical sophistication, a sense of audience, and a personal individualism marks these female characters.

4. The staging of female characters in many different scenes frequently shows men watching women and commenting on how they do and/or should behave. Although women are given autonomy and enact plot changes, they are always public objects. This dynamic is particularly evident in *The Tempest*, where we literally see woman as subject to dominant masculine surveillance in the form of Prospero as father, monarch and magus.

5. Comic reconciliation and festive celebration are allied to reversals of gender norms: an unusually radical association. Reconciliation is through the female line: engineered by Paulina in *The Winter's Tale*, and the return of two women believed dead; through the marriage of Miranda and Ferdinand in *The Tempest*; through Marina's recovery and reconciliation with her father in *Pericles*; and Innogen's restoration in *Cymbeline*.

6. Chaste marriage is symbolically linked to familial reconciliation, and thereby metonymically to social and political stability: a potentially more conservative reading than the previous one. Chastity is tested and 'proved' in all the plays: most radically in *The Winter's Tale* and *Cymbeline* through a husband's jealous extremism, but asserted in the characters of all the virginal young heroines whose marriages predicate future stability. Theme and narrative trajectory coincide in validating chastity as an essential personal and political good.

7. Characterisation is created through dialogue, staging, character juxtaposition and linguistic register, as much as through individual monologues. In contradistinction to the tragedies, where soliloquies engage audiences and reveal character, we need to be alert to the nuances of dialogue and exchange in these plays to develop a sense of character.

Methods of Analysis

1. This chapter has used the methods of the previous chapter on characterisation.
2. We have also:
    a. looked at how female characters are positioned in relation to each other and to the male characters of the play, both structurally and within individual scenes;
    b. considered the structural function of female characters at key moments of plays: turning points and resolutions;
    c. linked thematic and dramatic concerns to the language and function of individual characters.

Suggested Work

Cymbeline

1. Look at the characterisation of Innogen in the opening scene with both her husband and father.
2. Innogen appears in three scenes in Act 1 (1.1, 1.3, and 1.6): comment on her stage dominance but eventual victimisation by the plot.
3. Comment on the characterisation and function of the queen (see, for example, 1.1.151–181 and 1.5.1–85; in which she plots the war against Rome and displays her interest in poisons).
4. Look at 3.4, the scene in which Pisanio reveals Posthumus's mistrust of Innogen. How does she respond? What kind of crisis scene and what kind of life-change does she initiate?

The Winter's Tale

1. The scene outside the jail between Paulina and Emilia, 2.2, is a short one, focussing on a debate between two women about childbirth. How does the scene play out? What is its significance within the structure of the drama?
2. Look at 3.2.170–240, after Hermione has collapsed: how is Paulina's characterisation demonstrated? What changes?
3. Look at the rest of 5.1 when Florizel and Perdita arrive at Leontes' court: why does Perdita remain silent? Comment on Paulina's words and function in this scene. Look again at the final scene's characterisation of all three women: how do they interact? How are they defined? Why do men's words end the play?

Pericles

1. Look at the earlier part of the scene where Marina is first brought to the brothel: how are setting and other characters used to establish her character?
2. Look now at Scene 21, where Marina is brought in to 'cure' Pericles' melancholy: how does her characterisation help convince us of his revival? Comment on Marina's language and song.
3. Finally, look at Scene 22 and the reunion of Thaisa and Marina with Pericles: how and why is familial reunion figured as the final resolution?

The Tempest

Miranda is the only human woman in the play: look at all the four scenes in which she appears and speaks: 1.2 (on stage for the whole scene, albeit asleep some of the time); 3.1 (which we have analysed here); 4.1.1–163; and 5.1.171–end. Why does she appear so infrequently, and how does her symbolic effect resonate given this?

Look at each of her speeches and her place in each dialogue, and think about both what she says and how she says it: is her innocence consistent? Does it change at all?

Look at the marriage masque in 4.1.58–143: here female gods appear performing in words and music a celebration designed by Prospero. We will be looking at this in greater detail in Chapter 8, but look at the words of the gods, and think about how female language and symbolism is used in a marriage masque designed by a male magician: what message is being conveyed? How do the gods' words and characterisation relate to Miranda's place in the narrative?

6

Masters, Servants and Slaves: Society and Politics

Shakespeare's late plays examine relationships between classes, paralleling events, language and actions occurring amongst the elite and servant classes. They ask questions about who has the right to hold power; about how and to what extent marriage is an essential part of aristocratic political alliances and negotiations; about who and what kind of person should have power over other individuals or nations; about what kind of autonomy a nation can have; about abuses of power because of status; about how women are confined by patriarchal political and familial conventions; and about how anxieties about female sexuality both define and poison political relationships between men. This chapter draws explicit attention to the ways those questions are fuelled and reinforced in parallel or subplots to intensify the audience's understanding of the main plot's key questions. Let us turn first to some extracts from *The Tempest*: each of these scenes follow on from each other, and in different but successive and cumulative ways raise similar questions about ruling, leadership and rights.

Analysis: *The Tempest*, 1.2.306–364

PROSPERO   Shake it off. Come on;
      We'll visit Caliban, my slave, who never
      Yields us kind answer.
MIRANDA   'Tis a villain, sir,

	I do not love to look on.	
PROSPERO	But as 'tis,	310
	We cannot miss him. He does make our fire,	
	Fetch in our wood and serves in offices	
	That profit us. What ho, slave! Caliban!	
	Thou earth, thou, speak!	
CALIBAN [within]	There's wood enough within.	
PROSPERO	Come forth, I say; there's other business for thee.	315
	Come, thou tortoise, when?	

Enter Ariel like a water-nymph

	Fine apparition! My quaint Ariel,	
	Hark in thine ear [*whispers*]	
ARIEL	My lord it shall be done.	[*Exit*]
PROSPERO	Thou poisonous slave, got by the devil himself	
	Upon thy wicked dam, come forth!	320

Enter Caliban

CALIBAN	As wicked dew as e'er my mother brushed	
	With raven's feather from unwholesome fen	
	Drop on you both! A south-west blow on ye	
	And blister you all o'er!	
PROSPERO	For this be sure tonight thou shalt have cramps,	325
	Side-stitches that shall pen thy breath up. Urchins	
	Shall, for that vast of night that they may work,	
	All exercise on thee. Thou shalt be pinched	
	As thick as honeycomb, each pinch more stinging	
	Than bees that made 'em.	
CALIBAN	I must eat my dinner.	330
	This island's mine by Sycorax my mother,	
	Which thou tak'st from me. When thou cam'st first,	
	Thou strok'st me and made much of me; wouldst give me	
	Water with berries in't, and teach me how	
	To name the bigger light, and how the less,	335
	That burn by day and night; and then I loved thee,	
	And showed thee all the qualities o' th' isle,	

	The fresh springs, brine-pits, barren place and fertile—	

<pre>
              The fresh springs, brine-pits, barren place and fertile—
              Cursed be I that did so! All the charms
              Of Sycorax, toads, beetles, bats light on you!   340
              For I am all the subjects that you have,
              Which first was mine own king, and here you sty me
              In this hard rock, whiles you do keep from me
              The rest o' th' island.
PROSPERO   Thou most lying slave,
              Whom stripes may move, not kindness, I have used thee— 345
              Filth as thou art— with humane care, and lodged thee
              In mine own cell, till thou didst seek to violate
              The honour of my child.
CALIBAN   O ho, O ho! Would't had been done!
              Thou didst prevent me—I had peopled else
              This isle with Calibans.
MIRANDA   Abhorrèd slave,   350
              Which any print of goodness wilt not take,
              Being capable of all ill! I pitied thee,
              Took pains to make thee speak, taught thee each hour
              One thing or other. When thou didst not, savage,
              Know thine own meaning, but wouldst gabble like   355
              A thing most brutish, I endowed thy purposes
              With words that made them known. But thy vile race—
              Though thou didst learn—had that in't which good natures
              Could not abide to be with; therefore wast thou
              Deservedly confined into this rock,   360
              Who hadst deserved more than a prison.
CALIBAN   You taught me language; and my profit on't
              Is I know how to curse. The red plague rid you
              For learning me your language!
</pre>

This is part of the play's long second scene in which Prospero's empire is surveyed: he lectures Miranda on the past; he instructs Ariel to monitor Alonso and the courtiers; he insists on going to check on Caliban; and finally Ariel brings in Ferdinand who is manacled by Prospero. The sequential scenic structure displays Prospero's position as the island's supreme political ruler, albeit through magic, force and terror. It is our first meeting with Caliban.

What do we see? Prospero has suggested that Miranda and he move from their cave to wherever Caliban abides ('we'll visit Caliban', l.308). Caliban is hidden from the audience at first, as Prospero and he shout out at each other. Our first sight of Caliban on stage will be visually memorable: is he the 'savage and deformed slave' the 1623 cast list describes? Prospero's 'Come, thou tortoise, when?' (l.316) is a half line of five syllables, suggesting he and Miranda pause waiting for Caliban to emerge: instead Ariel arrives for further secret instructions. Caliban's refusal to come out until the third shout demonstrates a slave's physical resistance to a master's demands, while the master is given cause for his increasingly short temper. Caliban's recalcitrance is his only physical power.

Prospero's language betrays his perspective on the relationships between a master and slave, and the difference between his treatment of his daughter and his servants and slave. Prospero names Caliban 'slave' (ll.308, 313) and makes clear that his work and labour ensure the Europeans' survival ('as 'tis / we cannot miss him / ... / [he] serves in offices / That profit us', ll.310–13). Their social and economic interdependence, and Caliban's necessary subordination, are explicitly ideological. Prospero's speech combines short sharp commands ('Come forth, I say, l.315), peppered with insults ('Thou earth, thou', 'Thou poisonous slave', ll.314, 319). Each command includes a personal attack, through descriptive adjectives, name-calling, or slurs about parentage ('got by the devil himself / Upon thy wicked dam', ll.319–20). These linguistic tactics typify early-modern colonialists' treatment of non-Europeans.

The dialogue is fast-paced, as each character completes the other's lines, competing to put across their version of their relationship and authority. Prospero's completion of Caliban's lines begins in each case with an insult ('Thou most lying slave', and 'Abhorrèd slave', ll.344, 350), a repetitive refrain Prospero uses to reinforce Caliban's subject position, connoting his anger. Even in the midst of a longer speech, Prospero breaks out of his rhetorical logic to hurl an insult: for example, 'I have used thee— / *Filth as thou art*—with humane care' (ll.345–6). His curses list a succession of increasingly painful tortures on Caliban's body: he will have cramps, and urchins will pinch and sting his body (ll.326–30). The successive insults, curses and imagined violence create a tense atmosphere, and an impassioned argument about colonial identity and power.

Prospero typically uses declarative and exclamatory sentences ('thou shalt have...', 'I endowed thy purposes'... 'thou most lying slave'), a grammatical reflection of his position of power over Caliban, since he can literally command his actions. Prospero's communication is didactic, autocratic and hierarchical. His final speech counterbalances the angry insults and threats of torture: we learn Caliban has tried to rape Miranda, so Prospero's angry treatment of Caliban becomes credibly that of a distraught, irate father. However, because we learn this only after we watch Prospero's violence, our sympathy for Caliban's as victim is established. This complicates our responses to both characters.

We hear Caliban before we see him. This aural introduction identifies him as recalcitrant and mouthy, albeit in thrall to a master: 'there's wood enough within' (l.314). He answers his master's call, but voices his own opinion. Caliban's second speech coincides with our first sight of him as he enters the stage. His curses are lyrical and poetic ('As wicked dew as e'er my mother brushed / With raven's feather from unwholesome fen / Drop on you both!' ll.321–3), and in regular iambic pentameters, contrasting Prospero's rougher verse here. Despite his servile social (and racial) status, his language suggests a social and intellectual elevation, particularly within the conventions of Renaissance drama, when low-born characters tended to speak prose, and high-born poetry. Caliban's curses use concrete natural images from the world of the island: dew, ravens' feathers, fens. His third response to Prospero begins with a material assertion of his own needs and identity, 'I must eat my dinner' (l.330), segueing immediately into his defence of his rights to the island compared to Prospero's ('This island's mine by Sycorax my mother, / Which thou tak'st from me', ll.331–2). Caliban's autonomous identity and physical and political rights are displayed to us successively in these three opening speeches.

In juxtaposing this land-claim based on his mother's rights with Prospero's arrival on the island, Shakespeare reminds us of Prospero's figuration as a father-substitute for Caliban. Caliban recalls the time as one of innocence: a time of mutual exploration and knowledge in which Prospero physically and intellectually nourished him, whilst

Caliban showed him 'all the qualities o'th' isle' (l.337). The elegiac quality of the memory contrasts his political analysis of their current relationship: 'I am all the subjects that you have, / Which first was mine own king' (ll.341–2). However, the grounds for Caliban's equal political claim are side-stepped by Prospero. He refuses to engage in Caliban's language, but instead accuses him of a different crime. Caliban says Prospero stole his land, Prospero that Caliban tried to take his daughter. In claim and counter-claim daughter and land are made proxy equivalents, and Caliban's language of 'rights' to the land remains uncontested but ignored.

Other than minor physical resistance, Caliban's only power is language: 'You taught me language, and my profit on't / Is I know how to curse' (ll.362–3). He asserts an oppositional view to Prospero both through the poetic quality of his curses and descriptions, and his articulation of a theory of property ownership. Caliban, echoing Prospero's earlier account in this same scene to Miranda, asserts a back-story of usurpation. The parallel story forces us to recognise that the play asks who has the right to rule (whether it be Milan or an uninhabited island)? The play tests all its characters with ideas about rulership: should rule be based on birth, merit, inheritance, priority of settlement, or divinity?

Miranda's attack on Caliban ('Abhorrèd slave, / Which any print of goodness will not take', ll.350–51), implies one answer to this conundrum: Caliban is naturally slavish and no education will or can better his 'savage' (l.356) instincts ('thy vile race', l.357). Her civilising teaching and nurturing were wasted. The confrontation here between Prospero and Miranda, and Caliban distils early-modern disillusioned encounters between Europeans and native Americans: an initial wonderment is displaced by the grim realities of two different cultures clashing and failing to understand each other's perspectives.

This encounter with Caliban, set between Prospero's management of Ariel and the forthcoming meeting between Ferdinand and Miranda, reminds us of the diversity of those whom Prospero rules. It also acts as a salutary warning about the legitimacy and effectiveness of Prospero's leadership of the island, and continues to ask questions about who should rule, and when and where.

In the next scene, such questions are posed again in a different but supplementary way by Prospero's old friend Gonzalo.

Analysis: *The Tempest*, 2.1.141–162

GONZALO (*to Alonso*) Had I plantation of this isle, my lord,—
ANTONIO   He'd sow't with nettle-seed.
SEBASTIAN   Or docks, or mallows.
GONZALO   —And were the king on't, what would I do?
SEBASTIAN 'Scape being drunk for want of wine.
GONZALO   I' th' commonwealth I would by contraries   145
          Execute all things, for no kind of traffic
          Would I admit; no name of magistrate;
          Letters should not be known; riches, poverty,
          And use of service, none; contract, succession,
          Bourn, bound of land, tilth, vineyard, none;   150
          No use of metal, corn, or wine, or oil;
          No occupation; all men idle, all,
          And women too, but innocent and pure;
          No sovereignty—
SEBASTIAN   Yet he would be king on't.
ANTONIO   The latter end of his commonwealth forgets the beginning. 155
GONZALO   All things in common nature should produce
          Without sweat or endeavour. Treason, felony,
          Sword, pike, knife, gun, or need of any engine
          Would I not have; but nature should bring forth   160
          Of its own kind all foison, all abundance
          To feed my innocent people.

This occurs in the scene where we first see Alonso and his courtiers on the island. Antonio and Sebastian are typically pessimistic, suggesting Alonso's son must be dead, that his daughter is lost to an African, and continue to behave as cynical courtiers. Attempting to change the subject, perhaps as a means of distracting the king from his lost son, perhaps in genuine excitement, Gonzalo imagines establishing a colony ('had I plantation of this isle, my lord', l.141) in this apparently uninhabited space. The plantation he imagines will be opposite to usual social organisations ('by contraries / Execute all things', l.145). His vision of 'no traffic' (trade), 'no name of magistrate', and '[no] riches, poverty, use of service...contract, succession... tilth' (ll.147–50) eliminates the economic and commercial ties of early modern and feudal society. The language invokes that of a classical golden age, an Eden-equivalent, repeated in Montaigne's *Essays*, from which Shakespeare quotes here. Many of Shakespeare's original audience would have recognised this reference to a pastoral pre-civilised world both to describe the New World and to imagine an alternative one. Gonzalo's plantation has resonances of an egalitarian social and political structure, no taxes ('tilth'), communal ownership of land, no servants or slaves, and no formal agricultural production. It becomes increasingly fantastic: by rejecting the use of metals, corn and wine, he denies the plantation tools, food and drink; and by rendering all people idle and with 'no sovereignty' (l.154) he suggests political anarchy rather than the freedom with which he begins.

His second speech combines imagery from the Bible's Eden (*Genesis* 3:19) with that from Ovid's version of the golden age in his *Metamorphoses*. In this proto-paradise nature will offer up food in abundance without the necessity of labour; and war and conflict will be eliminated. This vision is mocked by Sebastian and Antonio, both for its contradictions (he would be king, but have 'no sovereignty'), and for its idealism (the idle will be 'whores and knaves', l.164). The audience are given two perspectives on the dilemma of Europeans newly arrived on hitherto undiscovered land. Is the land a place for a new vision of social and political order, or a space to practice older habits of ideology and political attitudes? In both cases, the land is a blank slate on which European debates about settlement and colonisation are imposed. This uninhabited land is actually populated, as the audience know. Prospero and his daughter reside here, and so do two islanders who preceded them, Ariel and Caliban. However, although Gonzalo's speech raises radical possibilities of alternative social and political organisation, it is located in the scene and play as simply a fantasy. The play suggests we need to find more pragmatic solutions to the questions of who should rule and how.

In the third extract from *The Tempest*, Caliban has been gathering wood, but believing that Trinculo is one of the tormenting spirits sent by Prospero, hides under his cloak to escape. Trinculo spots the shape, comically investigates whether it is a fish, man or monster, and ends up hiding under the gabardine with Caliban to escape the storm. It is at this point that Stephano enters. This extract omits the middle part of the scene.

Analysis: *The Tempest*, 2.2.41–75 and 154–182

	Enter Stephano, singing, [a bottle in his hand]	
STEPHANO	I shall no more to sea, to sea,	
	Here shall I die ashore—	
	This is a very scurvy tune to sing at a man's funeral.	
	Well, here's my comfort. (*Drinks*)	
	(*Sings*)	
	The master, the swabber, the boatswain and I,	45
	The gunner and his mate,	
	Loved Moll, Meg, and Marian, and Margery,	
	But none of us cared for Kate;	
	For she had a tongue with a tang,	
	Would cry to a sailor, 'Go hang!'	50
	She loved not the savour of tar nor of pitch,	
	Yet a tailor might scratch her where'er she did itch:	
	Then to sea, boys, and let her go hang!	
	This is a scurvy tune too, but here's my comfort.	
	[*He*] *drinks*	
CALIBAN	Do not torment me! O!	55
STEPHANO	What's the matter? Have we devils here? Do you put tricks upon's with savages and men of Ind? Ha? I have not scaped drowning to be afeard now of your four legs; for it hath been said, 'As proper a man as ever went on four legs cannot make him give ground'; and it shall be said so again while Stephano breathes at' nostrils.	60
CALIBAN	The spirit torments me! O!	
STEPHANO	This is some monster of the isle with four legs, who hath got, as I take it, an ague. Where the devil should he learn our language? I will give him some relief, if it be but for that. If I can recover him and keep him tame, and get to Naples with him, he's a present for any emperor that ever trod on neat's-leather.	65
CALIBAN	Do not torment me, prithee! I'll bring my wood home faster.	70

STEPHANO He's in his fit now, and does not talk after the
wisest. He shall taste of my bottle. If he have never drunk
wine afore, it will go near to remove his fit. If I can recover
him and keep him tame, I will not take too much for him;
he shall pay for him that hath him, and that soundly.   75

***

CALIBAN I'll show thee the best springs; I'll pluck thee berries;
I'll fish for thee, and get thee wood enough.   155
A plague upon the tyrant that I serve!
I'll bear him no more sticks, but follow thee,
Thou wondrous man.
TRINCULO A most ridiculous monster, to make a wonder of
a poor drunkard!   160
CALIBAN I prithee let me bring thee where crabs grow,
And I with my long nails will dig thee pig-nuts;
Show thee a jay's nest, and instruct thee how
To snare the nimble marmoset. I'll bring thee
To clust'ring filberts, and sometimes I'll get thee   165
Young scamels from the rock. Wilt thou go with me?
STEPHANO I prithee now, lead the way without any more
talking. Trinculo, the King and all our company else
being drowned, we will inherit here. [*To Caliban*] Here,
bear my bottle. Fellow Trinculo, we'll fill him by and by   170
again.
CALIBAN [*Sings drunkenly*] Farewell master; farewell,
farewell!
TRINCULO A howling monster; a drunken monster!
CALIBAN No more dams I'll make for fish   175
    Nor fetch in firing
  At requiring,
Nor scrape trenchering, nor wash dish;
    'Ban, 'Ban, Ca-Caliban
Has a new master—get a new man!   180
Freedom, high-day! High-day, freedom! Freedom, high-
day, freedom!
STEPHANO O brave monster! Lead the way.   *Exeunt*

This scene parallels the first encounter between white Europeans and native islanders that Caliban recollects (1.2.330–43). Both Stephano and Trinculo voice the view that the strange native ('some monster of the isle with four legs', l.63; or 'a man or a fish?', l.24), will make money for them if they take him home. Trinculo argues 'were I in England now... and had this fish painted, not a holiday-fool there but would give a piece of silver' (ll.28–9), whilst Stephano says 'If I can recover him, and keep him tame, and get to Naples with him, he's a present for any emperor' (ll.67–8). The representation of native peoples as freak-show fodder, 'savages and men of Ind' (l.57) to be 'tamed', is the bathetic parallel to the main plot's representation of the relationship between Caliban and Prospero. Stephano's exuberant self-confidence and folly, intensified because he is drunk, create a comic situation as he encounters the four-legged gabardine on stage. His wondering, 'where the devil should he learn our language?' (l.64), illustrative of his skewed drunken perspective and the implausibility of the whole situation, creates traditional knockabout comedy. It suggests simultaneously his displaced and amazed perception and our superior pre-knowledge of Caliban and his knowledge of their language. The audience's perception of this gap between how the newcomers see Caliban, and what we know, is crucial to the scene's comic effect.

Stephano's misperception of Caliban as a malleable native is ironically both true and untrue. Caliban goes on to make the same mistakes he made with Prospero (albeit bribed here by alcohol). He eagerly offers them the secrets of the island (ll.153–7, 161–6), both natural and political, and his services, implying a natural inclination to service and subordination. However, unlike Caliban and Prospero's pre-history, his relationship with Stephano and Trinculo is played out on stage as part of the action. His initial assumption that they are Prospero's enforcers, gives way to wonder at more new Europeans. As their relationship develops, Caliban becomes the brains behind their decision to stage a rebellion against Prospero. Although Stephano immediately claims inheritance of the leadership of the barren island in the king's absence (l.169), it is Caliban who voices a political stance: cursing Prospero as a 'tyrant' (l.157) and in exuberantly singing a liberationist song, delineates a slave's typical chores (fishing, wood collection, making the fire, and scraping and cleaning dishes). Nevertheless, his song is sadly self-limiting: although he uses the term 'freedom', he characterises his new situation in old terms ('Has a new master—get a new man!' l.180). At this point, Caliban's version of freedom is simply that of better conditions of service.

Stephano and Trinculo illustrate the most gung-ho characterisation of English colonialists: they offer alcohol as a means of subduing native people, and suggest selling and abusing Caliban's body to European markets. Nevertheless, as the plot progresses it proves to be Caliban who understands the island. His knowledge of the natural plants, of Prospero's behaviour and habits, the islands' spirits and Prospero's books enable him to guide and lead men on the island: native knowledge is more insightful than that of the European under-classes.

Let us now turn to look at two extracts from *The Winter's Tale*.

Analysis: *The Winter's Tale*, 2.3.95–157

PAULINA	It is yours;	95
	And, might we lay th'old proverb to your charge,	
	So like you, 'tis the worse. Behold, my lords,	
	Although the print be little, the whole matter	
	And copy of the father— eye, nose, lip,	
	The trick of's frown, his forehead, nay, the valley,	100
	The pretty dimples of his chin and cheek, his smiles,	
	The very mould and frame of hand, nail, finger.	
	And thou, good goddess Nature, which hast made it	
	So like to him that got it, if thou hast	
	The ordering of the mind too, 'mongst all colours,	105
	No yellow in't, lest she suspect, as he does,	
	Her children not her husband's.	
LEONTES	A gross hag!	
	And losel, thou art worthy to be hanged,	
	That wilt not stay her tongue.	
ANTIGONUS	Hang all the husbands	
	That cannot do that feat, you'll leave yourself	110
	Hardly one subject.	
LEONTES	Once more, take her hence!	
PAULINA	A most unworthy and unnatural lord	
	Can do no more.	
LEONTES	I'll ha' thee burnt!	
PAULINA	I care not;	
	It is an heretic that makes the fire,	
	Not she which burns in't. I'll not call you tyrant;	115

	But this most cruel usage of your Queen,	
	Not able to produce more accusation	
	Than your own weak-hinged fancy, something savours	
	Of tyranny, and will ignoble make you,	
	Yea, scandalous to the world.	
LEONTES [*To Antigonus*]	On your allegiance,	120
	Out of the chamber with her! Were I a tyrant,	
	Where were her life? She durst not call me so	
	If she did know me one. Away with her.	
PAULINA	I pray you, do not push me; I'll be gone.	
	Look to your babe, my lord; 'tis yours—Jove send her	125
	A better guiding spirit. What needs these hands?	
	You, that are thus so tender o'er his follies,	
	Will never do him good, not one of you.	
	So, so; farewell, we are gone.	*Exit*
LEONTES [*To Antigonus*]	Thou, traitor, hast set on thy wife to this.	130
	My child? Away with't! Even thou, that hast	
	A heart so tender o'er it, take it hence	
	And see it instantly consumed with fire.	
	Even thou, and none but thou. Take it up straight.	
	Within this hour bring me word 'tis done,	135
	And by good testimony, or I'll seize thy life,	
	With what thou else call'st thine. If thou refuse	
	And wilt encounter with my wrath, say so;	
	The bastard brains with these my proper hands	
	Shall I dash out. Go, take it to the fire,	140
	For thou set'st on thy wife.	
ANTIGONUS	I did not, sir:	
	These lords, my noble fellows, if they please,	
	Can clear me in't.	
LORDS	We can; my royal liege,	
	He is not guilty of her coming hither.	
LEONTES	You're liars all!	145
FIRST LORD	Beseech your highness, give us better credit.	
	We have always truly served you, and beseech	
	So to esteem of us; and on our knees we beg,	
	As recompense of our dear services	
	Past and to come, that you do change this purpose,	150
	Which being so horrible, so bloody, must	

	Lead on to some foul issue. We all kneel.	
LEONTES	I am a feather for each wind that blows.	
	Shall I live on to see this bastard kneel	
	And call me father? Better burn it now	155
	Than curse it then. But be it; let it live.	
	—It shall not neither	

This extract plays out Paulina's belief that by bringing Hermione's newly-born baby into Leontes' presence she will force Leontes to realise his jealousy was a terrible mistake, repent his anger, and release Hermione. Paulina completely misreads him, and is thereby indirectly the catalyst which prompts Leontes to send the baby to be abandoned, and his wife to trial. Paulina enters early in the scene and it is worth reading the whole scene to understand the dynamics of the argument. This particular part illustrates Leontes' relationship with, and attitude to, his courtier servants.

Paulina's argument is premised on the physical appearance of the child ('Behold...', l.97): she matches each feature to that of Leontes ('the whole matter / And copy of the father, eye, nose, lip', ll.98–9). Her list-like labelling of the baby's face suggests she displays the child to her audience, and matches these features against those of Leontes in a physical gesture. She addresses Leontes directly from the beginning ('it is yours', l.95). Paulina's description is transposed into an exclamatory disquisition, ironically suggesting that if the baby's mind is equally like Leontes', the child will potentially become as jealous. By imagining the possibility of a woman suspecting her children do not belong to her husband, she indirectly and involuntarily invokes Leontes' suspicions of Hermione and his fears about his genealogical heritage. Her speech's rhythm in these last two lines (ll.105–7) veers away from the regular iambic pentameter in which she has lovingly listed the baby's attributes, with 12 syllables in each line. The irregular rhythm signposts her anger: content and rhythm have drifted from her intention to encourage Leontes to love the baby, and instead have disastrously evoked Leontes' anger. Once she stops talking about the baby and refers to Hermione's imprisonment and Leontes' jealousy, both characters retreat into trading insults.

Leontes' reply is not directed at Paulina, but to her husband Antigonus ('*thou* art worthy to be hanged / *That will not stay her tongue*', ll.108–9), a swerve from the intensity of Paulina's direct address, signalling his supercilious rudeness, his refusal to listen, and the intersection of his misogyny and patriarchal perceptions. It also underlines his refusal to physically contemplate the baby. Leontes insults Paulina, implying both her low birth ('losel', l.108) and her gendered age ('gross hag'), linking these directly to political rebellion ('worthy to be hanged', l.108). He commands his courtiers, who initially resist him. Antigonus's jokey answer to Leontes' demand that he silence his wife, ('hang all the husbands / That cannot do that feat, you'll leave yourself / Hardly one subject', ll.109–11) tries to deflect Leontes' anger, but unwittingly implies that women cannot be controlled, feeding Leontes' misogynistic viewpoint. Leontes' only addresses Paulina directly once ('I'll ha'thee burnt', l.113), in a line which is monosyllabically spit out, as though he cannot help himself.

The physical positioning of characters in the scene, Paulina with the baby, Leontes on his throne, or pacing around amongst his courtiers, reflects the plot's paradoxes. Visually and narrationally, for the audience, the baby and Paulina are central: and like Paulina, we see Leontes' reactions and jealousy as irrational. However, from Leontes' point of view, the baby is simply physical evidence of Hermione's betrayal. So he ignores both her physical presence, and anything Paulina says. Situation and dialogue intersect to reinforce this paradox.

Paulina, in contrast to the male courtiers, speaks her mind precisely: accusing Leontes of being tyrannous (a charge he takes up in the trial scene), fanciful and 'ignoble' (l.119). She inverts his implied accusation of witchcraft, arguing that the heretic is the one who sets the fire, not 'she who burns in't', (l.115). Leontes' language and behaviour assume absolute obedience from his subjects, and an exact equation between his perceptions and legality. By contrast, Paulina suggests that his actions and beliefs characterise tyranny and absolutism, and are against God (via her inverted definition of heretic). Their argument becomes one not just about the baby and Hermione, but also one about due process, fairness and law.

Once Paulina has left the stage, leaving the baby behind, the male courtiers are forced to respond to Leontes. His initial attack on Antigonus ('thou traitor, hast set on thy wife to this', 'even thou and none but thou', ll.130 and 134), reiterates his perception that any personal disagreement with him is treachery. Leontes believes a man should control his wife, and owe complete obedience to his monarch above all others. His successive orders to Antigonus to burn the child are mixed with threats underlining how power is enforced with violence ('or I'll seize thy life', l.136). The male courtiers speak communally, reinforcing each other's 'innocence' of the charge Leontes imputes (that Antigonus put his wife up to the attack). Antigonus and the Lords deny Paulina, and swear loyalty to their monarch (ll.147–8), but in swearing fealty, beg him to change his mind: 'on our knees we beg / As recompense of our dear service / Past and to come, that you do change this purpose', (ll.148–50). Their physical submission to Leontes (they frame the beginning and end of their plea with references to kneeling) contrasts its absence in Paulina, their language of respect her outspoken truth-telling. The Lords' deferential language and actions work on Leontes, who credits them when he will not Hermione or Paulina (albeit on a different matter). His self-doubt emerges for the first time: 'I am a feather for each wind that blows / ... But be it; let it live / It shall not neither' (ll.153–6). The proverbial metaphor (feather in the wind), posits a Leontes who is more torn and divided than he has appeared in his encounter with Paulina. Leontes is less intemperate with his male courtiers and servants: when they follow the conventional modes and language of courtly deference and submission, he listens. Their plea to Leontes is based on concepts of fealty, duty and service, not on the 'rights' of Hermione or the child. Paulina based her arguments on ideas of love, justice and honour. Men and women courtiers here represent divergent political worldviews: the former an absolutist model of hierarchical government and unswerving obedience; the latter a more open model where justice and rights dominate over social status or position. Leontes' thinking can only be influenced within the frame of his hierarchical masculine political system. Paulina's actions and language have no immediate political or narrational impact.

At the end of the trial scene this moment is strangely mirrored: news of Mamillius's death recalls the physical appearance of a daughter denied by her father. Leontes is unmoved by the daughter whom he sends to her death, but moved to repentance by the death of his son. The plot plays out through tragedy the possibility that Leontes could have embraced salvation when his children were alive: a dead son hauntingly reminds us of a lost daughter who promised potential reconciliation. Paulina's desperate attempt to break through Leontes' jealousy fails: but the plot tragically vindicates her as Leontes is punished by the loss of his son and wife. The later rediscovery of a daughter and resurrection of a wife, enables Paulina's reconciliatory advocacy to be reincorporated into the main plot's resolution: her rebellious viewpoint is validated 16 years later.

Let us now turn to Autolycus.

Analysis: *The Winter's Tale*, 4.4.724–747

OLD SHEPHERD	Are you a courtier, an't like you, sir?	
AUTOLYCUS	Whether it like me or no, I am a courtier. Seest thou not the air of the court in these enfoldings? Hath not my gait in it the measure of the court? Receives not thy nose court odour from me? Reflect I not on thy baseness court-contempt? Think'st thou, for that I insinuate, or toze from thee thy business, I am therefore no courtier? I am courtier cap-à-pie; and one that will either push on or pluck back thy business there; whereupon I command thee to open thy affair.	725

730 |
OLD SHEPHERD	My business, sir, is to the King.	
AUTOLYCUS	What advocate hast thou to him?	735
OLD SHEPHERD	I know not, an't like you.	
CLOWN	Advocate's the court-word for a pheasant—say you have none.	
OLD SHEPHERD	None, sir; I have no pheasant, cock nor hen.	
AUTOLYCUS	How blessed are we that are not simple men! Yet nature might have made me as these are, Therefore I will not disdain.	740
CLOWN	This cannot be but a great courtier.	
OLD SHEPHERD	His garments are rich, but he wears them not handsomely.	745
CLOWN	He seems to be the more noble in being fantastical. a great man, I'll warrant—I know by the picking on's teeth.	

This extract occurs at the very end of the long sheep-shearing festival scene, after Camillo has offered to escort Florizel and Perdita away from Bohemia to Sicilia. Autolycus overhears the old shepherd's intentions to deliver a 'box' to the king to show Perdita is not his child, and to explain how Florizel deceived him by dressing as a commoner. Autolycus, who hitherto has shown a concern only for his own interests, worries that this will provide an 'impediment ... to the flight of my master' (l.705), whips off his false beard, and 'becomes' a courtier. This is his fourth physical disguise or identity of the act: in 4.3 he is dressed raggedly, but pretends he has been robbed in order to steal money and clothes from the clown; earlier in 4.4 he appears 'with a false beard' as a tinker and ballad-seller; Camillo forces him to exchange clothes with Florizel (4.4.642) so that Florizel and Perdita can escape, but Autolycus retains the beard; and when he takes off the beard he appears fully 'a courtier' (l.724). In his initial song (which we discuss in Chapter 9), he tells us he used to serve Florizel 'and in my time wore three-pile but I am now out of service' (4.3.14). His continued loyalty to Florizel here enables him to con the Shepherd and his son to flee Bohemia with him, and directly influence the play's closure, since they hold the proof of Perdita's true identity. Autolycus's version of 'service' is a complicated mixture of self-interest and loyalty: his sense of identity a mixture of service and clothing ('three-pile' is a reference to the velvet he wore). This act includes a variety of characters in disguise: Florizel as a commoner so he can woo Perdita; Polixenes and Camillo as commoners to spy on Florizel; Florizel and Perdita are disguised respectively as a tinker and a young man. Autolycus is the only character who dons multiple disguises, but in each case clothing is used to connote a different identity and status: class is denoted by garb and performance, as Autolycus says 'seest you not the air of the court in these enfoldings?' (l.726) Autolycus weaves a narration about courtly identity to the shepherd's scepticism: 'hath not my gait in it the measure of the court? Receives not thy nose court odour from me? Reflect I not on thy baseness court-contempt?' (ll.726–8) Courtiers walk, are perfumed and act superciliously. This characterisation convinces the clown but not the old shepherd, ('this cannot be but a great courtier' versus 'his garments are rich, but he wears them not handsomely, (l.744–5)'. The clown's view that 'he seems to be the more noble in being fantastical'l.743–4) expresses both a commentary on his exaggerated appearance and a satire on the dress of courtiers. The debate created comically here resonates with the play's broader questions: what is nobility – are we 'naturally' noble, or virtuous, or is it something we can learn or put on? The elevation of the shepherds to gentlemen in 5.2 is also later signalled by the clothes they are given.

Autolycus's grammar shifts to a formal delivery: his list of rhetorical questions create authority, although their content remains banal (do I not smell like a courtier?). The disjunction between form and content creates humour, although the shepherds can see something is not quite right, they are not sure what that is. Autolycus's use of the word 'advocate' is a malapropism (for advocacy), which neither listener understands. The shepherds decide 'advocate' is a pheasant, and reply accordingly. Semantics illustrate the gap between Autolycus's knowingness and the shepherds' innocence, but also the gap between Autolycus and the 'real' courtiers like Camillo and Florizel, whose language does not make these kinds of rhetorical, semantic or grammatical slips.

Autolycus's previous service to Florizel defines his identity: he is currently a vagrant because no longer in service. His in-between status places him outside society, even other characters who change status through cross-dressing still behave as part of the social elite. Autolycus is careless of others' opinions, celebrating his thieving, whoring and gambling in his songs: asking us to share his delight in trickery. Other outsider characters (be it Hermione, Perdita, Paulina or Florizel) work towards being reincorporated into the social fabric. Although Autolycus's identity is forged by his outsider status, and celebrates trickery as essential to the economics of living, he also seeks service and identity at the centre of power, pleading with the shepherds in 5.2 that they intervene for him with the prince.

Conclusions

1. The range of social classes intersecting with the dominant action suggests social relationships are central to the plots and narrative. Characters' dependence on status, gender and economics determines initial power relationships. The plays test such relationships through conflict and drama and ask questions: Who

should hold authority? What is (and should be) the relationship between master and servant? What relationships between different social groups should a society acknowledge and foster? Are there limits to freedom? What should they be and who should decide these?
2. Contemporary social and political practices and the play-world share a number of features:
   - dynastic marriage is assumed to be a social and political good, albeit tested via personal or political adversity;
   - political authority is questioned, provoking discussions about who should or can rule;
   - professional knowledge and authority is an alternative to political power through birth;
   - individual liberty and its relationship to duty is debated;
   - ideas of natural law are invoked as an alternative to divine law;
   - service is contested;
   - Machiavellianism as a mode of self-interested political practice is condemned;
   - different models of land ownership, rulership and authority are debated.
3. These themes are dramatised through conflict between characters and narrational scenic oppositions and juxtapositions. The audience are actively engaged in a dramatic enquiry through the doubling and mirroring of plot motifs and character types across class and gender. Subplots echo the action and themes of main plots, acting as a comic or darker commentary on the main action. Subplots are not 'comic relief', but integral to the play's overall shape and meaning: the interleaving of main plot and subplot in the ordering of scenes enhances the main plot through parallels and juxtapositional commentary.
4. 'Commentator' figures from the non-elite classes include, Paulina and Autolycus in *The Winter's Tale*, Pisanio and Giacomo in *Cymbeline* and the fishermen in *Pericles*.
5. The 'low' characters typically speak prose. An intriguing exception to this is Caliban, the quality of whose verse marks him as more elite than his enslaved status. 'Low' characters conventionally speak prose and belong in comedy, in classical and renaissance dramatic theory. Shakespeare fuses this convention with native English clowning, where traditionally 'there is no slander in an

allowed fool' (*Twelfth Night* 1.5.88): these 'foolish' or outsider characters indirectly speak truths about the main plot.
6. Shakespeare's endings focus on the coincidence of familial, dynastic and sovereign identity through dramatic resolution, offering a predominantly conservative model of political and social order – with some remarkable exceptions, including:
    - Paulina (a woman and a servant) is the agent through whom political and familial change occurs;
    - young women (not young men) hold political power, although they pass it on through marriage to their husbands;
    - Antonio and Sebastian are not included in the dynastic and social inclusionism of the Milan–Naples reconciliation;
    - Caliban is left as lord of his island; alternatives to dominant models of rulership are examined and debated.
7. Shakespeare sets the questions as dramatic and narrative problems, most of which are resolved in the plays' closures. His characteristically dialectical method enables directors, actors and audience to be engaged in these political debates and to come to their own conclusions.

Methods of Analysis

We have:

1. focussed on character, language and imagery as an initial way of understanding scene, action and character;
2. looked particularly at structural elements, such as subplots, parallel plotting, endings, dramatic framing, and different characters' symbolic function, enabling us to see how themes and questions develop, and how questions asked by one element of the plot, can be answered or asked in different ways in other plots;
3. placed direct textual analysis into a broader frame, in the context of three broader questions: what does this tell us about the political, social and economic structures and ideologies of this fictional world? What place does this particular extract have within that broader debate? What kinds of ideas does Shakespeare want us to think about?

Suggested Work

There are many passages which a reader could consider when debating ideas of service, slavery and politics (for example some extracts in Chapters 2 and 3 on endings and turning points). In particular, students may find it useful to consider the following extracts.

Cymbeline

In Act 3 Scene 1, Cymbeline and the queen articulate explicit British resistance to Roman imperial rule. How does character inform language and political position? How far are Cymbeline's political views influenced by the queen's? How is femininity figured? Look at the end of the play to help answer these questions.

How is the marriage of Innogen to Posthumus figured? In what way do the dynamics of the plot generate sympathy for him despite his 'low birth'? What kind of language does Giacomo use about Posthumus in their meeting in Rome (1.4)? How do their meetings (1.4 and 2.4) articulate the social, political and gendered tensions which inform the play?

The Tempest

Look at the successive usurpation attempts: Prospero's account of his brother's 16 years earlier, 1.2.61–151; Sebastian and Antonio's discussion of a plot to usurp Alonso, 2.1.197–294, followed up at 3.3.11–15; Stephano and Trinculo's debate with Caliban and attempt to usurp Prospero, 3.2.1–122 and 4.1.193–253. Look at how each character has differing desires and ambitions, and how they are thwarted. What is the effect of the tripling of attempts at usurpation?

The Winter's Tale

To what extent is Autolycus's 'liberty' a fantasy of freedom: a safety-valve for the political claustrophobia of the social elite? To what extent is Paulina's liberty to speak out suppressed by the ending? Look at the scene in which Leontes' and Perdita's reunion is described (5.2) by servants and messengers: comment on their characterisation, and this perspective of the court and reunion. Why does knowledge come to us through men?

Pericles

Look at the scene between the fishermen, their language and outlook. How does this scene integrate with the rest of the play? Look again at the brothel scenes, and the representation of Boult and the Bawd: how are their needs figured? Are they simply foils for Marina's 'natural' nobility?

7

Stage Properties

Stage properties and stage furniture are the items and objects which characters mention, carry, or are referred to in the original stage directions, and are integral to the performance and meaning of plays. In the late plays stage properties coalesce and fuse literary, dramatic and narrative moments. We will look at one example from each of three late plays to debate how Shakespeare uses stage properties as symbolic icons, visual cues and physical memories which echo and resound throughout the play's visual and textual references. This attention to the physical aspects of performance helps visualise a dramatic text as a playscript, and see how the written text acts as a set of stage directions about stage properties and actors' bodies.

Let us now turn to a key scene from *Cymbeline*.

Analysis: *Cymbeline*, 2.2.1–51

	Enter Innogen in her bed and a lady[1]	
INNOGEN	Who's there? My woman Helen?	
HELEN	Please you, madam	
INNOGEN	What hour is it?	
HELEN	Almost midnight, madam.	
INNOGEN	I have read three hours then. Mine eyes are weak.	
	Fold down the leaf where I have left. To bed.	
	Take not away the taper, leave it burning;	5
	And if thou canst awake by four o' th' clock,	

---

[1] Oxford Edition: *A trunk is put in position. A bed [is put forth] with Innogen in it, reading a book. Enter to her, Helen, a lady*

	I prithee call me. Sleep hath seized me wholly [*Exit Helen*]	
	To your protection I commend me, gods.	
	From fairies and the tempters of the night	
	Guard me beseech ye.	10
	[*She sleeps.*]	
	[*Giacomo comes from the trunk*]	
GIACOMO	The crickets sing, and man's o'er-laboured sense	
	Repairs itself by rest. Our Tarquin thus	
	Did softly press the rushes ere he wakened	
	The chastity he wounded. Cytherea,	
	How bravely thou becom'st thy bed, fresh lily,	15
	And whiter than the sheets! That I might touch,	
	But kiss, one kiss! Rubies unparagoned,	
	How dearly they do't! 'Tis her breathing that	
	Perfumes the chamber thus. The flame o' th' taper	
	Bows toward her, and would underpeep her lids,	20
	To see th' enclosed lights, now canopied	
	Under these windows, white and azure-laced	
	With blue of heaven's own tinct. But my design—	
	To note the chamber. I will write all down:	
	[*He writes in his tables*]	
	Such and such pictures, there the window, such	25
	Th'adornment of her bed, the arras, figures,	
	Why, such and such; and the contents o' th' story.	
	Ah, but some natural notes about her body	
	Above ten thousand meaner moveables	
	Would testify t' enrich mine inventory.	30
	O sleep, thou ape of death, lie dull upon her,	
	And be her sense but as a monument	
	Thus in a chapel lying. Come off, come off;	
	As slippery as the Gordian knot was hard!	
	[*He takes the bracelet from her arm*]	
	'Tis mine, and this will witness outwardly,	35
	As strongly as the conscience does within,	
	To th' madding of her lord. On her left breast	
	A mole cinque-spotted, like the crimson drops	
	I' th' bottom of a cowslip. Here's a voucher	
	Stronger than ever law could make; this secret	40
	Will force him think I have picked the lock and ta'en	

> The treasure of her honour. No more. To what end?
> Why should I write this down that's riveted,
> Screwed to my memory? She hath been reading late,
> ↘ The tale of Tereus. Here the leaf's turned down   45
> Where Philomel gave up. I have enough.
> To th' trunk again, and shut the spring of it.
> Swift, swift, you dragons of the night, that dawning
> May bare the raven's eye! I lodge in fear.
> Though this a heavenly angel, hell is here.   50
>   *Clock strikes*
> One, two, three. Time, time!
>
>   [*Exit into the trunk*]

What do we see happening here? The explicit and implicit stage directions paint a scene of hushed and intimate darkness, drawing attention to the scene's physical stage properties: the bed, the trunk, the candle, the book, the notebook, and the bracelet. Detailed stage directions are rare in Shakespeare's plays, partly because the dialogue builds in many implicit stage directions. We shall use this extract to analyse how Shakespeare typically uses dialogue to tell actor, director and audience what is happening physically on stage.

If we look only at the explicit stage directions published in the 1623 folio edition, we can see the scene's skeletal shape. The original stage directions were: '*Enter Innogen in her bed and a lady*' (l.0); '*Sleeps. Giacomo from the trunk*' (l.10); '*Clock strikes*' (l.50); '*exeunt*' (l.51). We know, therefore, that both a bed and a large trunk must be on stage. Innogen remains relatively static on the bed for the whole scene, while Giacomo is first concealed in the trunk, but ranges and walks around the stage and bed during his 40-plus lines. The bed is visually central to the scene: both because it must be placed centrally for Giacomo to be able to walk around Innogen and comment on her body, and because it is central to the impact of the whole scene: a vulnerable woman exposed to both Giacomo and our view. Stage property and actor within it are metonyms for female vulnerability to the masculine gaze and to competitions between men (Giacomo bet's with Posthumus that he will be able to seduce his wife in 1.5). Innogen is a passive token in the wager, beholden to both men's desire. By locating her in a bed, as she prepares for sleep, Shakespeare portrays her private self: we watch her undressed and reading.

However, by using the trunk as a Trojan horse, Shakespeare suggests bedrooms and beds themselves are places of potential physical invasion. The bed becomes a location for potential dramatic conflict, a metonym of the stage space itself. The stage property of the bed thus functions not only as a practical location for a sleeping Innogen, but a proxy metonym for the female body, female vulnerability and the stage space. In addition, the 'trunk' invades the woman's 'bedroom' so both stage properties metonymise the bodies of a man and a woman respectively. Stage properties stand for the scene's symbolic narrative meaning: a man is taking advantage of a sleeping woman, and will be using that advantage to imply they have had sex. Sex and sexuality are implicit throughout: the men wagered on Innogen's chastity, and through Giacomo's explicit description of Innogen's body his actions are deliberately eroticised. Once the bed appears on stage, the narrative tension is raised, as the audience know from the previous scene that Giacomo is in the trunk. Although Innogen feels her bedroom is a safe place of retreat, we know its very privacy is the source of her vulnerability. The woman in bed open to the viewers gaze is integral to the scene's meaning. The audience are voyeurs as Giacomo is, and his languid tally of Innogen's physical characteristics encourage the viewer to linger on her passive body. What effect does this have on the audience's response? Giacomo's invasive accounting of Innogen simultaneously draws us into what he is viewing and distances us from his abuse. His language self-consciously invokes Tarquin (l.12), the Roman emperor who raped Lucretia, the subject of a narrative poem by Shakespeare, and of many contemporary images. The story of Lucretia was frequently used as a model for female chastity: because she killed herself rather than live with the 'shame'. Her husband helped overthrow the Roman monarchy, enabling the establishment of the Roman Republic. By allowing Giacomo to characterise himself as the villain of that story, Shakespeare suggests both bed and situation are iconically and thematically linked to rape as a political trope for freedom. This whole play problematises the dependence of the ancient British political world on imperial Rome. Here, that political problem is reduced iconically and symbolically to the sexual politics of a bedroom scene. The bed and the woman symbolise a threatened Britain, the trunk and Giacomo a corrupting Rome.

The book set aside by Innogen ('fold down the leaf where I have left', l.4), is picked up and fondled by Giacomo ('She hath been reading late, / The tale of Tereus. Here the leaf's turned down / Where Philomel gave up', ll.44–6). This story, familiar from Ovid's *Metamorphoses*, again introduces rape as an explicit reference within this scene. Philomela is raped by Tereus, deputised by her father to protect her on a journey, who cuts out her tongue to prevent her reporting the rape. The physical book, read by Innogen, its pages folded down, telling of rape, is physically literally handled by Giacomo. The book and the bed as physical objects stand in for body and voice of a woman. The silenced Philomela echoes the sleeping and silenced Innogen here and throughout the play as Innogen's voice is successively silenced by husband, father and brothers. However, just as Innogen was reading the book of Philomela who can sing but not speak, so the audience 'read' Innogen's victimisation, positioned to her as she is positioned to Philomela. By making us see how sexual assault is a competition between men, an invasion of female space and a complicity of silence, the physical stage properties draw attention to our role. We have an analogous interpretative position to Innogen, and the audience's usual silence during a performance further riffs on this parallel: however, our political and interpretative responses are activated.

The 'taper' (l.5) which Innogen asks to be left burning provides the light whereby Giacomo can itemise the features of her body and write them in his notebook. The stage furniture is essential to our perception that light is filtered and at night, enhancing the scene's secrecy and intimacy. Giacomo's notebook ('I will write all down', l.24) physically itemises Innogen's body in writing: a symbol of his control over her body and fate so he can take 'proofs' back to her husband. Visual and verbal knowledge (confirmed in writing) are 'read' by Posthumus as proof of carnal knowledge. The notebook itself bears the truth of the event (he only wrote and noted, did not rape), but provides the means whereby he can imply much more. The power of knowledge and its usage is symbolically encoded in Giacomo's notebook as proof of knowledge: a theme explored throughout all the late plays.

The most invasive act is Giacomo's stealing of Innogen's bracelet from her sleeping body. The bracelet was given to her by Posthumus in the opening wooing scene, and pledged as a token of faith. Although the word 'bracelet' is not mentioned here, we know this is what Giacomo takes because we see him deliver it to Posthumus in Rome. Giacomo integrates stage directions into his dialogue, via an imperative: 'Come off, Come off; / As slippery as the Gordian knot was hard.' (ll.33–4). '*This* will witness outwardly' (l.35) suggests that he holds it up for the audience to see. The bracelet, like bed and book, symbolises the body of the woman from whom it has been stolen, and implies her lost virtue. Giacomo depends on this conventional metonymy of woman and jewel when he carries the bracelet to Rome, and it is one to which Posthumus also falls victim. However, the audience know that this conventional reading is wrong, and is deliberately manipulated by Giacomo. The use of stage properties from this scene show us how symbols are misread and suggests the damage misreading has on human relationships, trust and families. Physical stage props are used both to represent conventional connotations, and suggest ways such 'readings' can be both wrong and damaging.

How are stage directions embedded in the dialogue? One way is through different sentence types. Interrogatives ('Who's there? My woman Helen?, l.1) which, by asking and answering, locate characters, time and place. Exclamations ('That I might touch, / But kiss, one kiss!', ll.16–17) are used to tell us what characters are feeling and doing. Declaratives ('I will write all down', l.24) express intention and describe action. Imperatives ('come off, come off') direct action. Conditionals ('why should I write this down', l.43), explain and lead decisions and actions. The other way in which stage directions are embedded is through prepositions (there, here, up, down, yonder, by, thus, these, this) which are scattered throughout the dialogue: 'our Tarquin *thus*', l.13; 'perfumes the chamber *thus*', l.19; 'under *these* windows' l.23; '*there* the window / , *Such* the adornment of the bed'; '*thus* in a chapel', l.33. These denotative prepositions show Giacomo is moving around the stage noting features of room and body, and thus delineate his detailed surveillance of Innogen, rendering his language, his eyes and his body (he kisses her) equally invasive. Internal stage directions illuminate character, action and performance, and supplement the ways stage properties function to deepen our sense of character and thematic development in the plot.

Let us now read the extract from *Pericles*.

Analysis: *Pericles*, Scene 5, ll.155–204

SECOND FISHERMAN	Help, master, help! Here's a fish hangs	155
	in the net like a poor man's right in the law; 'twill hardly	
	come out. Ha, bots on't, 'tis come at last, and 'tis turned	
	to a rusty armour.	
PERICLES	An armour, friends? I pray you, let me see it.	
	Thanks, fortune, yet that after all my crosses	160
	Thou giv'st me somewhat to repair my losses,	
	And though it was mine own, part of my heritage	
	Which my dead father did bequeath to me	
	With this strict charge even as he left his life:	
	'Keep it, my Pericles; it hath been a shield	165
	'Twixt me and death', and pointed to this brace,	
	'For that it saved me, keep it. In like necessity,	
	The which the gods forfend, the same may defend thee.'	
	It kept where I kept, I so dearly loved it,	
	Till the rough seas, that spares not any man	170
	Took it in rage, though calmed have given't again.	
	I thank thee for't. My shipwreck now's no ill,	
	Since I have here my father gave in's will.	
MASTER	What mean you, sir?	
PERICLES	To beg of you, kind friends, this coat of worth,	175
	For it was sometime target to a king.	
	I know it by this mark. He loved me dearly,	
	And for his sake I wish the having of it,	
	And that you'd guide me to your sovereign's court,	
	Where with it I may appear a gentleman.	180
	And if that ever my low fortune's better,	
	I'll pay your bounties, till then rest your debtor.	
MASTER	Why, wilt thou tourney for the lady?	
PERICLES	I'll show the virtue I have learned in arms.	
MASTER	Why, d'ye take it, and the gods give thee good on't!	185
SECOND FISHERMAN	Ay, but hark you, my friend; 'twas we	
	that made up this garment through the rough seams of	
	the waters. There are certain condolements, certain	
	vails. I hope sir, if you thrive, you'll remember from	
	whence you had this.	190
PERICLES	Believe't, I will.	

	By your furtherance I am clothed in steel,	
	And spite of all the rapture of the sea	
	This jewel holds his building on my arm.	
	Unto thy value I will mount myself	195
	Upon a courser whose delightsome steps	
	Shall make the gazer joy to see him tread.	
	Only, my friend, I yet am unprovided	
	Of a pair of bases.	
SECOND FISHERMAN	We'll sure provide. Thou shalt have my	200
	best gown to make thee a pair; and I'll bring thee to the	
	court myself.	
PERICLES	Then honour be but a goal to my will,	
	This day I'll rise, or else add ill to ill.	*Exeunt*

Pericles wanders on to stage (the shore of Pantapolis) after a shipwreck, having lost men and possessions. Fishermen are drawing up their nets, debating the weather and politics. The physical labour of pulling up nets is implicit in their call to help untangle the nets or pull the fish out. The net and its contents give immediate visual veracity to the fishermen's labour: and the rusty armour they pull from it prompts a physical and narrational turning point for Pericles. Once he hears that the difficult fish is actually armour, Pericles changes, his delivery enlivened from the despair articulated at the scene's opening. The initial appearance of the armour creates a comic disjunction between what the fisherman hoped was a valuable fish and the physical actuality of clunky armour: 'bots on't...'tis turned to a rusty armour' (l.157). The stage property begins as a potentially lucrative fish then becomes useless rubbish.

However, Pericles converts this rubbish into a meaningful object, giving it a history, and aligning it to his personal identity, both past and future. The armour will 'repair my losses' (l.161), because it 'was mine own' and because 'my dead father did bequeath [it] to me' (l.163). He validates a genealogical history for the armour by directly quoting his father's words, giving the armour a talismanic quality, enabling him to define himself through both his father and his own past. Pericles' words enact some of the magic of drama itself, which gives inanimate objects life and meaning. The rusty dead armour that was dragged to shore in the net has become, with the power of recognition and language, a proxy for Pericles' identity, history and reason for living. But what we see literally acts as a constant counterpoint to Pericles' talisman. The stage property thus works in two directions, simultaneously: awakening Pericles to a sense of himself and purpose, but remaining visually ridiculous to the audience (and the fishermen), denoting Pericles' clutching at the vestiges of a lost past. The stage property's function enhances the dramatic tension between past and future through visual and material means.

However, as the scene progresses, the armour garners greater resonances. Pericles does not just use it as a memento on which to ponder his past and his heritage: he puts it on and changes his identity and destiny. The object which was pulled from the sea, meaningless to the fishermen, can clothe Pericles, 'with it I may appear a gentleman' (l.180), and '*show* the virtue I have learned in arms' (l.184). Armour outwardly signals to viewers the inner gentleman and acts as external proxy for his virtue. Pericles' claim, however, is always visually and narrationally undercut. The armour is rusty, generating a comical not a serious figure, visually suggesting Don Quixote, who archaically rode to quests in rusty armour. The second fisherman's dialogue punctures Pericles' chivalric modelling. The fisherman's assertion of agency in the production of the rusty armour reminds Pericles and us that this particular armour has its own 'new' identity: ''twas we that made up this garment through the rough seams of the waters' (l.187). This is a plea for 'certain condolements' (l.188), a resonant malapropism which puns both the 'dole' of a reward, and the 'condolences' for death and loss. But more resonantly, it asserts the changed nature of the armour: not only is it rusty, but it has been through different hands, its history has changed. Its journey through water, its changed quality from steel to rust, its plucking from the sea, all tell us this is not the armour it once was, as Pericles is not the man he once was. His desperate clutching of the rusty armour and its former significance is at once heroic and tragic. We admire his bravery and fortitude, but bewail his folly. The comic undercutting of his heroic remembrances is affected both through the visual effect of the armour on the audience and by the fishermen's clunky wit and understandable desire to have a reward if one is to be found. Stage property and characters therefore share a narrative function.

What is armour? Armour in early-modern plays usually signalled martial and aristocratic valour and identity. Pericles' belief that wearing the armour will restore his past identity and status echoes Hamlet's recognition of the ghost of his father on the battlements by his armour. In many ways he is not wrong, since it is the armour, however rusty it might be, which enables him to fight in the tournament at King Simonides' court and win his wife Thaisa (Scene 9). However, its rusty outward appearance continually reminds the audience that Pericles does belong in the world of chivalry. His outsider status is a visual and narrative reminder that the world invoked by Gower (the medieval poet-narrator used as the play's chorus) is a self-consciously archaic world. The rusty armour carries visual resonances of precisely this conundrum: what place do ancient virtues and values have in a newly commercialised and competitive world? Each member of the audience must arrive at their own answer. However, the ultimate success of Pericles' quest seems to reward his 'virtue'. The romance-ending, which reunites his lost family despite their successive and tragic trials, idealistically suggests that even in rusty armour, a gentleman's natural qualities will ensure a happy ending.

The Christian imagery implicit in this scene reinforces this sense of a providential destiny. The armour, like Pericles, has been washed in the sea, and emerges in a new identity. The baptismal resonances are implicit: St Paul enjoined Christians to 'put on the whole armour of God, that ye may be able to withstand in the evil day, and having done all, to stand' (*Ephesians* 6.11). Pericles' rusty armour resonates with baptismal renewal and purposeful quest. Its chivalric and historic past renders it personally meaningful to Pericles, but its newly acquired rust and baptismal status becomes the means through which Pericles begins to gesture at a renewed and reconfigured sense of destiny. It is the familial and the personal which prove virtue, not status. Of course, at the end of the play this rediscovered virtue turns out to belong to a royal family after all. However, this ending does not detract from the radical visual and narrational suggestions (personal virtue, not status, counts) achieved through the successive resonances of the stage property.

Let us now look at a scene from *The Winter's Tale*.

Analysis: *The Winter's Tale*, 3.3.1–56

Enter Antigonus, [carrying the] baby, [and] a Mariner
ANTIGONUS Thou art perfect, then, our ship hath touched upon
　　　　　　The deserts of Bohemia?
MARINER　　　　　　　　　　　　Ay, my lord, and fear
　　　　　　We have landed in ill time—the skies look grimly
　　　　　　And threaten present blusters. In my conscience,
　　　　　　The heavens with that we have in hand are angry,　　5
　　　　　　And frown upon 's.
ANTIGONUS Their sacred wills be done. Go, get aboard;
　　　　　　Look to thy barque; I'll not be long before
　　　　　　I call upon thee.
MARINER　　　　　　Make your best haste, and go not
　　　　　　Too far i' th' land; 'tis like to be loud weather.　　10
　　　　　　Besides, this place is famous for the creatures
　　　　　　Of prey that keep upon't.
ANTIGONUS　　　　　　　　　Go thou away,
　　　　　　I'll follow instantly.
MARINER　　　　　　　　I am glad at heart
　　　　　　To be so rid o' th' business.　　　　　　　　　　*Exit*
ANTIGONUS　　　　　　　　　　　Come, poor babe.
　　　　　　I have heard, but not believed, the spirits o' th' dead　15
　　　　　　May walk again. If such thing be, thy mother
　　　　　　Appeared to me last night, for ne'er was dream
　　　　　　So like a waking. To me comes a creature,
　　　　　　Sometimes her head on one side, some another;
　　　　　　I never saw a vessel of like sorrow,　　　　　　　　20
　　　　　　So filled and so becoming. In pure white robes,
　　　　　　Like very sanctity, she did approach
　　　　　　My cabin where I lay, thrice bowed before me,
　　　　　　And, gasping to begin some speech, her eyes
　　　　　　Became two spouts; the fury spent, anon　　　　　　25
　　　　　　Did this break from her: 'Good Antigonus,
　　　　　　Since fate, against thy better disposition,
　　　　　　Hath made thy person for the thrower-out
　　　　　　Of my poor babe, according to thine oath,
　　　　　　Places remote enough are in Bohemia;　　　　　　　30

There weep, and leave it crying; and for the babe
Is counted lost for ever, Perdita
I prithee call't. For this ungentle business
Put on thee by my lord, thou ne'er shalt see
Thy wife Paulina more.' And so with shrieks					35
She melted into air. Affrighted much,
I did in time collect myself, and thought
This was so, and no slumber. Dreams are toys;
Yet for this once, yea, superstitiously,
I will be squared by this. I do believe					40
Hermione hath suffered death, and that
Apollo would, this being indeed the issue
Of King Polixenes, it should here be laid,
Either for life or death, upon the earth
Of its right father. Blossom, speed thee well!					45
   [*He lays down the baby and a scroll*]
There lie, and there thy character; there these,
   [*He lays down a bundle*]
Which may, if fortune please, both breed thee, pretty,
And still rest thine. [*Thunder*] The storm begins—poor wretch,
That for thy mother's fault art thus exposed
To loss, and what may follow! Weep I cannot,					50
But my heart bleeds, and most accurst am I
To be by oath enjoined to this. Farewell;
The day frowns more and more—thou'rt like to have
A lullaby too rough. I never saw
The heavens so dim by day.
[*Storm, with a sound of dogs barking and hunting horns*]
                    A savage clamour!					55
Well may I get aboard!—This is the chase;
I am gone for ever!   *Exit pursued by a bear*

There are four stage properties here. The 'babe' must be a constructed doll of fabric and cloth; the 'character' (l.46) and gold (l.47) which Antigonus leaves with Perdita to both aid her survival and provide her with a future identity; and the 'bear', which must be a man in a bear head or suit. The bear is technically not a stage property, but an actor using a stage property that has become a costume.

Babies are metaphorically and actually present on stage at a number of key moments in the play: the promise of young Mamillius is eulogised by courtiers in the play's opening; Hermione's pregnant body waddles around the stage in the second scene, and provides the visual prompt for Leontes' outburst of jealous rage; the young princess, barely a few days old, is laid on the ground before Leontes' throne to win back his love and sanity; Hermione appears in her trial dishevelled from giving birth, the absent baby present in the accusations of adultery, and the physical evidence of her body; finally, the baby appears again here. The promise of a future, and the continuation of life implicit in a birth is dismantled and dissected in the first half of this play. Leontes exposes the fragility of trust between a man and a woman in a sexual relationship: how can we know our child is our own, and why does this matter? The physical presence of the baby is a concrete material reminder to us and Leontes of his pain and simultaneously his mania. Hermione's cumulative and logical appeals to trust and faith, and her physical dishevelment, convince the audience of her innocence. The physical baby pulls the parents further apart: proving to Leontes that he is right and to Hermione the tragedy of the masculine demand for absolute knowledge and proof of paternity.

When Antigonus brings the baby to the fictional shores of Bohemia, the court's ambivalence towards Hermione and the baby is expressed through him. Antigonus had been banished with the baby from court before the trial, so he has no knowledge of the reading of Apollo's judgement, and Mamillius and Hermione's deaths. When he speaks here of the dream in which Hermione appeared to him, he assumes she has been executed ('suffered death', l.41) and that Polixenes is the baby's father. Representative of the male courtiers most loyal to Leontes, Antigonus carries out Leontes' command to abandon the baby 'upon the earth / Of its right father', ll.44–5). Paternal identity is seen to establish 'right' identity: no maternal link is acknowledged. The horror of breaking this maternal connection is made visually clear to the audience (as throughout Act 3), through Antigonus's misreading of Hermione's appearance to him in a dream as evidence of her guilt. The stage property symbolises the divergent interpretations of the break between Hermione and Leontes, which has tended to split on gendered lines. To Leontes and Antigonus the baby is the supreme evidence of Hermione's guilt; but to herself and her women it is proof of her honesty and faith.

Antigonus's language and action express sympathy for the baby and its situation: he uses diminutives ('Blossom, speed thee well'; 'pretty'; 'poor wretch', ll.45–8); he weeps; and worries what will happen to her. Shakespeare engenders pathos through both situation and Antigonus's responses, connoting tragic and romance outcomes. In romances and fairy tales abandoned babies die or are eaten by wolves and bears, but are sometimes rescued by shepherds. Both these possible outcomes happen here. The baby as stage property enables tragic potential to turn into hope: abandonment happens, but baby and money are discovered safely by shepherds at the end of the scene.

The bear appears as if from nowhere, although the Mariner warns Antigonus that the land is 'famous for the creatures / Of prey that keep on 't' (ll.11–12). Antigonus refers to the strange sounds and the storm through which they have come. Weather, land, and nature are all anthropomorphised, threatening him and the child. The nightmare in which Hermione 'shrieks' at him conspires with the 'deserts of Bohemia' to create an image of a barren, terrifying place and experience. The land that in Act 4 presents as the location of an apparent pastoral idyll, is in fact violent, uncertain, full of nightmarish fears and actual wild beasts. But why does a bear appear? Antigonus dies a grisly death: his cries as he runs off ('this is the chase'), underlining the bloody reality. His death is the last of the play, marking the final tragedy before the swerve to pastoral comedy. The shepherds who arrive on stage immediately after this extract, summarise the peripeteia: 'thou metst with things dying, I with things newborn' (ll.109–110). Antigonus's death is a proxy punishment for Leontes' hubristic jealousy: no other male adult courtier or leader dies. Images of bears were associated with Russia, and Antigonus has just dreamed of Hermione, who desired that her father, the Emperor of Russia, were alive to be able to avenge her (3.2.117). The huge wild bear destroying Leontes' chief courtier as punishment for the failure to protect Perdita works on both a plausible narrative level (there are wild bears in forests) and on a symbolic narrative level (Hermione has been revenged).

Bears feature in folk tales and popular European winter celebrations: as winter festivities end, young men dress up as bears, trees and wolves to 'play' out the savagery of winter in a carnivalesque celebration. The play's title and structure invoke folk-tale connotations. The appearance of the bear just as the plot turns from winter to summer, from tragedy to comedy, from Leontes' worldview towards that of his daughter, suggests the bear is a symbolic fulcrum shifting us from tragedy to pastoral, from a kind of gritty political realism, to a romantic dream world evoked in popular romance and fairy-tale.

Conclusions

1. Shakespeare's choice of significant stage properties in the plays illustrates his dramaturgical skills and imagination. He uses a select number of stage properties, which can carry the significance of a whole scene, and resonate throughout the play.
2. The intersection of script and the visual arrangement of stage properties show how stage properties were used both to symbolise and coalesce some of the thematic complexities of the plays. We have seen how this occurs with the cumulative actual and potential appearance of the 'baby' in *The Winter's Tale*; in the changing resonances of the rusty armour in *Pericles*; and the arrangement of the bed and its furnishings in *Cymbeline*. Each stage property resonates with different themes, often both reinforcing and questioning the way that characters and audience think.
3. Stage properties are used to help guide and intensify the audience's emotional response, and they do this in key ways. Shakespeare uses several conventional emblematic meanings of visual prompts, as way of complicating our responses to scene and character: for example, the bed symbolises a place for both lust *and* marital chastity; armour symbolises both military valour *and* aggression. Shakespeare enables the audience to both see and feel the paradoxical and contradictory readings and interpretations of behaviour and actions on which the plots of the late plays and comedies pivot. Stage properties are a central visual hook into complex ways of seeing situations.
4. Objects have both literal and symbolic cultural value: stage properties and stage furniture can access and test these, particularly via internal generic and rhetorical means (think about the bear, and attitudes to the rusty armour). The bracelet in *Cymbeline* which is a

precious jewel, also symbolises the perfection of married love, and metonymically the female genitals and body. The scene's focus on the theft of this bracelet from the woman's sleeping body self-consciously asks the audience to think about the characters through the medium of the stage properties and furniture. Giacomo's invasion of bedroom and theft of the bracelet feel as violent as a physical rape, although no such actual violence occurs. Stage properties allows us to see the violence beneath Giacomo's supposedly civilised discourse and the wager he and Posthumus have set up.

5. Conventional objects or furniture can be transformed through the material and aesthetic experiences on stage and through story. Pericles' rusty armour is a good example of this.
6. Stage furniture is used in combination with plot to enhance, complicate and deepen characterisation. Innogen's bed, book, candle and bracelet construct her identity: attention to the objects linked with characters illuminates and broadens our understanding of how Shakespeare creates character.
7. We have observed how characters comment upon stage properties as objects of symbolic resonance. Shakespeare is thus asking us to recognise the textual and visual integration of meanings and connotations: drama is both textual and visual.
8. Stage properties are fully integrated into the narrative, often acting simultaneously at a number of levels. They are symbolic icons of key themes; triggers for a key peripeteia in the plot; the means for differential character reactions; and the visual centre of action on stage in a key scene. If we only look at a text-based analysis of the play, we lose the symbolic and visual nuances which stage property analysis offers.

Methods of Analysis

1. We identified the key stage properties invoked by a particular scene, both explicitly through published stage directions, and implicitly through the scene's action and dialogue.
2. We considered the ways in which the stage property resonated within the scene's action and how that integrated to actual and symbolic references elsewhere.

3. We thought about ways objects have a variety of cultural and visual meanings, and how those impact on the representation and use of the object within the play.
4. We considered how objects help definitions and distinctions of character.
5. We tried to integrate our understandings of an individual stage property to the broader themes of the play or scene.

Suggested Work

The Tempest

- Look at Miranda and Ferdinand's chess game (5.1.189): what is important about this stage property and at this point in the narrative? How does the couple's conversation illuminate what the prop is doing?
- Look at the banquet scene which we discussed in Chapter 2: how are stage properties integral to the scene's visual and emotional meaning? What kinds of cultural and symbolic meanings are used? How does this affect the audience's response?
- How do these props integrate with the play's key themes?

The Winter's Tale

- Look at the flowers, hay bales, songs and gifts handed out in the shepherds' festival in 4.4: how do these construct character, atmosphere, and audience response?
- Paulina's gallery and the statue are stage properties. Look at 5.3 from the point of view of stage properties. What is the significance of an apparently inanimate stage property coming alive? Is this just a joke about stage properties, or does it signal something deeper about the magic of theatricality?

Pericles

- Look at Scene 1 (ll.40ff) when Gower reveals the decapitated heads of Antiochus's daughter's failed suitors. What is the effect of these props? How do they resonate?

- Look at the banquet scene after the joust (Scene 7): how are props used to generate atmosphere, character and resonance?
- Other resonant props in the play include: the baby (Scenes 10 and 11); the bed in which Pericles' wife apparently dies in childbirth and one from which Pericles later cannot rise (Scenes 11 and 21); letters (Scenes 9 and 10); and gold. Consider how these function using some of our approaches from the chapter.

Cymbeline

- Think about Cloten's head (as the heads from *Pericles*) and body in 4.2.
- We discuss the Jupiter scene (5.4) in Chapter 8: remember to deepen your reading of that scene with some thinking about how stage properties are used to enhance its spectacular and dramatic effects.

8

Spectacle and Theatricality

Shakespeare's late plays overtly display large-scale spectacles combined with elements of self-conscious meta-theatricality. This was a popular mode in plays written and performed in the post-1608 Jacobean theatre, a fashion encouraged by the growth in popularity of courtly masques, and the King's Men's acquisition of a second, indoor, theatre at Blackfriars in 1608. How does Shakespeare use spectacle and theatricality? And what impact do they have on character, plot and theme?

Our first scene is from *Cymbeline*.

Analysis: *Cymbeline*, 5.3.124–214

Solemn music. Enter, as in an apparition, Sicilius Leonatus, father to Posthumus, an old man, attired like a warrior, leading in his hand an ancient matron, his wife, and mother to Posthumus, with music before them. Then, after other music, follows the two young Leonati, brothers to Posthumus, with wounds as they died in the wars. They circle Posthumus round as he lies sleeping

SICILIUS	No more, thou thunder-master, show	
	Thy spite on mortal flies.	125
	With Mars fall out, with Juno chide,	
	That thy adulteries	
	Rates and revenges.	
	Hath my poor boy done aught but well,	
	Whose face I never saw?	130

	I died whilst in the womb he stayed,	
	Attending nature's law,	
	Whose father then—as men report	
	Thou orphans' father art—	
	Thou shouldst have been, and shielded him	135
	From this earth-vexing smart.	
MOTHER	Lucina lent not me her aid,	
	But took me in my throes,	
	That from me was Posthumus ripped,	
	Came crying 'mongst his foes,	140
	A thing of pity.	
SICILIUS	Great nature, like his ancestry	
	Moulded the stuff so fair	
	That he deserved the praise o' th' world,	
	As great Sicilius' heir.	145
FIRST BROTHER	When once he was mature for man,	
	In Britain where was he	
	That could stand up his parallel,	
	Or fruitful object be	
	In eye of Innogen, that best	150
	Could deem his dignity?	
MOTHER	With marriage wherefore was he mocked,	
	To be exiled, and thrown	
	From Leonati seat and cast	
	From her his dearest one,	155
	Sweet Innogen?	
SICILIUS	Why did you suffer Giacomo,	
	Slight thing of Italy,	
	To taint his nobler heart and brain	
	With needless jealousy,	160
	And to become the geck and scorn	
	O' th' other's villany?	
SECOND BROTHER	For this from stiller seats we came,	
	Our parents and us twain,	
	That striking in our country's cause	165
	Fell bravely and were slain,	

	Our fealty and Tenantius' right	
	With honour to maintain.	
FIRST BROTHER	Like hardiment Posthumus hath	
	To Cymbeline performed.	170
	Then, Jupiter, thou king of gods,	
	Why hast thou thus adjourned	
	The graces for his merits due,	
	Being all to dolours turned?	
SICILIUS	Thy crystal window ope, look out,	175
	No longer exercise	
	Upon a valiant race thy harsh	
	And potent injuries.	
MOTHER	Since, Jupiter, our son is good,	
	Take off his miseries.	180
SICILIUS	Peep through thy marble mansion, help,	
	Or we poor ghosts will cry	
	To th' shining synod of the rest	
	Against thy deity.	
BROTHERS	Help, Jupiter, or we appeal,	185
	And from thy justice fly.	
	Jupiter descends in thunder and lightning, sitting upon an eagle. He throws a thunderbolt. The ghosts fall on their knees	
JUPITER	No more, you petty spirits of region low,	
	Offend our hearing. Hush! How dare you ghosts	
	Accuse the thunderer, whose bolt, you know,	
	Sky-planted, batters all rebelling coasts?	190
	Poor shadows of Elysium, hence, and rest	
	Upon your never-withering banks of flowers.	
	Be not with mortal accidents oppressed;	
	No care of yours it is, you know 'tis ours.	
	Whom best I love, I cross, to make my gift,	195
	The more delayed, delighted. Be content.	
	Your low-laid son our godhead will uplift.	
	His comforts thrive, his trials well are spent.	
	Our Jovial star reigned at his birth, and in	
	Our temple was he married. Rise, and fade.	200

	He shall be lord of lady Innogen,	
	And happier much by his affliction made.	
	This tablet lay upon his breast, wherein	
	Our pleasure his full fortune doth confine:	
	[*He gives the ghosts a tablet which they lay upon Posthumus' breast*]	
	And so away; no farther with your din	205
	Express impatience, lest you stir up mine.	
	Mount, eagle, to my palace crystalline.	
	He ascends into the heavens	
SICILIUS	He came in thunder, his celestial breath	
	Was sulphurous to smell; the holy eagle	
	Stooped, as to foot us; his ascension is	210
	More sweet than our blest fields; his royal bird	
	Preens the immortal wing and cloys his beak	
	As when his god is pleased.	
ALL THE GHOSTS	Thanks, Jupiter.	

This sequence occurs as Posthumus, dressed as a Roman, lies chained, captured by the Britons. In the previous scenes' successive battles between Romans and Britons, Posthumus fought for the Britons to help rescue the king, switching clothes at the battle's end to ensure capture. Grief and despair at his betrayal of country and wife have rendered him passive.

What does he dream and what do we see? His whole family appear as warriors, bloodied as though they died in a war: father, mother and brothers. '*Solemn Music*' accompanies their entrance, which heralds the strangeness of the vision, conjoining war-torn humans and classical gods. '*With music before them*' and '*after other music*' suggests different music for parents and children. The haunting music and the strange appearance of the ghosts who '*circle... round as he lies sleeping*' signal their other-worldly status. The sleeping character surrounded by speaking figures is a conventional dramatic mode of figuring the contents of a dream. The descent of Jupiter (explicitly from above) would have used stage machinery to lower the divine-looking and impressive character. He is a literal '*deus ex machina*' described by Aristotle and English Renaissance critics as one way of ending a play. Jupiter's arrival here is not the end of the play, but performs a riff on that convention. The god is part of a dream sequence enabling a character to change direction so he can help bring the story to a satisfactory close.

Shakespeare reinvents and revivifies the tired dramatic mode, at the same time as he gets away with using it.

The spectacle is revelatory for its two audiences, us and Posthumus. Once Posthumus wakes from the dream vision, he is a new man: once he reads the prophecy (ll.232–8), he jokes with the gaoler, puts aside his despair and prepares for a future. The spectacle is literally transformative. The experience of watching and listening (analogous to the audience's experience) is other-worldly, magical, impossible, and life-changing.

The ghosts' metre is the form and rhythm of popular ballads which use lines of alternate tetrameter and trimeter beats (four and three stresses respectively, in eight and six syllabic lines). Ballads' usual rhyme scheme is ABCB, and with a few notable exceptions this is the rhyme here. The ballad is quintessentially a populist English poetic mode, often set in a rural environment, enabling a story to be sung, often with a mournful or tragic twist, by a male or female character. The ballad mode implies that music continues to play alongside the textual recitation. The ghosts' story, which is Posthumus's family history, narrates and gives flesh to his tragic heritage through the distinct yet conjoined voices of mother, father and brothers. The popular metrical form helps construct a sense of Posthumus's identity as located and rooted in English history. This is subliminal to the content, but significantly marks the moment of his self-definition and conversion from his Roman clothing and identity. That conversion is central to the abandonment of his jealousy, his return to Innogen, and their joint inheritance of the British throne. Poetic mode, rhythm, rhyme and tone fuse with the narrative trajectory and character development.

The ballad-dialogue's rhythm acts in a musically polyphonic way. Sicilius and the Mother use slightly divergent rhyming and line schemes, albeit with alternate lines rhyming. Sicilius's first verse of 13 lines falls into three parts with rhymes of ABCBD; ABCB; ABCB. The fifth line of that first 'verse' acts as a choral recitative, recurring formally in the Mother's first two verses of five lines, which also rhyme ABCBD (ll.137–41; 152–6). In each case the fifth line has only five beats compared to the six of other lines. The rhyme and rhythmic echoing of maternal and paternal voices sets up an unconscious dialogue between the two voices which simultaneously merges and separates their perspectives: an effect achieved musically and performatively. The brothers' rhymes are all verses of six lines rhyming ABCBDB, creating a communal unity and distinguishing them formally from the parental voice and mode. In the final two verses of 12 lines (before Jupiter descends), there are two six-line stanzas rhyming ABCBDB, the rhyme associated with the brothers' voices. However, these lines are spoken across the four characters: the first six lines are spoken by the father (ll.175–8) and mother (ll.179–80); the second six by the father (ll.181–4) and brothers (ll.185–6). This constructs a metrical and musical harmony which echoes the family history they describe. Despite the horror of their visual appearance as bloody ghosts, the musical, metrical and poetic message acts as a subliminal counterpoint. The sophisticated arrangement of voices and poetry enact a doubled message. Shakespeare's convergence and divergence of voice, representation and metre finds a way of representing the confusions and insights offered by dreams.

The pattern of rhymes is equally musically effective. Semantic emphasis falls on rhymes, noting the rhyming words, and making connections between them. In the parent's verses the final fifth shorter line resonates because it does not fit the stanza's rhythm or rhyme. The three fifth lines in the parent's verses are: 'Rates and revenges' (l.128); 'a thing of pity' (l.141); and 'sweet Innogen' (l.156). These three semantic fields echo into Posthumus's consciousness and help him reflect on his past and the possibility of Innogen's innocence. The main rhymes offered by the ballad rhythm, when listed, create semantic fields which resonate in listeners' consciousness: flies / adulteries; saw / law; art / smart; throes / foes; fair / heir; he / be / dignity; throne / one; Italy / jealousy / villainy; twain / slain / maintain; performed / adjourned / turned; exercise / injuries / miseries; cry / deity / fly. Links created between the words within each rhyme scheme invoke many of the play's continuing themes: questions of who has a right to rule; the role of art and theatre; the role of adversity in character development; and the opposition between British and Roman values and history. These rhymes echo and last beyond the physical singing and localised meaning of the verses, acting as unconscious suggestions of a moral and providential ordering of events.

What is actually said and how does it resonate? Posthumus's family's bloody past, their lives lost in war before he is born, and his mother's through childbirth, rendered him an orphan. Their message, appearance and story emphasise that history creates our identity: a message that the whole play reiterates about British history and identity. *Cymbeline*'s story is one of resistance to outside invasion and a developing sense of pride in Britishness. Posthumus's father's appeal to Jupiter produces an answer: Jupiter 'descends' to earth to promise resolution, albeit in an enigmatic way. Providence and divinity reward the just in the end: dramatic structure replicates the Christian story and promise of rebirth, albeit through a pre-Christian narrative.

Jupiter's descent is self-evidently meant to be spectacular, frightening (*'in thunder and lightning... he throws a thunderbolt'*), and awe-inspiring (*'the ghosts fall on their knees'*). Actual gods terrify mortals, and their words and intentions remain difficult for humans to interpret, although the final impact of their intervention in human affairs is both benevolent and ethical. The virtuous are rewarded, the sinful die. He speaks in regular iambic pentameter: the 21 lines are all ten-beat lines of predominantly iambic not trochaic emphasis. Such metrical regularity runs the risk of creating a dirge-like sound, but here, in combination with character and spectacle, enhances instead the sense of a divine judgemental voice. The regular rhyming scheme slows the delivery, forcing a slight pause on each rhymed word. The speech is in alternate rhymes of ABAB, consisting of four rhymes like this and ending with an additional line which enables a closure on a rhyming couplet. The regularity of the rhymes suggests a sense of an ordered world and events, both of which have hitherto seemed arbitrary and inequitable. Jupiter's rebuke to the ghosts ('Be not with mortal accidents opprest', l.193) is a rebuke to both characters and audience, who have seen a succession of tragedies in the plot. Instead, by promising Posthumus his protection (because born under a 'Jovial star' and married in his temple), Jupiter aligns him with the workings of divine intention. Providential design follows characters who turn to virtue and who suffer 'affliction' (l.203). Both narrative design and promised reward echo and invoke the Christian promise. It is also a generic turn from tragedy to comedy, towards an inclusive transformative ending.

Finally, the sequence here is a whole performance in itself: a tiny play of just under a hundred lines within the overall play which we are watching. It is structurally perfect, with a beginning, middle and end: the visual parade of the ghosts onto the stage; followed by the family's exposition of the past and their exhortation to Jupiter; and Jupiter's entrance prompting the dramatic turning point, provoking fear and awe in the on-stage audience, and the finale. This miniature structure echoes Aristotle's ideas in *The Poetics* about how dramatic structure resolves plot by moving from peripeteia towards catharsis through emotional shock. This play-within-a-play explicitly displays ideas about drama's effects, structure and content. This is a bit of a joke: the audience can see that the dream sequence, arrival of a god with thunder and lightning, and his untying of the plot tangle are a succession of self-conscious dramatic clichés. However, at the same time, the clichés set Posthumus on his path to recovery, and the play towards its resolution. By placing the device within a dream, Shakespeare breathes life back into the cliché, locating it within Posthumus's mind as well as making it theatrically visible. It is a gentle reflective commentary on how dramaturgy works as both plot and effect: and as such acts as a meta-theatrical observation on story, playing and audience. Song, music, spectacle, recognition, providence and resolution are all part of that dramatic construction, each playing a part in the total dramatic experience.

Let us now turn to a different theatrical experience: the Chorus of *The Winter's Tale*.

Analysis: *The Winter's Tale*, 4.1.1–32

Enter Time, the Chorus

TIME I, that please some, try all; both joy and terror
Of good and bad, that makes and unfolds error,
Now take upon me, in the name of Time,
To use my wings. Impute it not a crime
To me or my swift passage, that I slide   5
O'er sixteen years, and leave the growth untried
Of that wide gap, since it is in my power

>   To o'erthrow law, and in one self-born hour
>   To plant and o'erwhelm custom. Let me pass
>   The same I am, ere ancient'st order was,   10
>   Or what is now received. I witness to
>   The times that brought them in; so shall I do
>   To th' freshest things now reigning, and make stale
>   The glistering of this present, as my tale
>   Now seems to it. Your patience this allowing,   15
>   I turn my glass, and give my scene such growing
>   As you had slept between; Leontes leaving,
>   Th'effects of his fond jealousies so grieving
>   That he shuts up himself. Imagine me,
>   Gentle spectators, that I now may be   20
>   In fair Bohemia; and remember well,
>   I mentioned a son o' th' King's, which Florizel
>   I now name to you, and with speed so pace
>   To speak of Perdita, now grown in grace
>   Equal with wond'ring. What of her ensues   25
>   I list not prophecy, but let Time's news
>   Be known when 'tis brought forth. A shepherd's daughter,
>   And what to her adheres, which follows after,
>   Is th' argument of Time. Of this allow,
>   If ever you have spent time worse ere now;   30
>   If never, yet that Time himself doth say
>   He wishes earnestly you never may.   *Exit*

What do we see here? Time describes his appearance as winged (l.4) and holding an hour-glass (l.16), classical and Renaissance visual conventions for representing Time as an allegorical and personified figure. This is his only appearance, yet his entrance at this pivotal moment points both backwards and forwards to the play's action. The physical rendering of 'time' as a character has several effects. It displaces us from direct engagement with the characters and story to date, since none of the other characters have been remotely figurative and abstract: the representational mode has shifted from realism to abstract allegory, from enactment to narration. This pauses the action and enables reflection. The narrator figure reminds us that this is a (winter's) 'tale', a story working its effects, creating a momentary distancing effect. Act 3 had ended with the shepherds' discovery of Perdita, so the audience knows that she survives, but know nothing of what happened afterwards or in Sicilia. The choral interruption is a relief: we welcome an interlude to the succession of wrenching tragedies. However, we are also eager to know what happens next. The chorus's suspension of action paradoxically enhances and releases narrative tension, and does so in a self-conscious manner.

In Greek drama, the Chorus was the commentator on action and plot, a mediator between characters and audience, a communal representation of the relationship between fictional representation and the reception of the audience. The Chorus would usually speak at the front of the stage, physically signalling a liminal position between audience and play. In most cases choral figures remain anonymous and unnamed. In Shakespeare's plays where choruses appear (for example, *Romeo and Juliet* and *Henry V)* the speaker prefix is anonymised as 'chorus', spoken by one of the actors who may have taken another part. In *Henry IV* and *The Winter's Tale*, the chorus takes an allegorical name (Rumour and Time respectively). Time as an allegory in painting or poetry was often represented as old, carrying a scythe or more benignly an hour-glass, sometimes referred to as 'Father Time'. The connotations of a controlling, paternalistic figure remind us of Leontes' controlling desires and actions: but are linked here to a supra-human force which suggests that events are out of human control. Although the convention was for a masculine Time, there is nothing in the speech which gives a gender to this figure.

There are two discrete conceptions of time in the play: that of historical events predicated by humans and their follies, and that of forces beyond our control, such as nature, God, and our natural aging. Up until now, action has been predicated into tragedy by one man's extreme emotions and perceptions. Time's arrival introduces a supra-historical sense of time, divorced from human agency, and suggests through his intervention and appearance that micro-history can change and tragedy can be reversed. As Time upends his hourglass (l.16), literally at the mid-point of his speech, time moves visually and physically in a different direction.

The displacement of action from the characters and plot to this external figure, who is both narrator and a force of nature, renders human action insignificant. Although Time is not a god, the effect on action and audience is similar to that of Jupiter's appearance in *Cymbeline*. The action stops, pauses, and moves forward in a different direction. The paradoxical duality of Time is echoed in the oxymoronic statements Time voices ('joy and terror / good and bad'; 'plant and o'erwhelm', l.9), and in his descriptions of how 'the freshest things now reigning' (l.13) will soon be stale.

When the action recommences, 16 years have passed, so the interruption serves as a plot conjunction. However, the next scene between Camillo and Polixenes discursively repeats much of this material, so it is not dramatically essential to use a chorus to explain the passage of time. It is the interruption which is important, the time for reflection, the pause for thought and questions: what has time also done to us?

What does Time say that further illuminates this pause? The speech's opening couplet ('I, that please some, try all, both joy and terror / Of good and bad, that makes and unfolds error', ll.1–2) establishes Time as an emphatic and self-consciously powerful agent. The opening pronoun, 'I' posits a controlling force in contradistinction to 'some' and 'all' (of us), yet one which suggests our ineluctable mutuality. Time will 'try' us all: the conventional phrase becomes one of providential intention. It suggests implicitly that there is a hidden hand of design behind life's trials. He repeats the personal pronoun as subject or pronoun 17 times in 32 lines, implying a supra-historical continuity that no individual humans can possess. The opening phrase links both fiction and life: a story, like Time, tests its characters; Aristotelian emotions of joy and terror are evoked by both. Time as character crosses between fiction and life: he is talking about Leontes and Hermione, but also about us. The adverbial prepositions which are used here place Time's appearance and current speech very much in the present: he uses 'now' at the beginning of three lines (ll.3, 15 and 23), as a way of both signalling his control of the action and the present tense. Although Time implies prescience, he does not prophesy a future, carefully heightening tension through anticipation. In this way this Chorus differs from those of both Greek tragedies and *Romeo and Juliet* (say), which narrate the action to come. This Chorus keeps us guessing.

Time speaks directly to the audience ('Imagine me / Gentle spectators', ll.19–20), explicitly invoking our role in creating theatrical spectacle: it is only through our imagination that the characters can be transported in time and space ('as you had slept between', l.17) to Bohemia. Personified Time and the theatre share this magical ability to compress and distort space and history, but only with our help. Time's final words invoke the audience's experience of 'spent time' (l.30) in opposition to his control of the passage of time, suggesting that understanding both experiences of time are valuable to our sense of the world. Directly addressing us ('you' ll.30, 32) he suggests that watching condensed time on stage will be more profitable than 'worse' spent time, and that Time's investment in human experience is essentially benevolent.

Time's speech is predominantly in iambic pentameters of rhyming couplets, aurally marking the scene as different from the rest of *The Winter's Tale*. Time's choral function suspends action and changes the pace. Rhyming couplets achieve the same paradoxical effect: speeding the delivery of each alternate line, as the speaker races to the rhyme, but slowing down as the rhyme is reached to savour the connection between the two rhyming words. The resultant subliminal stop–start effect is barely perceptible but intrinsic to rhyming couplets, and perfectly matches the dualistic conception of Time. Metrical timing here has an integral connection to the broader sense of how time on stage is always altered, condensed and stretched. Time's reference to the audience's theatrical experience 'spent time' implies a debate about both theatrical timing and "real life" leisure time, lending a metatheatrical dimension to his words and thinking. Language, metre and representation all fuse.

Let us now move on to the final extract in this chapter, Ceres' masque in *The Tempest*.

Analysis: *The Tempest*, 4.1.57–142

PROSPERO   Well.
   Now come, my Ariel. Bring a corollary,
   Rather than want a spirit. Appear and pertly!
      Soft music
   No tongue! All eyes! Be silent.

Enter Iris

IRIS Ceres, most bounteous lady, thy rich leas　　　　　60
Of wheat, rye, barley, vetches, oats, and peas;
Thy turfy mountains, where live nibbling sheep,
And flat meads thatched with stover them to keep;
Thy banks with pionèd and twillèd brims,
Which spongy April at thy hest betrims,　　　　　65
To make cold nymphs chaste crowns; and thy broom-groves,
Whose shadow the dismissèd bachelor loves,
Being lass-lorn; thy poll-clipped vineyard,
And thy sea-marge sterile and rocky-hard,
Where thou thyself dost air: the Queen o' th' sky,　　　70
Whose watery arch and messenger am I,
Bids thee leave these, and with her sovereign grace,
Here on this grass-plot, in this very place,
To come and sport. Her peacocks fly amain.
[*Juno's chariot appears suspended above the stage*]
Approach, rich Ceres, her to entertain.　　　　　75

Enter [Ariel as] Ceres

CERES Hail, many-coloured messenger, that ne'er
Dost disobey the wife of Jupiter;
Who with thy saffron wings upon my flowers
Diffusest honey-drops, refreshing showers;
And with each end of thy blue bow dost crown　　　80
My bosky acres and my unshrubbed down,
Rich scarf to my proud earth: why hath thy queen
Summoned me hither, to this short-grassed green?
IRIS A contract of true love to celebrate,
And some donation freely to estate　　　　　85
On the blessed lovers.
CERES　　　　　　　Tell me, heavenly bow,
If Venus or her son, as thou dost know,
Do now attend the Queen? Since they did plot
The means that dusky Dis my daughter got,
Her and her blind boy's scandalled company　　　90
I have forsworn.

IRIS	Of her society
	Be not afraid. I met her deity
	Cutting the clouds towards Paphos, and her son
	Dove-drawn with her. Here thought they to have done
	Some wanton charm upon this man and maid, 95
	Whose vows are, that no bed-right shall be paid
	Till Hymen's torch be lighted; but in vain.
	Mars's hot minion is returned again;
	Her waspish-headed son has broke his arrows,
	Swears he will shoot no more, but play with sparrows, 100
	And be a boy right out.
CERES	High'st Queen of state,
	Great Juno, comes; I know her by her gait.
	[*Juno's chariot descends to the stage*]
JUNO	How does my bounteous sister? Go with me
	To bless this twain, that they may prosperous be,
	And honoured in their issue. 105
	[*Ceres joins Juno in the chariot, which rises and hovers above the stage.*] *They sing*
JUNO	Honour, riches, marriage-blessing,
	Long continuance, and increasing,
	Hourly joys be still upon you!
	Juno sings her blessings on you.
CERES	Earth's increase, foison plenty, 110
	Barns and garners never empty,
	Vines and clust'ring bunches growing,
	Plants with goodly burtden bowing;
	Spring come to you at the farthest,
	In the very end of harvest! 105
	Scarcity and want shall shun you;
	Ceres' blessing so is on you.
FERDINAND	This is a most majestic vision, and
	Harmonious charmingly. May I be bold
	To think these spirits?
PROSPERO	Spirits, which by mine art 120
	I have from their confines called to enact
	My present fancies.
FERDINAND	Let me live here ever;
	So rare a wondered father and a wife

	Makes this place paradise.	
	Juno and Ceres whisper, and send Iris on employment	
PROSPERO	Sweet, now, silence!	
	Juno and Ceres whisper seriously.	125
	There's something else to do. Hush, and be mute,	
	Or else our spell is marred.	
IRIS	You nymphs, called Naiads, of the windring brooks,	
	With your sedged crowns, and ever-harmless looks,	
	Leave your crisp channels, and on this green land	130
	Answer your summons, Juno does command.	
	Come, temperate nymphs, and help to celebrate	
	A contract of true love. Be not too late.	

Enter certain nymphs

You sunburnt sickle-men, of August weary,
Come hither from the furrow and be merry; 135
Make holiday; your rye-straw hats put on,
And these fresh nymphs encounter every one
In country footing.

Enter certain reapers, properly habited. They join with the Nymphs in a graceful dance, towards the end whereof Prospero starts suddenly, and speaks, after which, to a strange hollow and confused noise, they heavily vanish

PROSPERO	[*aside*] I had forgot that foul conspiracy	
	Of the beast Caliban and his confederates	140
	Against my life. The minute of their plot	
	Is almost come. [*To the Spirits*]—Well done, avoid. No more!	

This marriage masque is produced by Prospero to mark the solemnity of Miranda and Ferdinand's wedding, and is preceded by Prospero's lecture to them about curbing their sexual desire. Moments before this performance begins, he tells Ferdinand 'be more abstemious' (l.53), rebukingly suggesting the young couple must be kissing. We are reminded that they need to participate in the public part of their wedding, and that Prospero's oversight of their marriage extends to surveillance of their sexual conduct. The masque performance contextualises their sexuality within a mythic framework, and since it is designed by Prospero, defines his approval of their sexual conduct within the narrative of the masque.

The performance of this masque is framed by Prospero as master of ceremonies: his fussy orders to Ariel and to the audience (Miranda and Ferdinand) at the beginning suggest him bustling about anxiously getting everyone into position so his show will achieve his aims. It is the first time we have seen this front-of-house aspect to Prospero's theatrical talents. Previous magical or spirit shows (the Harpy banquet scene, or Ariel's song to Ferdinand), although arranged indirectly by Prospero, have not involved his direct presence. His initial instructions to Ariel, Miranda and Ferdinand are a succession of six imperative commands within two lines ('Come', 'Bring', 'Appear, and pertly!', 'No tongue! All eyes! Be silent!', ll.57–8). The cumulative effect is of haste, accelerating us towards the opening of the show, mimicking the anticipation and excitement before a show starts. During the performance there is a brief conversation between Prospero and Ferdinand, initiated by Ferdinand, to which Prospero's final response is again to quiet the audience through imperatives 'now, silence!' 'Hush, and be mute'(ll.124–6). Equally, his final instructions to the performers are a succession of imperatives ('Well done, avoid. No more.', l.142). During the performance Prospero frames and directs both actors and on-stage audience. We, the off-stage audience, are watching three performances: the masque, the masque's audience, and Prospero. This layered watching is made visible through the stage direction '*Prospero starts suddenly...*'. Prospero's complete immersion in his production and his daughter's wedding has displaced him from his hitherto control of all the stage action. His framing and direction is central to the masque, but ultimately the world of that performance is rendered transient by external events which are almost by not quite out of Prospero's control. The vision disappears when his mind is not concentrating, connoting both his magical powers and the dream-like quality of the performance.

This strange end to the wedding masque echoes the end of the Harpy banquet, where the image and reality of a festive occasion are physically broken up. In the Harpy banquet Prospero used such a break as part of the design of the performance to visually represent the communal laws broken by the 'three men of sin' in their usurpation of Prospero.

Here, by contrast, the sudden breaking up of a marriage celebration is not part of Prospero's design, although it is part of Shakespeare's. Prospero is thereby rendered weaker, less in control of his island and his art, more vulnerable and older. The breaking up of the vision of goddesses also suggests a breaking up of the vision of the island: here they have access to a momentary vision of perfection, but it is only momentary: real life and time ('the *minute* of their plot / Is almost come', ll.141–2) intrude. Prospero's first public directorial debut ends in chaos: what does this signify? It suggests the inevitability of entropy, presaging the melancholic farewell Prospero as magus makes to his magic and books in Act 5, and the actor's farewell in the epilogue. It signals the fragility of youth, marriage and love, so lucidly celebrated by Ceres and Juno and symbolised in the union of Miranda and Ferdinand. It literally shows that aesthetic objects, performance and art can only stop time momentarily, and exist in counterpoint to the 'real' world.

However, there are more positive messages about the impact of art and performance. We observe Ferdinand and Miranda watching as the primary audience of the masque. Ferdinand's mid-point observation about the show suggests that art can transform, inspire and civilise. Ferdinand's relationship with Prospero changes from this moment, not just because he becomes Miranda's husband, but also though art. Ferdinand's judgement of the show as a 'most majestic vision', created by 'so rare a wondered father and a wife' that 'Makes this place paradise', ll.123–4, gives precedence to Prospero, and posits a hierarchy in his new identity: son to Prospero first, and husband second. Ferdinand's perception of royal marriage as a fusing of relationships between men, rather than erotic connections between two young people, generates Prospero's endearment in response ('Sweet, now, silence!', l.124). Art is thereby the means whereby Ferdinand is transformed from besotted lover to responsible husband within the patriarchal order. Art is transformative and magical: but also educative and politically directed. The director's approval of his audience's response is explicit in that diminutive 'sweet', approving Ferdinand's acceptance of his proper place of submission to the father of his bride. By suggesting that the island is 'paradise' (l.124) and referring to his father and wife, Ferdinand's words connote himself as Adam, Miranda as Eve, and Prospero as God of Eden. Although it was something of an explorer's cliché to describe America as a second paradise, here the rediscovery of paradise is located in a marriage between the heirs of Naples and Milan. The play ends as they are set to return to Europe: the symbolism implying that the new Adam and Eve will establish a new world back in Italy. The political message is simultaneously conservative and radical: the family structure is rigidly patriarchal, consisting of a hierarchy of male head of state / male husband / wife. However, that family is used to symbolise ideas of political regeneration back in Europe, an implicit suggestion both that such regeneration is required and that political redemption is possible.

Female gods alone bless the wedding, creating a feminised semantic and imagistic frame, nominally directed by a male magician. Iris is the messenger of the Roman gods and of the rainbow, presaging the arrival of Juno and Ceres, queen of the gods, and goddess of fertility and the Earth respectively. Shakespeare (or Prospero) explicitly chose a female messenger, rather than the more well-known messenger of the gods, the male Mercury. The all-female cast direct the stage action, including the dance of the male reapers and nymphs, and all represent key elements of the female life-cycle: Juno goddess of marriage and childbirth; Ceres of fertility, spring, harvest and the earth; and Iris of nature. Female gods pattern forth the intersection of natural and human fertility and life cycles, echoed in the imagery of Iris's description of Ceres' lush rural empire (ll.60–70), and Ceres' sensuous description of Iris's physical appearance (ll.76–9).

The performance itself falls into three parts, broken by the short interlude of commentary: the initial conversation between the three goddesses, acting as a prologue to the 'show'; the first two songs; the interlude as Ferdinand comments on the performance; and the invocation by Iris of the dance and dancers. Let us consider each of these in turn.

The prologue-like conversation between the goddesses acts out the pretence that the actors are back-stage preparing for the performance. The metre is in iambic pentameter, separating it metrically from the sung performance that follows, although the whole 'show' is in rhyming couplets, giving it an overall linguistic coherence. The goddesses are worried Venus might turn up at the masque to create mischief (ll.87–9), but Iris assures them she has retired to her island at Paphos, frustrated, and that Cupid's arrows are broken. The dialogue posits a fragile opposition between Venus's connection to 'wanton' sexual love and the celebration of marriage. Juno's aim 'that they may prosperous be / And honoured in their issue' (ll.104–5) is set in opposition to the 'wanton mischief' (l.89) intended by Venus, and implied by Prospero in his earlier lecture to the couple on abstinence, and his concern for legitimacy. Legitimacy is allegorised by gods, advocated by Prospero, and refers simultaneously to marriage, political rights, and child-bearing within marriage.

The two songs sung by Juno and Ceres constitute the equivalent of the first act of a two-act performance, in which Iris's invocation to the reapers' dance is the second act. The songs are in a regular tetrameter, conventionally used in Shakespearean songs. Juno's opening sentence lists six nouns before the following verb: a cumulative succession of gifts ('honour, riches, marriage-blessing, / Long continuance and increasing, / Hourly joys') she donates to the couple. Ceres' song implies her gifts are those of the earth: successful harvests, luscious food, and plenty of children. However, she tropes this into a golden age in wishing for no winters ('Spring come to you at the farthest / In the very end of harvest', ll.114–15), echoing Gonzalo in his imagined commonwealth of Act 2 (analysed in Chapter 6). The pastoral, idealised world evoked by Juno and Ceres, in which human sexuality and marriage are explicitly integrated to the seasonal cycles of nature, proposes a rural idyll in which Miranda and Ferdinand symbolise and actualise the perfection of human sexuality and its integral place in the cycles of the natural world. The implicit evocation of Adam and Eve in Ferdinand's commentary implicitly connects the classical pastoral idyll with Christian symbolism. However, the pastoral fantasy of both the golden age and Eden is punctured by the memory of Caliban's rebellion: a physical reminder that the pastoral genre is an idealised fantasy.

The second act, Iris's call to the nymphs and reapers, is in iambic pentameters, distinguishing it from the goddess's songs. As messenger she acts as a mistress of ceremonies, bringing Ceres and Juno for the first song, and now the Naiads and 'sunburnt sickle-men' (l.134) for a *graceful dance* (l.138). The dance is explicitly linked to harvest time (the reapers are sunburnt and 'weary' in August, l.134): and the dances 'in country footing' (l.138) implicitly those performed during harvest time. Song, dance and celebration of the cycles of nature characterised both real harvest festivals and pastoral poetry: and both realism and idealism are invoked fictively, a doubleness acknowledging both the political situation in which Miranda and Ferdinand are bound, and the idealistic hopes associated with their union.

The goddesses emphasise the physical geography through prepositional stage directions three times. Iris calls to Ceres to arrive 'here on *this* grass-plot, *this* very place' (l.73). Ceres asks why she has been summoned 'to *this* short-grassed green' (l.83), and Iris calls on the Naiads to come to '*this* green land' (l.130). The repetition of the location and its rural appearance conjures a place of beauty and lushness. The green world of the island ('this very place') is simultaneously concrete to the performers on stage and symbolic. It is both very much inhabited by Miranda and Ferdinand, and yet symbolically 'green' to the audience in the theatre. Shakespeare's other green worlds (for example in *A Midsummer Night's Dream* or *As You Like It)* are places of fantasy, the exploration of sexuality and strange happenings. The green world the goddesses find on stage symbolically coheres with the performance they offer, and our island experience symbolically elides with the semantic and imagistic pastoral idyll evoked by Ceres and Juno.

Conclusions

1. Visual spectacle occurs at key dramatic turning points. Each spectacle occurs at a moment where key elements of the plot come together, fuse and move into another direction, towards some kind of resolution. Spectacle coincides with and is integral to dramatic plot, and frequently initiates familial reconciliation through marriage, parent–child recognition, and the agency of women.
2. Spectacle condenses and elongates the audience's experience of characters' emotions and acts as a psychological proxy for deepening understanding. By slowing down and speeding up time, literally on stage and metaphorically in audience's conceptions, spectacle enables audience and characters to contemplate time as both a philosophical and lived experience, a key theme in these late plays.

3. Visual spectacles often dramatise classical gods, and enable allegorical figures to represent key emotions, ideas and concepts to characters and audience. Gods or allegorical figures promise a providential resolution after vicissitude confirming the Christian promise, and enabling tragedy to turn to comedy. This is the narrative trope of romance, figured explicitly through supra-theatrical spectacle.
4. The masque form, popular in James I's court incorporated this combined mode of allegory, dance, music and providence, usually to celebrate directly the power of the monarch. Shakespeare's spectacles share the masque's mode and structure, and similarly confirm the restoration of rightful order and rule. The difference between Jacobean masques and the spectacles *within* these plays is that the rest of the play's action, plot and characters contextualise the spectacle. They deepen and question some of the simple assumptions of the masque's form and content: as we noticed in our analysis of Ceres' masque. Jacobean masques ended with a celebratory dance in which all members of cast and elite audience joined. These spectacles utilise an element of that inclusion, since the on-stage audiences are in each case a select elite. However, characters and plot break up the fragile harmony represented by the spectacle: real life always intrudes.
5. Spectacle can help the audience to 'read' the action in certain directions, both because the extended spectacle acts as a visual metaphor for the ideas, emotions and concepts which allegorical characters figure, and because it is contextualised within the wider plot.
6. Meta-theatrical consciousness, in both the audience and characters, is used to enable the audience to reflect simultaneously on the play's content and on how it works to move and inform us. By forcing us to think about how performance and representation work on an audience (because we see it happening to the on-stage audience), Shakespeare creates a self-conscious and sceptical audience in the theatre. However, neither audience becomes cynical about the power of art. We can simultaneously enjoy the spectacle, and acknowledge its fictive status. Meta-theatre enables the positioning of various critical perspectives on action and content, and can thus speak to divergent and different classes.

7. Visual spectacle and action intersect with language, music and song to create and produce a multi-media theatrical experience. The visual appeal of Shakespeare's dramatic skills evidences his continued active engagement as a fashionable practising playwright and business man in the King's Men in the period 1608–11.
8. The intersection and juxtaposition of 'spectacle' with more naturalistic scenic dialogue is closer to a modern musical than some of Shakespeare's earlier comedies. These juxtapositions enable a richer audience response, at a number of emotional and psychological levels, and more layered representations of character and character response to varying situations on stage.

Methods of Analysis

In addition to the linguistic and dramaturgical methods delineated in earlier chapters we have:

1. specifically considered how explicit and implicit stage directions construct and direct character and spectacle on stage;
2. identified the grammatical modes which can help us locate internal stage directions;
3. considered how allegorical figures create meaning;
4. debated the intersection of music, spectacle and language;
5. considered ways in which audience response is integrated, manipulated and made self-conscious as part of the dramatic experience.

Suggested Work

In each play we looked at there is at least one additional spectacle which you should analyse in detail. It is also worth looking at the spectacles from *Pericles*.

The Tempest

Look again at the scene of the Harpy banquet (analysed in Chapter 2). Consider the ways in which the visual and allegorical elements and the use of the on-stage audience achieve dramatic effects. How and why does a spectacle have to occur at this point of the play? Why is time slowed down at this point, and why might that be important?

The Winter's Tale

Look at two spectacles in the play: the summer festival in Bohemia (4.4) and the statue scene (5.3) and consider ways in which spectacle is integral to meaning and effect. Each integrates music, visual spectacle and language; has an on-stage audience; and acts as a key narrative turning point. Look at the staging, thinking carefully about stage directions, visual prompts, and the structuring of the event. How are we and the on-stage audience positioned? Do these differ? Comment on how language and metaphor create a coherent structure of feeling. Do the narratives of each spectacle have a political message?

Cymbeline

Look at Innogen's 'funeral' (4.2, we analyse the song in the next chapter): think about the visual and aural effects of this mini-spectacle. Why is it integrated into the main action?

Pericles

Look at Scene 21 (ll.68–237) from Marina's song to Pericles, his gradual awakening to her identity, his restored sanity, to the descent of the goddess Diana and her promise of providential reconciliations. Look at how language and action slow down time. What kind of language do Pericles and Marina use? What is the effect of her performance, and its history in her stay in the bawdy house? Comment on how daughters 'rescue' fathers successively in these late plays.

9

Music and Song

These plays use music and song as integral parts of the dramatic experience: representing themes, furthering and exploring plot, character and theatrical magic. Music and song are often linked to dramatic spectacle, to the appearance of supernatural figures, and to the magical resolution of conflict, but is equally distinct from these. We have little direct evidence of the actual music played in the original performances, partly because we do not have 'original' scripts approved by Shakespeare. There is some internal and contemporary evidence that Robert Johnson wrote some of the songs for *The Tempest*. We can also say with certainty that many of the contemporary court musicians (such as Ferrabosco, Campion, and Johnson) wrote and performed music at court masques and at many of the plays written for the indoor Blackfriars theatre for the King's Men, as well as the coterie theatres such as St Paul's Boys. They probably wrote to commission, and the songs and music additionally circulated in manuscript, or were published as part of song books, completely separate from the plays themselves. However, we do have the textual words and form of the song, the stage directions, and the placing within the narrative. Let us first turn to Cymbeline, and Innogen's funeral song.

Analysis: *Cymbeline*, 4.2.258–282

	Song
GUIDERIUS	Fear no more the heat o' th' sun,
	Nor the furious winter's rages.

	Thou thy worldly task hast done,	260
	Home art gone, and ta'en thy wages.	
	Golden lads and girls all must,	
	As chimney-sweepers, come to dust.	
ARVIRAGUS	Fear no more the frown o' the great,	265
	Thou art past the tyrant's stroke.	
	Care no more to clothe and eat,	
	To thee the reed is as the oak.	
	The sceptre, learning, physic, must	
	All follow this, and come to dust.	270
GUIDERIUS	Fear no more the lightning flash,	
ARVIRAGUS	Nor th'all dreaded thunder-stone.	
GUIDERIUS	Fear not slander, censure rash.	
ARVIRAGUS	Thou hast finished joy and moan.	
GUIDERIUS *and* ARVIRAGUS	All lovers young, all lovers must	275
	Consign to thee and come to dust.	
GUIDERIUS	No exorciser harm thee,	
ARVIRAGUS	Nor no witchcraft charm thee.	
GUIDERIUS	Ghost unlaid forbear thee.	
ARVIRAGUS	Nothing ill come near thee.	280
GUIDERIUS *and* ARVIRAGUS	Quiet consummation have,	
	And renownèd be thy grave!	

Enter Belarius, with the body of Cloten in Posthumus' clothes

This song is performed to a strangely grotesque visual tableau. It is a joint funeral for Innogen and Cloten. Innogen (whom the brothers believe to be a young man) is lying, covered in flowers (ll.221) near their mother's grave. Cloten's body is missing, so they lay his head beside Innogen. While the father tries to find Cloten's body, the brothers sing this song. Arviragus had found Innogen dead in their cave after hearing '*solemn music*' (l.187). The magical music heralds the narrative's apparent shift towards tragedy, and this plangent song (for which there is no contemporary musical setting) echoes the shift from fairy-tale pastoral to tragedy.

What does the lead-up to the song tell us about its delivery and purpose? Arviragus and Guiderius (unbeknownst to them, the true sons of the King Cymbeline) prepare to do appropriate honour to Innogen 'to sing him to the ground / As once our mother' (ll.237–8), albeit now in their older 'mannish' voices. Guiderius is too upset to sing ('I cannot sing. I'll weep and word it with thee' (l.241), and Arviragus concurs 'we'll speak it then' (l.243). Thus although the stage direction in the 1623 edition cites it as a 'Song', the characters clearly tell us it is spoken. Perhaps it is chanted to a lute or tabor. That this was the very song performed at their mother's burial mean that music and song provide a bridge into the past, suggesting familial continuity and shared communal emotions. Subliminally, it also suggests a family connection between the brothers and their family and Innogen's. The audience's familiarity with fairy-tale motifs, together with Cymbeline's story of lost sons at the beginning of the play and this scene's terrible tension, fuels the hint that she may be their sister.

The song's formal arrangement is in four stanzas of six lines each, three verses in tetrameter, and the final a faster trimeter, accelerating pace and rhythm. The first three verses are rhymed ABABCC, the final AAAABB. The syllabic count is occasionally seven per line, but maintaining a strong four stresses: for example 'care no more to clothe and eat' (l.267) is seven syllables, but has stress on care / more / clothe / eat. The rhyme scheme of the first three verses (also used in *Venus and Adonis*), was often used for longer ballads as a variant on the simpler ballad scheme of ABAB. The refrain 'come to dust' in each verse plays a semantic variation on meanings of death. The repetition of the word 'dust' at the end of each verse with that of the opening refrain of 'fear no more' evokes both the Christian burial ceremony and the Christian promise of salvation, despite the play's pre-Christian setting.

The song's elegiac quality lies partly in its direct address to the dead beloved: the intimate personal pronoun is used in each verse, 'thou', 'thy', and 'thee', and the vocative form of verbs ('fear no more', 'care no more', 'fear not'). The words and song are not specific to Innogen, but garner meaning because the young men have sung them at their mother's funeral. Their weight and significance comes from its previous history, the ritual which they establish by repeating the song at a second funeral. The generalised referents of the first three stanzas attempt to be inclusive about three different kinds of life experience. The first stanza describes a rural outdoors life where sun and storm forge human identity, with a faint hint of a pastoral idyll ('golden lads and girls all must / As chimney sweepers, come to dust', ll.262–3). The second stanza describes an urban and political life, the economic need to feed and clothe, and the civic life of the elite ('the sceptre, learning, physic, must / All follow this, and come to dust', ll.269–70). The third stanza makes explicit links between the rural evocation of the first stanza with the political and civic world of the second, by using natural imagery to denote the complexities of political and civic life. The continuity of imagery and referents gives coherence to the poetic frame. Walter Raleigh's anti-courtly poem 'The Lie', circulating at this time in the Jacobean court, uses the same rhyming scheme, and expresses a similar sceptical anger about the tyranny of courts, the elite and religious and academic institutions. The repeated refrain reminds the listeners that even great men and tyrants are equal to us in death.

The final stanza (ll.277–81) in its swifter beat and repeated rhythm is closer to a dirge than the lyrical if melancholic song of the first three stanzas. The content rattles off a series of charms to ward off evil spirits and witchcraft: giving credibility to the story's pre-Christian context.

Song and music displace us and the characters from immediate engagement in the onward progression of events. Music provides a pause for thought at the same time as being integrated into the action itself. Music's sound and words enable us to reflect more broadly on the play's bigger themes at the same time as it performs Innogen's funeral. Music is thus inward- and outward-facing: both integral to the narrative moment, and to the plot more generally.

Let us now move onto *The Winter's Tale*. Music characterises Act 4: all the play's music is to be found here, except the viol music which 'awakens' Hermione in Act 5. In this chapter we shall look at four songs, three in one continuous piece of action, framed by a debate about ballads, included as the second extract here. First is Autolycus's arrival on stage.

Analysis: *The Winter's Tale*, 4.3.1–30

Enter Autolycus, singing

AUTOLYCUS   When daffodils begin to peer,
   With hey, the doxy over the dale,
   Why, then comes in the sweet o' the year,
   For the red blood reigns in the winter's pale.

> The white sheet bleaching on the hedge, 5
> With hey, the sweet birds O how they sing!
> Doth set my pugging tooth on edge,
> For a quart of ale is a dish for a king.
>
> The lark, that tirra lirra chants,
> With hey, with hey, the thrush and the jay, 10
> Are summer songs for me and my aunts,
> While we lie tumbling in the hay.
>
> I have served Prince Florizel and in my time wore
> three-pile; but now I am out of service.
> > But shall I go mourn for that, my dear? 15
> > The pale moon shines by night,
> > And when I wander here and there,
> > I then do most go right.
>
> > If tinkers may have leave to live
> > And bear the sow-skin budget, 20
> > Then my account I well may give,
> > And in the stocks avouch it.
> My traffic is sheets–when the kite builds, look to lesser
> linen. My father named me Autolycus, who, being as I
> am littered under Mercury, was likewise a snapper-up 25
> of unconsidered trifles. With die and drab I purchased
> this caparison, and my revenue is the silly cheat.
> Gallows and knock are too powerful on the highway;
> beating and hanging are terrors to me. For the life to
> come, I sleep out the thought of it. A prize, a prize! 30

This is Autolycus's first appearance on stage, and he characteristically enters in song, signalling his festive role. The two songs have different rhythms the first, consisting mainly of the populist tetrameter, slipping at points into pentameters. The second song is more regular in its alternating lines of four and three beats, a standard ballad form. Both songs use typical ballad content: populist celebration of nature, and a ventriloquised narration of the experience of a lower-class character, and establish Autolycus as a roguish vagrant. His song serenades summer as a time of free love ('the doxy over the dale', and his 'aunts', ll.2, 11) and the cycle of seasons bringing fertility in summer. 'The red blood reigns in the winter's pale' puns on rein / reign, suggesting a curb to winter's frugality, and the supremacy of summer's passions. The washing drying on hedges, the songbirds echoing the singer's exuberance, and the experience of tumbling in the hay image forth summer in a rural setting, and Autolycus's place within that economy. The choral ('with hey, with hey') punningly echoes the sexual references of tumbling in the hay, and invokes a conventional upbeat dance atmosphere to song and scene.

Autolycus intersperses his songs with verbal commentary: possibly addressing the audience directly, at the front of the stage. His first direct address tell us he served Prince Florizel, 'but I am now out of service', and it is this reflection that perhaps prompts the melancholy of the second song, 'But shall I go mourn for that my dear?' The song's words seem to belong to a woman mourning her lover. This ventriloquised female voice enhances his effectiveness as a tinker selling songs and trinkets. His witty claim to 'traffic [in] sheets' references the sheets drying on hedges which he steals, the sheets he might invade when he has sex, and the sheet ballad music he sells. Gambling and whoring ('die and drab' l.26), have funded his current 'caparison' and profession. Clothes dominate his subsequent conversation as Autolycus enacts a fiction of robbery, conning the clown of his own clothes and money. Thus the action following the song enacts the knavery of which Autolycus sings. Music presages dramatic function and character, and self-conscious self-fashioning is integral to successful identity.

Analysis: *The Winter's Tale*, 4.4.219–233

Enter Autolycus [wearing a false beard, carrying his pack] singing

AUTOLYCUS	Lawn as white as driven snow,	
	Cypress black as e'er was crow,	220
	Gloves as sweet as damask roses,	
	Masks for faces and for noses,	
	Bugle-bracelet, necklace-amber,	
	Perfume for a lady's chamber,	
	Golden coifs and stomachers,	225

| | For my lads to give their dears,
| | Pins and poking-sticks of steel;
| | What maids lack from head to heel—
| | Come buy of me, come, come buy, come buy;
| | Buy, lads, or else your lasses cry; come buy.   230
| CLOWN | If I were not in love with Mopsa, thou shouldst
| | take no money of me; but being enthralled as I am, it
| | will also be the bondage of certain ribbons and gloves.

A mid-seventeenth-century setting for this song by John Wilson exists, which may have followed an original by Robert Johnson, who composed songs for *The Tempest*. The rhythm is the conventional tetrameter of four strong beats, often in a seven syllable line, with the exception of the final two lines which are five beats. The rhyming couplets generate a quick rhythm, with the minuscule pause on the second rhyme itself, enabling Autolycus's acting skills to emphasise the potential sexual innuendos to aid his sales (amber / chamber, ll.223–4). The cumulative list of luxury items (lawn, crepe, gloves, masks, jewellery, head gear, and needles) delineates shopping heaven for the early modern consumer. Autolycus is the perfect salesman: he has already tricked the clown out of his clothes and money, and the audience's ability to recognise him even in disguise is crucial to our appreciation of his role as trickster. The effectiveness of his disguise and performance is confirmed in the clown's failure to recognise the con-man, and in his response to the song: his beloved Mopsa will want to spend money ('the bondage of certain ribbons and gloves' l.233). The song's choral ending, repeating 'come buy, come buy' authenticates Autolycus's role, and simultaneously functions as a typical vignette of a rural fair. The shepherds and women bustle around the tinker and his wares, lending veracity to the overall representation. We are aware that Autolycus is engaged in a 'performance', and are doubly enthralled by the trickery and the salesmanship of his wares.

The next extract follows on thirty or so lines later, featuring a debate amongst the shepherds and Autolycus about the ballads he has for sale, a song sung in parts, and a finale song by Autolycus. It is worth reading the whole sequence.

Analysis: *The Winter's Tale*, 4.4.257–317

CLOWN	What hast here? Ballads?
MOPSA	Pray now, buy some. I love a ballad in print, a-life, for then we are sure they are true.
AUTOLYCUS	Here's one to a very doleful tune, how a usurer's wife was brought to bed of twenty money-bags at a burden, and how she longed to eat adders' heads and toads carbonadoed.
MOPSA	Is it true, think you?
AUTOLYCUS	Very true, and but a month old.
DORCAS	Bless me from marrying a usurer!
AUTOLYCUS	Here's the midwife's name to't, one Mistress Taleporter, and five or six honest wives that were present. Why should I carry lies abroad?
MOPSA	Pray you now, buy it.
CLOWN	Come on, lay it by, and let's first see more ballads. We'll buy the other things anon.
AUTOLYCUS	Here's another ballad, of a fish, that appeared upon the coast on Wednesday the fourscore of April forty thousand fathom above water, and sung this ballad against the hard hearts of maids. It was thought she was a woman and was turned into a cold fish for she would not exchange flesh with one that loved her. The ballad is very pitiful and as true.
DORCAS	Is it true too, think you?
AUTOLYCUS	Five justices' hands at it, and witnesses more than my pack will hold.
CLOWN	Lay it by too. Another.
AUTOLYCUS	This is a merry ballad, but a very pretty one.
MOPSA	Let's have some merry ones.
AUTOLYCUS	Why, this is a passing merry one, and goes to the tune of 'Two maids wooing a man'. There's scarce a maid westward but she sings it—'tis in request, I can tell you.
MOPSA	We can both sing it. If thou'lt bear a part, thou shalt hear; 'tis in three parts.
DORCAS	We had the tune on't a month ago.
AUTOLYCUS	I can bear my part; you must know 'tis my

260

265

270

275

280

285

290

	occupation. Have at it with you.	
	Song	
AUTOLYCUS	Get you hence, for I must go	295
	Where it fits you not to know.	
DORCAS	Whither?	
MOPSA	O, whither?	
DORCAS	Whither?	
MOPSA	It becomes thy oath full well,	
	Thou to me thy secrets tell.	
DORCAS	Me too; let me go thither.	300
MOPSA	Or thou goest to th' grange or mill—	
DORCAS	If to either, thou dost ill—	
AUTOLYCUS	Neither.	
DORCAS	What, neither?	
AUTOLYCUS	Neither.	
DORCAS	Thou hast sworn my love to be.	
MOPSA	Thou hast sworn it more to me;	305
	Then whither goest? Say, whither?	
CLOWN	We'll have this song out anon by ourselves: my father and the gentlemen are in sad talk, and we'll not trouble them. Come, bring away thy pack after me; wenches, I'll buy for you both. Pedlar, let's have the first choice—follow me, girls.	310

[*Exit with Dorcas and Mopsa*]

AUTOLYCUS	And you shall pay well for 'em.	
	Song	
	Will you buy any tape, or lace for your cape,	
	My dainty duck, my dear-a?	
	Any silk, any thread, any toys for your head,	315
	Of the new'st and fin'st, fin'st wear-a?	
	Come to the pedlar, money's a meddler	
	That doth utter all men's ware-a.	*Exit*

This sequence falls naturally into four parts: the debate and bartering about the ballads for sale (ll.258–85); the preparation and singing of the song in parts (ll.286–306); the clown's account of songs in popular culture (ll.307–10); and Autolycus's final words and song (ll.311–19). The excitement generated by the unveiling of the ballads suggests a community eager for new music and songs, more so than for the lawn, cambric and pins Autolycus is also selling. Mopsa is simultaneously naively innocent about the ballads' provenance and fantastic content (they are in print, so 'we are sure they are true', l.259) and astute about their currency, desiring what is both new and true. Dorcas's and her eagerly repeated 'Is it true, think you?' (ll.259, 264, 280) encourage Autolycus's narrations of the scandalous contents of ballads, analogous to true-life crime or tabloid news today. Autolycus's confirmation of their authenticity varies from contemporaneity, to authorial or witnesses' verification : 'very true, and but a month old'; or 'here's the midwife's name to't'; 'five justices' hands to't, and witnesses more than my pack will hold' (ll.265–81). His words give a flavour of the marketing of such ballads, who bought them, the variety of reading matter, and the enthusiasm for popular songs. The clown is the main customer, agreeing to buy three ballads (the one of the woman who gave birth to money bags; of a singing fish who used to be a woman; and 'Get you hence for I must go'). Ballads, like the sad tale which Mamillius promised to his mother, tell of fantastic events, magical monsters and improbable miracles. Ballads turn out to be, in their content and populist appeal, very like the plot of *The Winter's Tale* itself.

The second part of the extract involves detailed description of this song and its reception as they discuss how to sing it. The tune was usually published on the text of the ballad ('to Two maids wooing a man') an effective way of marketing and selling new ballads, since many different ballads could be sung to the same tune. 'There's scarce a maid westward but she sings it—'tis in request, I can tell you' (ll.287–9), successfully tempts the purchasers with its popularity and currency, predicating Mopsa into a directorial role. She tells Autolycus what part to sing and that they already know the tune ('we had the tune on't a month ago', l.292): suggesting a vibrant and quick-moving market. The setting for the song was circulated in Robert Johnson's *Airs, Songs and Dialogues*. Its form is simple, consisting of seven or eight syllables per line with fours stresses, and rhymed AAB; CCB; DDB; EEB, so that the refrain demanded by the female voices provides an aural and rhymed continuity to the song.

The three-part song figures a love triangle, with two women begging to accompany a man with whom they want to spend time. The man is disdainful and aggressive to the women; whilst they are both plangent and supplicatory. By dividing the single-lined refrain between their voices ('Whither? O whither? Whither?' l.297), the song suggests their mutual desperation and competition for the man. The final verse replicates this triangular competition with both women repeating the same words of fealty with a minor variation ('Thou hast sworn my love to be / Thou hast sworn it more to me', ll.304–5). The repeated onomatopoeic 'whither' sounds a musically wistful note, characterising the singer's loss. Mopsa and Dorcas self-consciously enact the story of the song without becoming the characters of the song. But the song's content and message construct a world where manliness is remote and inaccessible, and women compete for male favours. This invokes memories of Leontes' court and suggests that sexual and erotic love are fraught with competitive and jealous desires and political nuances. We are about to discover this is present even in this pastoral world as Polixenes unmasks his son.

The extract's third part illustrates how popular songs and performance affect behaviour. The clown's admiration of the song ('we'll have this song anon by ourselves' l.307), and decision to buy it, is predicated both by the performance and the idea of consumption. We literally watch how songs become personally talismanic and performance produces affective responses. We saw in Chapter 8 how spectacles affected and transformed the on-stage audience, creating a metatheatrical perception of how art works on us: songs and music work in the same way.

Autolycus's cynical comment to the audience as the Clown departs with Mopsa and Dorcas ('you shall pay well for 'em', l.311), signals via direct address and explicit commentary on the mechanics of marketing both that the Clown is in thrall to the two women and that he is making a nice profit. Autolycus's roguery, repeated in each of scene in which he appears, is never demonised and always performed with one eye on the audience for complicit laughs.

His final song ('Will you buy any tape…') evokes the archetypal chapman's cry as he sells his wares, (we are familiar with Thomas Campion's contemporary 'Cherry Ripe'). The jog-trot rhythm echoes the pacing up and down of the chapman, who has to walk to sell his wares. Back in character, Autolycus paces amongst the various classes of people on stage at the festival, simultaneously picking pockets and selling his wares. His song acts as a choral echo through the scene as it turns progressively away from the gentle world of pastoral to the nastier reality of family politics, class protectionism and monarchical absolutism. His finale 'money's a meddler / That doth all men's wares-a' (l.318) echoes punningly and proleptically through the scene. Florizel and Perdita's innocent pastoral love is denied by the greater power of money, status and politics. The triple pun connoted by "wares-a" suggests Autolycus's various dramatic roles: knowledge (awareness), warning, and selling. Autolycus's songs perform the voice of the traditional fool: they speak a truth to the audience no-one else voices. The songs provide a musical counterpoint to the visual and narrative action, so that the audience can see and understand several perspectives simultaneously.

Music is integral to many parts of the performance of *The Tempest*, from the initial discordant 'a confused noise within' as the boat hits the rocks in the opening scene, through the magical sounds which all characters hear during the play, the populist songs of Stephano and Trinculo, to the more formal songs and music played by Ariel and for Prospero. Music thus provides an aural environment through which audience and characters encounter the other-worldly nature of the island.

Let us here consider Ariel's songs and their place in the play.

Analysis: *The Tempest*, 1.2.374–404

Enter Ferdinand, and Ariel invisible, playing and singing
ARIEL *song*   Come unto these yellow sands,
              And then take hands;
              Curtsied when you have, and kissed
              The wild waves whist,
              Foot it featly here and there,
              And sweet sprites bear
              The burden. Hark, hark!   380
                    Burden dispersedly Bow-wow.
                    The watch-dogs bark.
                    [*Burden dispersedly*] Bow-wow.
                    Hark, hark! I hear

| | The strain of strutting Chanticleer
Cry Cock a diddle dow.
[Burden dispersedly] Cock a diddle dow. | |
| -------------- | ---- | ---- |
| FERDINAND | Where should this music be?—I' th' air or th' earth?
It sounds no more; and sure it waits upon
Some god o' th' island. Sitting on a bank,
Weeping again the King my father's wreck,
This music crept by me upon the waters,
Allaying both their fury and my passion
With its sweet air. Thence I have followed it,
Or it hath drawn me rather; but 'tis gone.
No, it begins again. | 390 |
| ARIEL *song* | Full fathom five thy father lies,
Of his bones are coral made;
Those are pearls that were his eyes;
Nothing of him that doth fade,
But doth suffer a sea-change
Into something rich and strange.
Sea-nymphs hourly ring his knell.
Burden Ding-dong
Hark, now I hear them, ding-dong, bell. | 400 |

Of all the music that must have originally accompanied the play's first performance, only two settings survive, both of Ariel's songs 'Full fathom five' and 'Where the bee sucks', both in manuscript attributed to Robert Johnson. Ariel's entrance '*invisible, playing and singing*' is the first we see of his magical powers: although we have earlier heard him narrate what he did to the ship. He is probably 'invisible' to Ferdinand but visible in some way to the audience, perhaps wearing a diaphanous costume, or walking along a balcony. Both music and appearance disperse the disturbing scene we have just witnessed between Prospero and Caliban, with implicit violence bubbling below the surface. The elision into an encounter in which Prospero wants Miranda to fall in love with Ferdinand must convince both her and us that the anger has been dissipated, and ethereal music helps achieve this. Equally, Ferdinand must be moved and transformed out of his grief by the music.

This is the first time we have met Ferdinand, and his absolute grief for his father must garner our sympathy at the same time as we also believe in his emerging love for Miranda. Music is the means through which this transformation occurs and is credible. Music is literally affective.

The melancholic lyrics of both songs create a visceral sense of the other-worldly atmosphere which Ariel always seems to introduce. The first song's incongruous invocation of dance movements across the 'yellow sands' and of a chorus ('burden') sung by 'sweet sprites' (l.379) displaces us and Ferdinand from the gritty reality of Caliban hauling wood and grief at lost fathers. However, the choral refrain of watchdogs barking and cocks crowing generates dissonant sounds: like the Harpy banquet scene of Act 3 Scene 2, animal sounds disturb musical harmonies. This juxtaposition suggests four interpretations, all of which relate more broadly to themes in the whole play. The first suggests a world where the human and animal must coexist; the second interpretation a world where the 'civilised' sounds of music are integrally related to the natural world; the third, a world where the 'civilised' is always destroyed by the animalistic impulses; and the final a world where the rational and physical (or bestial) are in opposition, while the bestial continually punctures our rational senses. The aural effect of the discordant sounds generates a sense in which music and harmony are being disturbed and destroyed: a subliminal aesthetic and political message which echoes throughout this first scene on the island.

Ferdinand's response to the music acts as stage directions for its delivery ('Where should this music be? I'th'air or th'earth?' l.388; 'But 'tis gone. / No, it begins again', ll.395–6). His comments stress the music's ethereal and indeterminate qualities: of the air or earth; spiritual or mortal? They are guides for directors and audience when to play music or song, and illustrate its integrity to the action. His words give a psychological validity to his ambulation: the music has compelled him to follow it, literally leaving his grief behind on the rocks.

Ariel's second song ('Full fathom five thy father lies') is sung directly to Ferdinand and resonates poetically and musically with the strange world which the island offers. The voice setting for Johnson's music is a counter-tenor, a relatively high male voice. The sound would therefore be slightly ethereal, and is usually sung by a counter-tenor or alto in modern productions. The first line's alliterated 'fs' create a sonorous effect echoed in the musical notes. The subsequent sibilant 's's in the last few lines echo the sounds of the sea washing his father's bones. The song's lyrics narrate the terrible death of Ferdinand's father: drowned at sea. However, they do so through fantastic literalised images: his bones have turned to coral, his eyes to pearl, 'nothing of him [remains]... but doth suffer a sea-change' (ll.400–401). These images are simultaneously distressing and wondrous: Ferdinand imagines the decay of his father's body, but the miracle of natural decay creates physical metamorphosis: jewels grow from decaying bones. The sea itself, which surrounds the island, and immersed them all, is a wider metaphor for transformation and new life, with subtextual Christian connotations. The combination of haunting music and resonant lyrics hangs over Ferdinand and the play. There is also a metaphoric message implicit in this haunting: new life will come from death, new knowledge from old, and a new world from the old world. The song's resonant connotations are paradigmatically central to the play's ideas of transformation, restoration and reconciliation.

The song's formal structure (mainly seven-syllable lines, with four strong beats per line, rhyming ABABCCDD) echoes that of many courtly songs and poems of the early seventeenth century, and is distinct from the ballad-form used later in the play by Stephano and Trinculo. The choral 'ding-dong' enables us to see instrumentation integrated music with the verbal structure and meaning. Rhymes create a semantic field emphasising the duality Ariel evokes, both death and transformation: lies / eyes; made / fade; change / strange; knell / bell. The two rhymes which are couplets (the last four lines) accelerate rhythm and meaning, emphasising Ferdinand's onward journey towards transformation, however 'strange' the experience.

Let us now look at Ariel's other song for which Johnson wrote the music.

Analysis: *The Tempest*, 5.1.88–94

Ariel sings and helps to attire him
ARIEL   Where the bee sucks, there suck I,
         In a cowslip's bell I lie;
         There I couch when owls do cry;   90
         On the bat's back I do fly
         After summer merrily.
         Merrily, merrily shall I live now
         Under the blossom that hangs on the bough.

Ariel has just been promised immediate freedom by Prospero, and this song is his only one about his own feelings. The natural imagery and exuberant tone provide us with an unadulterated sense of his character and desires. His self-conceit is to be congruent with all kinds of flying animals and creatures: insects, birds, and bats. Ariel's connection to the natural world has been implicit in his ability to mimic storms, winds and natural forces: but this has been filtered through Prospero's magic. The song's lyrics display Ariel's return to freedom is to a symbiotic connection with the natural world. Magic, identity and nature fuse in his character, which is integral to the island itself. The repetition of 'merrily' posits a joyous freedom which inversely comments on Ariel's service to Prospero. He has repeatedly ask for his 'liberty', but it is only though song and music he expresses what that freedom means. Music is literally expressive and illuminative of identity. His lyrics share themes with 'Full fathom five': just as he describes strange changes to bodies there, here he celebrates his own metamorphic qualities. Ariel is like quicksilver, here one minute, elsewhere the next: is he actually a bee or just like a bee; actually a bat, or just at one with a bat? The lyrics suggest that he can cross species' boundaries, that his nature as well as his modes of travel is fluid. The romance of a creature able to metamorphose is a fantasy common to many of the characters in the play: from Stephano and Trinculo who want to be kings, through Antonio and Sebastian who simply want more power, to Alonso and Prospero who want, respectively, a son and a kingdom back. Ariel's words, resonate with a broader significance than that of his own personal desires and future: the fantasy of freedom and change belongs to us all, and evokes Caliban's own song 'Freedom, high day!' (discussed in Chapter 6).

Finally, let us consider Stephano's song in Act 3 Scene 2.

Analysis: *The Tempest*, 3.2.114–24

CALIBAN	Thou mak'st me merry. I am full of pleasure;	
	Let us be jocund. Will you troll the catch	115
	You taught me but whilere?	

STEPHANO	At thy request, monster, I will do reason, any reason. Come on, Trinculo, let us sing.
	Sings
	Flout 'em and cout 'em
	And scout 'em and flout 'em,　　　　　　　　120
	Thought is free.
CALIBAN	That's not the tune.
	Ariel plays the tune on a tabor and pipe
STEPHANO	What is this same?
TRINCULO	This is the tune of our catch, played by the picture of Nobody.

Caliban has been fed alcohol by the two seamen, and gladly gives up the secrets of Prospero's power, suggesting they join up to overthrow him. He implies here they have already been singing this tune ('Will you troll the catch / You taught me but whilere' l.116), an informal stage direction suggesting that the whole drunken episode is punctuated by music during a performance. We have no record of notation with this song, but its lyrics belong to the category of drinking-men's songs, celebrating drink and masculine bonding. Its words are all synonyms of 'beat up', enabling the singers to work up their courage for a fight. The rhythm is simple alternate stresses, and the choral line echoes as a plangent refrain 'thought is free': both Ariel and Caliban demand freedom from Prospero. Thought itself does remain free, both those of rebels, and those belonging to men holding power. However, in this rendition, the men's drunken shouts of freedom are mocked both because they are spoken by inept drunkards (who subsequently fail in their project) and because Ariel interrupts the music. Only the audience see Ariel's interruption: the characters on stage are mystified by the origin of the music ('played by the picture of Nobody'). The mini-scene displays that thought is not free, because Prospero and Ariel are watching and intervening: the freedoms of the island and speech are illusory. Music here expresses identity, but is simultaneously a marker of broader themes: such broader connotations are thematic (as in Ariel's songs), structural (as in the function of music as a transporting device) and dramaturgical (as here).

Conclusions

1. All the late plays associate music with spectacle, magic and romance: music is linked either visually or thematically to spectacle and its effects of slowing down action and engendering reflection. However, the mood of each single piece of music is dependent on the immediate plot and emotion in the scene: music and song are never incidental but always integral to the action. Song and music intensify the textual drama.
2. The words of songs always resonate more widely than the simple expression of a single character's emotion. Lyrics speak to the audience about wider themes and ideas raised elsewhere. Music appeals to three different sensory response mechanisms (hearing, sight and emotion), and speaks on multiple levels simultaneously. It creates atmosphere and character, as well as providing judgment on emotion and character. Each song belongs to a particular part of the plot, so narrative comments on music and vice-versa. The connotations of music, lyrics, instrumentation and plot all generate subtly divergent responses.
3. Each song's genre, rhythm and rhyme is character-appropriate: helping locate character identity and class.
4. Songs are proxy markers of setting and mood, integrated within the scenes they are invaluable directorial and acting tools to gauge a scene's habitus, or change in mood. In analysing a new scene it is helpful to consider any music or song and its effects first, before considering what happens, when and where.
5. Whilst we do not definitively know the tunes to which most of these songs were set, it is clear that the playing of songs, music and tunes was integral to the theatrical performance. Music was central to courtly masques and productions in popular public theatres, often in the form of jigs and dances played before and after a performance. In the late plays this musical environment has been centrally integrated into the dramatic performance.
6. Song and music enable characters and audience to step out of the main plot, and use the space and time to reflect on the action. In some cases this is a self-conscious role (for example, Autolycus), but in many cases the pause-effect is generated by the music itself which interrupts action and words. Thus it is the audience

that perceives and experiences the pause, and it encourages our reflection. Interruption through music, like interruption through spectacle, generates reflection and potential peripateia.

7. The late plays enable the marshalling of spectacle, language, music, and emblem for the playwright, engendering a richer theatrical experience (the 'mis-en-scene' in cinematic terms).
8. Shakespeare utilises the complex possibilities inherent in using these three media, and juxtaposes music with plot, emblem with music, language and music to suggest dissonance (for example in the Harpy scene of *The Tempest*), and the divergence between characters' responses to a situation and the audience's possible judgement of it. We have observed this in *The Winter's Tale*'s songs, and Stephano's in *The Tempest*. However, this effect is intrinsic to the musical pause, and creates a doubled response in the audience: both immersed in the moment, and more broadly reflective (even if unconsciously).

Methods of Analysis

We have utilised many of the techniques and approaches of previous chapters. In addition we have:

1. considered explicitly how music is both integrated into the plot and stands alone;
2. looked at the metrical and linguistic constructions and effects of songs;
3. integrated our understanding of songs to that of plot, character and theme;
4. brought in external historical evidence about the play's music;
5. considered how music and song complement the play's visual and textual elements.

Suggested Work

You should research how different productions have written and used music to deepen the overall interpretation of a production. Look at productions on YouTube, as well as DVDs to which you have access, and consider how directors and performers have used the original stage directions and songs to develop a production's sense of the musical influence in a performance.

The Winter's Tale

Autolycus's final song 'Jog on, jog on the footpath way' (4.3.121–4) uses lyrics and metre to connote identity. Comment on its significance and how this is achieved. At what stage in the action is this delivered? What is the weight of it ending the scene?

In the long Act 4 Scene 4, music is specified for the dance of the satyrs 4.4.337ff: how does dance and music influence our interpretation of the political events and ensuing discussions?

The Tempest

Music occurs frequently: look at each instance and consider how it is used, signified, and relates to the play's other music. In addition to the songs discussed here and in Chapter 6, music is indicated at the following points:

- 2.1.182: Ariel *'playing solemn music'*, and at l.294 sings 'While you here do snoring lie';
- 3.3.17: music accompanying the banquet is *'solemn and strange'*, while *'soft music'* accompanies the re-entrance of the shapes;
- 4.1.58: Prospero's masque includes *'soft music'*; Juno and Ceres sing their lyrics; and the reapers perform a *'graceful dance'*, later interrupted by *'a strange hollow and confused noise'*;
- 5.1.52: Prospero demands 'heavenly music' as an 'airy charm' to reawaken Alonso and the courtiers.

How does music achieve its effects in each? How does it echo the scene's concerns, and act as a counterpoint to the action or characters? How is spectacle integrated with aural effects?

Cymbeline

In Act 2 Scene 2 Cloten woos Innogen, and calls musicians to his aid. Look at this whole scene, from Cloten's innuendos about musicians' 'fingering', to the lyrics of the song, 'Hark, hark, the lark at heaven's gate' (2.3.1–29). Why does this scene follow on immediately from the bedroom scene? How are masculinity and femininity figured in the discussion of music, its effects, and the lyrics themselves? Does Cloten ever play the music to Innogen? Why and how do events overtake his plans, and what is the significance of this?

Pericles

In Marina's reconciliation scene with Pericles she sings 'The Song' (Scene 21.65ff: although no lyrics are given). How does this music effect Pericles' transformation and recognition and act as a peripeteia, towards reconciliation? Pericles hears the music of the spheres (ll.216ff), predicating Diana's descent, the rediscovery of Thaisa, and the reunion of the lost family. How does music enhance and underline the play's political and social messages?

General Conclusions to Part I

1. Performance, theatricality and spectacle are integral to the dramatic experience of the late plays, and we both gain pleasure from our immersion in the performance, and learn from it, emotionally and intellectually. All the plays distil their key emotional moments and transformations through a multi-media fusion of music, spectacle and self-conscious theatricality. The successful marshalling of these theatrical moments is a testament to Shakespeare's dramaturgical talents: the play's internal meta-theatrical consciousness and display of how these spectacles work act as a brake on excess and ensures these moments do not fall into either camp performance or sentimentality.
2. All the plays' endings focus on reconciliation and associated themes which are shared with other comedies and romances: rebirth (of love, of the individual, of the family), the cyclical reintegration between human and natural, and the emergence of a comic resolution from potentially tragic events.
3. Femininity (both through daughters and wives) is figured as redemptive to masculine irascibility and sin. In *The Winter's Tale* female directorial creativity is celebrated in the theatricalised reunion scene by Paulina's stage management, but also in the mother / daughter reunion stage-managed by Shakespeare. In this way the dominance of patriarchal practices is queried.
4. Language and imagery are densely allusional, and integrated with character, plot, stage properties and iconographic performance. The elegance of this integration is a remarkable achievement, and

helps create a simultaneously sensory and intellectual response from the audience.
5. Setting and place are integral to the 'feel' of a scene and our theatrical experience of it: with minimal but critical stage properties and internal stage directions, these plays evoke time, space and place in concrete ways which help actors locate themselves on stage and audiences to see and feel the concrete conjuring of situations. But place is also used allusively to figure forth metaphorically the play's larger ideas and themes: other worlds, green worlds, summer or winter, Rome or Britain, the sea or land. Geography and place create identity but also test and displace it.
6. The plays are structured to engender critical responses to a variety of key questions by scenic juxtapositions, characterisation and audience positioning. These critical readings include questioning the validity of patriarchal authority, the power of art to move, and the relative importance of social status and birth.
7. Despite the formal emphasis on reconciliatory inclusion and change, and the intervention of a magical providence to achieve this, a political pragmatism rather than idealism marks the endings of most of the plays. We can see this in *The Tempest*'s acknowledgement that Antonio and Sebastian remain unchanged, and in Prospero's acceptance of 'this thing of darkness I acknowledge mine'; and in *Cymbeline*'s pragmatic reconciliation with Rome, leading Britain back into the empire. The old families continue to rule, albeit in a new guise.
8. The plays' endings – whilst focussing on themes of rebirth – also suggest mutability: the couple reunited at the end of *The Winter's Tale* and *Pericles* are heading towards old age, not youthful marriage. Natural seasonal cycles are implicitly patterned into the play's structures and imagery, integrating human and natural life: mutability is central to nature and our own lives within that.
9. The plays are intensely political: despite the emphasis on magic, gods, and providential intervention, all the plays feature families that rule courts or countries, and posit questions about both how to rule and who should rule. Should rulership be based on birth or ability, an aristocracy or a meritocracy? How and why should or do class and gender inhibit this? What is it to be a subject?

PART 2
THE CONTEXT AND THE CRITICS

10

Shakespeare's Literary Career

Shakespeare's literary career spanned the years from 1592 to 1616, the year of his death, encompassing the last decade of Elizabeth I's reign and the first decade of James I's. There is surprisingly sparse documentary evidence about his life: birth, baptismal and marriage records in Stratford; property records; a few court cases; references in a couple of literary memoirs; his name on the frontispiece of some of the published plays; and the posthumous publication of his complete works in 1623. From these scraps, biographers and fans have constructed a variety of myths about the man's life, views, affiliations and genius. Students who are interested in reading some of these speculations, as well as a closer discussion of the extant evidence, should consult the further reading section at the end of this book.

His plays and poems survive him, and are the best evidence we have for a discussion of his artistic and theatrical interests, concerns and development. The first recorded account of Shakespeare as a dramatist is in the scurrilous attack on him in Robert Greene's *Groatsworth of Wit*, published in 1592. A friend of Christopher Marlowe, Greene was a hack writer, and this publication was supposedly his dying farewell to his friends. He urged Marlowe to quit the evils of the public theatre before all playwrights were outshone by:

> an upstart crow, beautified with our feathers, that with his Tiger's heart wrapped in player's hide supposes he is as well able to bombast out a blank verse as the best of you, and being an absolute *Johannes factotum* [jack of all trades], is in his own conceit, the only shake-scene in the country.

The two references to Shakespeare are unmistakeable, wittily troping Shakespeare's words and name. The 'tiger's heart' reference quotes directly from *3 Henry VI*, amending 'woman's hide' to 'player's hide'; and the invented noun 'shake-scene' tropes the man's name into the active impact it is claimed he has had on the London stage scene. Greene's words suggest an element of professional jealousy: the accusation that Shakespeare has stolen Greene's words is eminently ridiculous, and surely spoken tongue in check, since Greene is doing precisely the same with Shakespeare's. This brief account vividly conveys the tight-knit theatrical community of the time: playwrights and writers watched each other's work, quoted it, borrowed from it, made jokes about it, and were in constant economic and professional competition. It also suggests Shakespeare's literary confidence (or arrogance, depending how you see it) and conveys some of the contemporary sense of awe at his 'shake-scening'.

What was Shakespeare doing in the early 1590s to cause this complex combination of envy and admiration? There are no records of what he was doing prior to this reference in 1592: but it is clear he must have been involved in some kind of theatrical and writing enterprise in order to have written the plays Greene references. In the late 1580s there were numerous theatre companies in London: companies had to have an aristocratic patron, because players were otherwise categorised as vagrants, and punished as such. Each theatre company was named after their patron, Lord Strange's Men, the Earl of Pembroke's Men, the Earl of Leicester's Company, and so on. Actors who played in each of those troupes in the early 1590s, later played in the same company for which Shakespeare worked. We know that by 1594 he was a member of the Lord Chamberlain's Men, because he, Will Kempe and Richard Burbage were all paid for a royal performance at Greenwich Palace on 26 and 28 December of that year. Shakespeare continued to work for this company for his whole career, a uniquely stable experience for a contemporary playwright. Most other playwrights were freelance, having plays commissioned by and selling them to a variety of companies. The Chamberlain's Men received royal patronage when James I ascended to the throne in 1603, becoming the King's Men.

Publications of Shakespeare's plays, in both quarto and folio, tended to foreground the company who had performed the play, rather than an author. For example, the publication of *Henry V* in 1600, followed the title with 'as it hath been sundry times played by the Right Honourable the Lord Chamberlain his servants'. However, the 1604 publication of *Hamlet* gave the author as 'William Shakespeare' and claimed it was 'newly imprinted and enlarged almost as much again as it was, according to the true and perfect copy': an acknowledgement that the 1603 version (which had no name on the frontispiece) was some kind of unauthorised (by author or company) version. The 1608 version of *King Lear* names both Shakespeare and the theatre company on the frontispiece. The name of the author could sell a play (in the case of *Hamlet* and *King Lear*), but so could the theatre company.

The theatre companies were businesses: Shakespeare himself was a 'sharer' in his company, meaning he was jointly responsible for its business success, its buildings, its employees and its finances. It was very much an urban, middling-income, non-aristocratic business. The King's Men was the most successful company from 1603 until the theatres were closed down in 1642 during the civil war, and Shakespeare and Richard Burbage (its leading actor) were the architects of both its business and aesthetic success. The first purpose-built theatre in London was erected in 1576 (called 'The Theatre'); a commercial enterprise organised by James Burbage, Richard Burbage's father, and the venue in which the Chamberlain's men performed in the 1590s. The Chamberlain's men did not own the land on which the Theatre stood in Shoreditch, and after a dispute about the rent owed on the land, the Chamberlain's Men dismantled the Theatre and used the timbers to build a new theatre, The Globe, on the south bank in Southwark in 1599.

Shakespeare's company had exclusive performance rights to the Globe, and were so financially successful that they funded the restoration of a permanent older indoors theatre closer to the city, known as 'Blackfriars Theatre', which reopened in 1608. The acquisition of an indoor theatre provided more repertory and performance flexibility for the company and its writers: it meant the company could perform all year, and were not restricted by the vagaries of the English weather. Indoor theatres were smaller than the outdoor ones (which could hold 1500–2000), accommodating an audience of only about

700. Consequently, tickets were more expensive, and audiences more elite: you could get a standing position for a penny at the Globe, while the lowest price at Blackfriars was 6 pence (the day-wage of a labourer). The smaller stage concomitant on a smaller space arguably invited both more intimate scenes, or more condensed moments on stage, as well as providing lighting and the fixtures for additional stage machinery, such as we see in the late plays we have discussed in this book. The Globe burned down in 1613 during a performance of *Henry VIII*, which necessitated a shift to indoors-only playing while it was rebuilt. By this time, Shakespeare himself had relinquished the close running of the business to his fellow sharers, and retired to Stratford for much of the year. Nevertheless, he remained a sharer in the company until his death in 1616.

Shakespeare's early career was also notable for the publication of his long poems *Venus and Adonis* and the *Rape of Lucrece* in 1593 and 1594, which he dedicated to the Earl of Southampton, in a probable search for aristocratic patronage. His sonnets circulated in manuscript, amongst aristocratic readers, and the Cambridge student play *The Return from Parnassus* features a young man who claims, 'I'll worship sweet master Shakespeare and to honour him will lay his *Venus and Adonis* under my pillow'. There is evidence, then, that despite his career in the public theatre, his literary ambitions encompassed genres more traditionally indulged in by courtly audiences. In late 1598 Francis Meres published an amalgam of literary reflections, including some on the contemporary literary scene, and describes how 'the sweet, witty soul of Ovid lives in mellifluous and honey-tongued Shakespeare, witness his *Venus and Adonis*, his *Lucrece*, his sugared sonnets among his private friends, etc.'. He goes on to delineate Shakespeare's dramatic successes:

> As Plautus and Seneca are accounted the best for comedy and tragedy among the Latins: so Shakespeare among the English is the most excellent in both kinds for the stage: for comedy, witness his *Gentlemen of Verona*, his *Errors*, his *Love's Labour's Lost*, his *Love Labour's Won*, his *Midsummer Night's Dream*, and his *Merchant of Venice*; for tragedy, his *Richard the 2*, his *Richard the 3*, *Henry the 4*, *King John*, *Titus Andronicus* and his *Romeo and Juliet*.

It is clear from Meres' catalogue that the diversity and range of Shakespeare's work and talent, as well as his status as equal to the great Greek and Roman dramatists, was recognised as much by his contemporaries as by posterity.

During his lifetime, Shakespeare, like most of his contemporary playwrights, did not supervise the printing and editing of his plays for publication, and this means dates of composition and performance are approximate. It also reflects a very different understanding of textual authority to ours. The company owned the play, and could put on any version of it they chose, make any cuts, add scenes, songs, prologues and epilogues. The evolution and different possible versions of the play-text was closer to today's web-based or interactive texts, than to Romantic conceptions of single-authored texts. Plays were written for a theatre company, approved and then stamped by the Master of Revels (employed directly by the monarch) for performance to certify they did not include any blasphemy or attack the monarch, and then performed. Publications of plays tended to happen when the play was no longer being regularly performed, and the theatre company had moved on to new plays. Copyright law did not exist at this time: the plays were owned by the theatre company, who could sell them on, publish them, or sit on them for future revivals. Theatre companies did revive plays: we have evidence that Shakespeare's plays were often performed at court on special occasions. Thus the Christmas celebrations of 1612 / 13, which extended into the festivities for the marriage of James I's daughter Elizabeth, included performances of *Othello, Much Ado About Nothing, The Winter's Tale* and *The Tempest*.

In the 1623 edition of all his dramatic works, *Mr William Shakespeare's Comedies, Histories, Tragedies*, 36 plays were published, 18 of which had previously been published in 'quarto' form. The term 'quarto' refers to the size of paper which the print sheets were folded into to form the book: a quarto book was about the size of a modern paperback or Kindle. A quarto book was relatively affordable and certainly portable. The publication of the 1623 work was in a larger format, called a 'folio' edition referring again to the size the paper on which the book was printed (a large sheet folded into two, it was bigger than an A4 sheet). Such a work was not portable, but designed to sit in someone's study or library. The cost of it unbound was about

15 shillings, or, with an elegant calf binding, one pound. Actors were paid a shilling a day when performing (20 shillings made up a pound): farm workers were paid about 6 pence (half a shilling) a day. So the price of the bound copy would represent a month's wage for an actor, and two months for a labourer. The plays in the folio edition are printed by genre, and there is no attempt to date the individual plays in the collection. Subsequent critical and bibliographical work, using both external evidence (such as references to the plays, citations from them, earlier publication, the first version of the play) and internal stylistic analysis have established an approximate chronology and ordering of the plays. The Oxford Shakespeare editorial project (first published in 1988, and a second edition in 2005) is the text from which the extracts in this book have been taken. Their dating of the plays and poems, and the publication of any version of them, is a reliable benchmark of the chronology of Shakespeare's career. We shall use that chronology as a starting point for discussing Shakespeare's more detailed literary and dramatic development through the plays themselves.

The editors of the first folio did not include *The Two Noble Kinsmen* or *Pericles* (now regarded as firmly within the Shakespearean canon) and this list includes those referenced in his lifetime but now lost. What else can we learn from this list? We can see from the publications of quartos some of the contemporary demand for reading Shakespeare's plays, as well as the kind of plays popular in the marketplace, at least in the eyes of the printers who produced them. The history plays were popular in the publications prior to 1623, speaking to a broader demand for English history at the time; some of the earlier plays are published three or more years after their first performance (for example, *The Merry Wives of Windsor*, *The Merchant of Venice*, *Troilus and Cressida*), perhaps suggesting that demand for reading earlier plays was generated by Shakespeare's increasing renown. If we look at the trajectory of Shakespeare's career there is some generic chronological clustering: English history plays in the first decade; comedies in the mid to late 1590s; tragedies in the early years of the 1600s; and a shift back towards comedies in the later part of his career. It is noticeable that tragedies and histories often include a generic description as part of their title. This suggests both that marketing a play's

Play	Now known as	Publications (1623 is the folio edition)	Oxford Editor's proposed dates
The Two Gentlemen of Verona		1623	1589–91
The Taming of the Shrew		1623	1590–91
The First Part of the Contention of the Two Famous Houses of York and Lancaster	2 Henry VI	1593, 1594, 1623	1590–91
The True Tragedy of Richard Duke of York and the Good King Henry the Sixth	3 Henry VI	1600, 1619, 1623	1591
The First Part of Henry the Sixth	1 Henry VI	1623	1592
The Most Lamentable Tragedy of Titus Andronicus	Titus Andronicus	1594, 1600, 1611, 1623	1592
The Tragedy of King Richard the Third	Richard III	1597, 1598, 1602, 1605, 1615, 1623	1592
Venus and Adonis		1593	1593
The Rape of Lucrece		1594	1594
*The Reign of King Edward the Third		1596	1594
The Comedy of Errors		1623	1594–5
Love's Labour's Lost		1598	1594–5
*Love's Labour's Won			1595

(*Continued*)

Play	Now known as	Publications (1623 is the folio edition)	Oxford Editor's proposed dates
The Tragedy of King Richard the Second	Richard II	1597, 1598, 1608, 1615, 1623	1595
The Most Excellent and Lamentable Tragedy of Romeo and Juliet	Romeo and Juliet	1597, 1599, 1609, 1623	1595
A Midsummer Night's Dream		1600, 1619	1595
The Life and Death of King John	King John	1623	1596
The Comical History of the Merchant of Venice, or otherwise called the Jew of Venice	The Merchant of Venice	1600, 1619, 1623	1596–7
The History of Henry the Fourth	1 Henry IV	1598, 1599, 1604, 1608, 1613, 1622, 1623	1596–7
The Merry Wives of Windsor		1602, 1619, 1623	1597–8
The Second Part of Henry the Fourth	2 Henry IV	1600, 1623	1597–8
Much Ado About Nothing		1600, 1623	1598–9
The Life of Henry the Fifth	Henry V	1600, 1602, 1619, 1623	1598–9
The Tragedy of Julius Caesar	Julius Caesar	1623	1599
As You Like It		1623	1599–1600
The Tragedy of Hamlet, Prince of Denmark	Hamlet	1603, 1604, 1611, 1623	1600–1601

Twelfth Night, or What You Will		1601
Troilus and Cressida		1602
Measure for Measure		1603–4
The Tragedy of Othello, the Moor of Venice		1603–4
*The Book of Sir Thomas More		1603–4
The History of King Lear	King Lear	1605–6
The Life of Timon of Athens	Timon of Athens	1606
The Tragedy of Macbeth	Macbeth	1606
The Tragedy of Antony and Cleopatra	Antony and Cleopatra	1606
All's Well That Ends Well		1606–7
Pericles, Prince of Tyre	Pericles	1607–8
The Tragedy of Coriolanus	Coriolanus	1608
The Winter's Tale		1609–10
Cymbeline: King of Britain	Cymbeline	1610–11
The Tempest		1610–11
*Cardenio		1612–13
All is True	Henry VIII	1613
The Two Noble Kinsmen		1613

		1623
		1609, 1623
		1623
		1622, 1623
		1608, 1619, 1623
		1623
		1623
		1623
		1623
		1609, 1611, 1619
		1623
		1623
		1623
		1623
		1623
		1634

*Plays now lost

genre was important, and that these genres were particularly popular, a view reinforced by the first folio's editors ordering of the plays along generic lines when they published the complete works.

The plays discussed in this book all belong to Shakespeare's later career, and all share thematic and dramaturgical features which mark them out as a distinctive group, sometimes called 'Romances' because they fuse both tragic and potentially tragic events with comic outcomes, transformations and resolutions. These plays also share a theatrical interest in spectacle, providential representations, and experimental linguistic and dramatic patterns. However, these particular elements can also be found in Shakespeare's earlier writings, as well as writings of some of his contemporaries (a point we will return to in the next chapter). For example, the fusion of a tragic conflict with plot twists and coincidences that result in familial reconciliation via the medium of a goddess-type figure was integral to plot and action as early as *The Comedy of Errors* (1594–5). The hard-won and discovered introspective language of the tragic heroes, most particularly Hamlet, but also Othello, is used and explored again by Leontes in *The Winter's Tale*. In the latter play, the language belongs to an older man in a different situation, the twisted and tangled semantics and grammar used to fashion and reflect a tortured mind. We can also see the continued fascination throughout his plays with masculinity. The sonnets' display of masculine sexual and identity anxiety, their combination of bravura, aggression and vulnerability is replicated in the plots of the comedies at the turn of the century, such as *Measure for Measure* and *Much Ado About Nothing*. In both those plays, such masculinity, although questioned, is never really tested by plot or dramaturgy. In all the late plays, as we have seen, the assumptions of masculinity as natural superiority, of patriarchy as a naturalised system of familial and political relationships, and of women as naturally subservient, are all fundamentally questioned through tragedy and a subsequent turn towards comic resolution. The tragedies, particularly *Othello,* figure forth both the vulnerabilities and the tragic consequences of a patriarchal ordering of the world. *The Winter's Tale* acts as counterpoint, answering a 'what if...?', turning from the tragedy of a wife killed by irrational jealousy, and creating a second half to the story through a shift in time and perspective. *Antony and Cleopatra* shares some of the experimental scenic and time shifts which we find in *Cymbeline* and *The Winter's Tale*, evidencing a dramaturgical practice which not only eschews, but deliberately flouts the unities of time and place which his contemporary Ben Jonson so espoused. In these late plays, as in *Antony and Cleopatra,* scenic shifts of place and time are used to create visceral and imagistic, almost cinematic, contrasts and experiences for the audience. Our understanding of dramatic plot and character is achieved through a combination of theatrical effects: visual, spectacular, musical, scenic structures and textual means. We do find such elements in earlier plays, think of *A Midsummer Night's Dream,* or *As You like It,* for instance, but not the sustained use of multi-media modes that we do throughout these late plays. The use of pastoral to delineate place; to consider how character and identity can change or be tested in a different place; and to show how 'other' spaces can help us reflect on our present place, are all typical of the late plays. But these dramatic modes are also present in some of the earlier comedies, such as *Love's Labour's Lost, A Midsummer Night's Dream* and *As You Like It.*

Another aspect of Shakespeare's late career was collaborative writing: we know that he co-wrote two later plays with John Fletcher, who inherited the role of chief playwright once Shakespeare retired from the King's Men. The two plays on which they collaborated, *Henry VIII* and *The Two Noble Kinsmen,* share many similarities with the late plays. They indulge in spectacular set pieces, they use music and visual organisation of character in pageantry as a way of signalling ideas, and they draw on popular romance and fairy-tale as a way of talking about broader political and historical issues. Collaborative writing was common in the period, and it was additionally common for other writers to add scenes, prologues or speeches for particular performances or revivals. The text was not sacred. We do not really know whether the texts we have today are written solely by Shakespeare, or have scenic and speech additions made by other playwrights for particular performances.

It is thus possible to see through these brief examples how the late plays utilise and reflect on themes and dramaturgical practices from all stages of Shakespeare's career: language and interiority; tragic form; the transformative effects of comedy; a concern with the political and intellectual history of England and Britain; the fraught issue of gender and sexuality; the connections between character, class and language; and the expressive effects of music, spectacle and song.

The publication of Shakespeare's complete works by his executors John Hemminge and Henry Condell in 1623 was a monumental effort, but we know little about the details of the process: did they use the approved scripts which the King's Men had possessed since the first authorised performance of each play? What kind of editing did they do? Had Shakespeare revised the plays as they went along? Did they include additions and emendations of editors, scribes, prompters? The truth is we do not know, and probably never will. The texts we have to use and reflect on are themselves works-in-progress, open to our interpretation and performance. It is worth reading what Shakespeare's executors said about the enterprise of publishing his works, because they speak to us too.

To the great Variety of Readers.
From the most able, to him that can but spell: there you are numbered. We had rather you were weighed. Especially, when the fate of all books depends upon your capacities: and not of your heads alone, but of your purses. Well! It is now public, and you will stand for your privileges we know: to read, and censure. Do so, but buy it first. That doth best commend a book, the Stationer says. Then, how odd soever your brains be, or your wisdoms, make your licence the same, and spare not. Judge your six-pen'orth, your shillings worth, your five shillings worth at a time, or higher, so you rise to the just rates, and welcome. But, whatever you do, buy. Censure will not drive a trade, or make the Jack go. And though you be a magistrate of wit, and sit on the Stage at *Black-Friars*, or the *Cock-pit*, to arraign plays daily, know, these plays have had their trial already, and stood out all appeals; and do now come forth quitted rather by a Decree of Court, then any purchased letters of commendation. It had been a thing, we confess, worthy to have been wished, that the author himself had lived to have set forth, and overseen his own writings. But since it hath been ordained otherwise, and he by death departed from that right, we pray you do not envy his friends the office of their care, and pain, to have collected and published them; and so to have published them, as where (before) you were abused with diverse stolen, and surreptitious copies, maimed, and deformed by the frauds and stealths of injurious impostors, that exposed them: even those, are now offered to your view cured, and perfect of their limbs; and all the

rest, absolute in their numbers, as he conceived them. Who, as he was a happy imitator of nature, was a most gentle expresser of it. His mind and hand went together: and what he thought, he uttered with that easiness, that we have scarce received from him a blot in his papers. But it is not our province, who only gather his works, and give them you, to praise him. It is yours that read him. And there we hope, to your divers capacities, you will find enough, both to draw, and hold you: for his wit can no more lie hid, then it could be lost. Read him, therefore; and again, and again. And if then you do not like him, surely you are in some manifest danger, not to understand him. And so we leave you to other of his friends, whom if you need, can be your guides: if you need them not, you can lead your selves, and others. And such readers we wish him.

John Heminge.
Henrie Condell.

There are a number of remarkable things about this preface. It is addressed to us, 'the great variety of readers', creating a sense of inclusion and universalism ('from the most able to him that can but spell'). It emphasises the importance of books to education and culture, but also to the marketplace ('read and censure: do so, but buy first'). It speaks directly to a knowledgeable and critical audience ('magistrate of wit [who] sit on the stage at Blackfriars or the Cockpit to arraign plays daily'), but also disarms such critics by arguing that these plays 'have had their trial already': the marketplace of performance has already had an impact on the plays and judged them worthy. The implication is that through the testing of performance, the texts of the playscripts have been improved as well as approved. The other feature of this preface is that it establishes key characteristics of the myth of Shakespeare the writer, which remain with us today. They describe him as 'a happy imitator of nature... a most gentle expresser of it. His mind and hand went together; and what he thought, he uttered with that easiness that we have scarce received from him a blot in his papers'. The myth of Shakespeare the writer as a conduit of genius, so attractive to the Romantics and even today, is first given voice by his executors in 1623 (although excessive commendation was often pinned to such publications). The preface purports also to throw some light on the status of previous publications and versions of the plays: 'you were abused with divers stolen and surreptitious copies, maimed and deformed by the frauds and stealths of injurious impostors'. This implies that at least some of the quarto publications of plays were not approved by either Shakespeare or the King's Men, and that this Folio alone 'only gather his works and give them to you'. The frontispiece of the 1623 folio reads 'published according to the true original copies' beneath the title: so all the para-textual information validated a direct connection between texts published in 1623 and authorial hand, filtered through the reliable hands of the other sharers in the King's Men, Hemming and Condell. Of course the editors are quite frank here that they are embarked on a commercial enterprise, and that the presentation of a legitimated text was evidently essential to the 'brand'. But it also tells us that this 'brand' was already valuable and valued. Publication of the complete works of a dramatist had only previously been accorded to Ben Jonson, who had organised the publication of his own *Works* in 1616, to the derision of many of his contemporaries. The fine collection, the print run, and the emphasis on the value of critical reading, reached out with confidence to contemporary and future fans asking us to 'read him, therefore; and again; and again', and to find help, if we fail to understand the first time, amongst 'other of his friends... [as] guides'. Critics, audiences, readers and students have been amongst those friends ever since.

11

Jacobean Contexts

Shakespeare's work is popularly regarded as timeless: but in any reading of the plays we are immediately confronted with a fundamental difficulty with this view. The language, however rich and resonant, self-evidently belongs to a seventeenth-century world: a world with different outlooks, values and modes of expression to ours. The more we learn about that world, the easier it is to understand Shakespeare's plays. We have talked a bit about the conditions under which Shakespeare wrote and performed his plays in the previous chapter: here we will broaden that discussion to think more about the specific literary, social, political and cultural contexts in which the late plays were produced.

The features which distinguish them from many of Shakespeare's earlier plays can be grounded in that context: first, they foreground theatricality and spectacle both for visual entertainment and philosophical debate; and second they fuse and juxtapose the tragic and comic in sometimes confusing ways. Earlier plays used both these dramatic modes, but the persistent appearance of them consistently over the last years of Shakespeare's writing career suggest a deeper exploration and celebration of a new way of writing and performing.

The reopening of the Blackfriars Theatre in 1608 as the permanent indoor home for the King's Men coincided with the failed performance of an English version of a much talked-about Italian play by Guarini, *Il Pastor Fido*, called *The Faithfull Shepherdess*. It was adapted by John Fletcher, later to become Shakespeare's collaborator on *The Two Noble Kinsmen*, and to succeed him as chief playwright for the King's Men. The play was put on by the Children of the Blackfriars a few months before the King's Men took over the theatre. Despite its theatrical failure, the play was printed in 1609 with a preface to the reader. Fletcher defended the play, its ideas and its distinctive representative mode, articulating a theoretical manifesto: the title-page described it as 'a pastoral tragi-comedy', a generic description used previously by Samuel Daniel about his *The Queen's Arcadia* (1605) and in the Stationer's register description of John Marston's *The Malcontent* as a 'tragicomedia' in 1604. Marston's play fuses satirical edginess with tragedy and comedy and was first performed by the boys company of St Pauls: but purchased by the King's Men in 1605 or 1606, and with a new induction by John Webster, became one of the company's popular staples. These writers had been reading the Italian poets and playwrights Cinthio and Guarini, whose view was that dramatic and romance modes combining comedy and tragedy were best suited to modern audiences. Guarini's *Compendium of Tragicomic Poetry* (published in Italian in 1601) defined tragicomedy thus:

> He who composes tragicomedy takes from tragedy its great persons but not its great action, it verisimilar plot but not its true one, its movement of the feelings, but not its disturbance of them, its pleasure but not its sadness, its danger, but not its death; from comedy it takes laughter that is not excessive, modest amusement, feigned difficulty, happy reversal, and above all the comic order.

Drama should be decorous ('laughter that is not excessive'), and dramatists should compose comedy appealing and acceptable to an elite audience. The narrative trajectory should move towards a 'comic order': in other words, one of reconciliation, restoration and inclusion. In Guarini's view, such plays are finally comedies: just as the editors of the folio felt when they placed the last plays in that category in the First Folio. The Roman playwright Plautus coined the term 'tragic-comedy', when Mercury, in the play *Amphitryon*, claims he will 'make it a mixture' of tragedy and comedy because slaves, kings and gods all appear in the one story. This idea of mixed genre went against classical and neoclassical models of drama: Sir Philip Sidney's *Defence of*

Poetry, written in about 1580, articulates one idea of what we should find in tragedies and comedies:

> the Comedy is an imitation of the common errors of our life, which he [the poet] representeth in the most ridiculous and scornfull sort that may be: so as it is impossible that any beholder can be content to be such a one. Now as in Geometry, the oblique must be known as well as the right, and in arithmetic, the odd as well as the even, so in the actions of our life, who seeth not the filthiness of evil, wanteth a great foil to perceive the beauty of virtue. This doth the Comedy handle so in our private and domestical matters, as with hearing it, we get as it were an experience what is to be looked for... and not only to know what effects are to be expected, but to know who be such, by the signifying badge given them by the Comedient. And little reason hath any man to say, that men learn the evil by seeing it so set out, since as I said before, there is no man living, but by the force truth hath in nature, no sooner seeth these men play their parts, but wisheth them in Pistrinum [a place of punishment for slaves], although perchance the lack of his own faults lie so behind his back, that he seeth not himself to dance the same measure: whereto yet nothing can more open his eyes, then to see his own actions contemptibly set forth. So that the right use of Comedy, will I think, by nobody be blamed; and much less of the high and excellent Tragedy, that openeth the greatest wounds, and showeth forth the Ulcers that are covered with Tissue, that maketh Kings fear to be Tyrants, and Tyrants manifest their tyrannical humours, that with stirring the affects of Admiration and Commiseration, teacheth the uncertainty of this world, and upon how weak foundations gilden roofs are builded: that maketh us know, *Qui sceptra Saevus duro imperio regit, Timet timentes, metus in authorem redit* ['An evil ruler's heavy sceptre makes him afraid of those who fear him, and the fear returns to its author.'].....

Our Tragedies and Comedies, not without cause cried out against, observing rules neither of honest civility, nor skilful Poetry... For where the Stage should alway represent but one place, and the uttermost time presupposed in it, should be both by Aristotle's precept, and common reason, but one day; there is both many days and places, inartificially imagined... where you shall have Asia of the one side, and Afric of the other, and so many other under Kingdoms, that the Player when he comes in, must ever begin with telling where he is, or else the tale will not be conceived. Now you shall have three Ladies walk to gather flowers, and then we must believe the stage to be a garden. By and by we hear news of shipwreck in the same place, then we are to blame if we accept it not for a Rock. Upon the back of that, comes out a hideous monster with fire and smoke, and then the miserable beholders are bound to take it for a Cave: while in the mean time two Armies fly in, represented with four swords and bucklers, and then what hard heart will not receive it for a pitched field. Now of time, they are much more liberal. For ordinary it is, that two young Princes fall in love, after many traverses she is got with child, delivered of a fair boy: he is lost, groweth a man, falleth in love, and is ready to get another child, and all this is in two hours space: which how absurd it is in sense (*A Defence of Poetry*, ed. J.Van Doorsten, Oxford University Press, 1966, pp. 45, 65.)

Sidney's view of comedy and tragedy are representative of his age: comedy shows the faults of common men, while tragedies shows those of the high-born, and both forms have didactic ends. His models for good drama are all classical: and by contrast he attacks English playwrights for their transgression of representational conventions of space and time. His parodic account of the story of a play reads remarkably like the plot of one of Shakespeare's late plays. However, the suspension of disbelief which he describes in a parodic way is absolutely essential to any viewing of dramatic action and performance. As Time advocates in the opening to Act 4 of *The Winter's Tale*, audience, actors and writer have an implicit contract in which disbelief is suspended, and in which we agree that there are certain recognisable conventions which we all use as short hand to help us understand the story and ideas. This contract extends not only to the suspension of disbelief (in Sidney's version taking a stage to be a garden and then a rock at sea), but to an acceptance of the breaking of generic conventions as well: a comedy can become a tragedy and vice versa.

In *Hamlet* this contract is debated at length in the scene where Hamlet hears that players have arrived at court (2.2). A long discussion ensues about acting styles, audience affect, and how genres work. Hamlet's world-weary summary of the conventions of character acting and plot outcomes show that contemporary audiences were well versed in expectations arising from such conventions:

> He that plays the king shall be welcome – his Majesty shall have tribute of me; the adventurous knight shall use his foil and target; the lover shall

not sigh gratis; the humorous man shall end his part in peace; the clown shall make those laugh whose lungs are tickle o' th' sere; and the lady shall say her mind freely, or the blank verse shall halt for't.'

(2.2.317–23)

Such expectations are implicitly to be found also in Polonius' parodic celebration of the arriving tragedians: 'The best actors in the world, either for tragedy, comedy, history, pastoral, pastoral-comical, historical-pastoral, tragical-historical, tragical-comical-historical-pastoral; scene individable, or poem unlimited. Seneca cannot be too heavy, nor Plautus too light' (2.2.391–5). Players and players' companies can perform anything, although the implication is that they lack special talents to do any one thing excellently. Thus, mixed genres are satirised.

Despite such knowing satirical representations of 'tragical-comical-historical-pastoral', the Italian model of tragicomedy became very fashionable in London after 1607. Perhaps it appealed to a native English dramatic tradition of fusing tragedy and comedy, a mixing of high and low styles and representation which dates back to the medieval mummers' plays. Pastoral tragic-comedy in particular was popular at court, increasingly so after Shakespeare's retirement. Samuel Daniel dedicated his tragicomedies to his patron Queen Anne of Denmark, James I's wife, and Beaumont and Fletcher's works for the King's Men increasingly relied on the pastoral tragic-comedy as a mode and place for escapist political fantasies.

When Fletcher published *The Faithfull Shepherdess* in 1609 his preface 'To the Reader', explicitly named and defended the genre as a 'pastoral tragicomedy': 'A tragicomedy is not so called in respect of mirth and killing, but in respect it wants deaths, which is enough to make it no tragedy, yet brings some near it, which is enough to make it no comedy.' Although Fletcher's play has a relatively static plot (and this might explain its lack of success), in his later career he allowed pastoral tragicomedy to evolve into more complicated plot and action in collaborative writing both with Shakespeare, and his longer-term writing partner, Francis Beaumont. Their *Philaster*, played by the King's Men probably in 1609 or 1610, was set in Sicily; the plot centred around the impossible love of the daughter of the King of Sicily for Philaster, a man hated by her father, who wants his daughter to marry the King of Spain. The young lovers are plotted against by one of the King's advisers, who convinces Philaster his beloved has betrayed him with another man. Both lovers are wounded, both condemned to death, but saved and restored to the Sicilian throne by citizens who do not want a Spanish king imposed on them. It is clear that the play owes a debt to *Cymbeline*, and that both the story and political message are one shared by Shakespeare's other late plays. Equally, we can see that they share with Beaumont and Fletcher, Guarini and Daniel, a dramatic and intellectual interest in the boundaries between comic and tragic outlooks and structures. The late plays in particular enable providentialist endings to reincorporate shattered hopes and pasts: using comic resolution to mend tragic conflict. Guarini's 'happy reversal' ensures the reassurance of a 'right order' re-established. However, his emphasis on how tragicomedy acts to ameliorate the high passions of characters and audience in tragedy, whilst perhaps true of *The Tempest* and *Cymbeline*, does not satisfactorily describe either characters or audience of *The Winter's Tale*. The heightened situation and emotions of the court of Sicilia, and the intensely plotted and realised tragedy of Leontes' madness, Hermione's trial and death and Mamillius's death break Guarini's rules of decorum. So whilst the fashion for, and interest in, tragicomedy does give us a context for these late plays, it does not fully explain them, or Shakespeare's achievements.

During James I's reign tragicomedy, tragedy, and city comedy were the most popular genres. City comedy belonged more to the boys' companies and some of the populist theatres, and tragedy and tragicomedy popular in both the elite and populist theatres. Tragicomedy offered two innovative strengths. First, it allowed a dramatist the freedom to mingle characters of different classes traditionally only allowed in the comic mode. Secondly, it offered the opportunity to use plot in unconventional ways. Love did not have to end in either marriage or death, but perhaps both; comedies did not have to be only about the young, but perhaps the middle-aged as well; plot turning points could be much more radically effective if generic expectations and rules were broken. Shakespeare uses both these opportunities in the late plays, enabling him to radically explore many of the ideas of his previous plays in new dramatic and expressive ways.

James I's court saw the development of another dramatic and spectacular mode in this same period: that of the court masque. The masque was a highly wrought combination of text, music and visual performance. They were performed at court on special occasions, such as weddings, ambassadorial visits, feast days and so on. The parts were always taken by members of the court, including members of the royal family: Prince Henry, for example, performed in Ben Jonson's *Oberon* in 1611.

Ben Jonson and Inigo Jones collaborated on many masques, fusing text with visual stage spectacle and design in these intellectual and artistic events. In many ways the court masque as it developed under the Stuart monarchs was a precursor to opera and ballet: highly stylised, designed, and utilising the most current stage technology and machinery. They were expensive to stage because of the building of sets and stage machinery and the costumes prepared for aristocratic performers, and consequently tended to be commissioned only by royalty and aristocracy. Ben Jonson and Samuel Daniel were the most prolific writers of masques: the former for James I himself, and the latter for his queen. The structure of masques evolved into a tripartite form, the presentation of a conflict, the appearance of an 'anti-masque' which threatened civic or rational order, and the resolution of conflict and the defeat of the 'anti-masque' by the forces of right order, generally figured as the monarch and what he represented. The masque would end in a dance, in which both performers and audience would dance, led by the monarch. The end of the masque conjoined the aesthetic closure with a political closure, celebrating the monarch's resolution of conflict as the right ending. The invention and development of masques under James I thus coincided with a Stuart political message that the monarch's power and political influence was absolute: their aesthetic message elided into the political one.

The evolution of a distinctive and popular courtly genre in tragicomedy, the technical innovations consequent upon moves to an indoor theatre and increased seat receipts, and the courtly fashion for masques, all coincided with Shakespeare's dramaturgical innovations in the late plays. These innovations, so often seen as marking out his late work as unique in his career, and making it distinctively 'late' and sophisticated, cannot be judged as separate from the Jacobean theatrical experience of which they were an integral part. While Shakespeare's work remains distinctively his, the turn towards tragic-comedy and romance sources was a turn also made by Samuel Daniel, John Fletcher and Francis Beaumont; and the turn towards spectacle and music was shared with Ben Jonson and Inigo Jones in their court masques.

The Political and Social Context of the Late Plays

We have mentioned political debates and discussions throughout our analysis of the plays, both in our discussion of how plays open and end, and on character. We have observed how debates are raised through the play's dramaturgy in the form of questions: who has the right to rule? Is there ever a justification for war? Is there a justification for the usurpation of a leader? What rights if any do men have over women? What fault-lines do we find in a patriarchal society? What is the place of a 'natural' aristocracy? What is liberty? What role do arranged marriages play in political diplomacy? Is political absolutism possible or desirable? What moral rights and status do indigenous populations have? Do political states have the right to populate other states? What is the place of women in a political world?

All these questions belong to the realm of political philosophy and are not specific only to Jacobean or seventeenth-century England. However, all these questions did have particular political currency at this time, and it is helpful to consider each question and its location within political debate in the seventeenth century.

The question about who has the right to rule was also raised by the question of who would succeed Elizabeth I in the first years of the century. Parliament and advisers repeatedly urged her to name a successor, since she did not have a child. Elizabeth I feared that naming a successor would initiate plots and counter-plots against her life and throne. Although the civil wars of the Wars of the Roses had come to an end over a century before, the national psyche kept them alive through history plays, and popular reading of chronicles. Elizabeth I's political position was questioned by Catholics who rebelled during her reign, by her cousin Mary Queen of Scots (who was the mother of James I), and by the invasion of the Spanish Armada, which had the backing of the Pope. The Catholic Church had never recognised

Henry VIII's divorce from Catherine of Aragon (his wife before Anne Boleyn, Elizabeth I's mother), and therefore continued to see Elizabeth as illegitimate with no right to the English throne. Such international political jockeying produced political treatises defending Elizabeth's legitimacy, and parliamentary declarations confirming it. Nevertheless, it also engendered a fragility about succession, authority and rule which continued to haunt the Stuart succession as well. In addition, a tradition of talking about republicanism evolved out of these debates, emerging first in Scotland, and often coded through discussions about Classical Greece and Rome. We can see this fashion replicated in the many plays about classical Roman and Greek political states in the first decade of the seventeenth century: *Julius Caesar, Coriolanus, Antony and Cleopatra,* and Ben Jonson's *Sejanus,* and *Catiline*. So although the Stuart succession was confirmed, the Pandora's box of political debate about who had the right to rule, and different types of political states had already been opened.

The question of national justification for war was debated by parliament and advisers with both Elizabeth I and James I: many vocal Protestants wanted an active military strategy against Spain and the Pope, and intervention in the religious war in the Low Countries (now Belgium and the Netherlands), where individual Englishmen did fight. However, both monarchs refused to intervene in European religious wars, maintaining a political position of non-intervention. The military operation in which they were both continually embroiled was that of Ireland: the ongoing attempt to convert Irish Catholics from Elizabeth's reign onwards was combined with a policy of settling English 'planters', and constitutional debates about the respective political rights of English and Irish inhabitants of Ireland. Such debates were both parliamentary and pamphlet-based, and although the dominant Stuart view of monarchical legitimacy dominated, divergent views were expressed and debated.

Debates about usurpation, despite the stability of the Stuart succession, were surprisingly current in an academic and philosophical environment. George Buchanan, a Scottish lawyer and fierce Calvinist, who had been a tutor of Montaigne and then James I as a boy, wrote a work dedicated to James called *De Jure Regni apud Scotos,* (*The Law of Ruling in Scotland*) in 1579, which argued that a monarch only ever ruled with the consent of the people, and that it was lawful to resist or in certain circumstances, to kill tyrants. Although Buchanan had died long before James inherited the English throne in 1603, his work had been published in Edinburgh, Antwerp and London, and was widely discussed in radical circles. Parliamentary debates in 1610 which fiercely contested James I's idea of the king's 'prerogative' drew on many of Buchanan's ideas about the legal position of parliament as constitutional ballast to the executive power of the monarch. James I and his son Charles I were equally dismissive of these arguments, and the increasingly vitriolic relationship between monarch and parliament on precisely these issues later set England on the path to civil war in the 1640s.

The next two questions are linked, and we can consider them together: what rights if any do men have over women; and what fault-lines do we find in a patriarchal society? James I wrote a work addressed to his eldest son, Henry, in 1598, *The True Law of Free Monarchies*, which was reissued when he came to the English throne in 1603. He wrote:

> By the law of nature the King becomes a natural father to all his lieges at his coronation. And as the father of his fatherly duty is bound to care for the nourishing, education and virtuous government of his children: even so is the King bound to care for all his subjects. As all the toil and pain that the father can take for his children, will be thought light and well bestowed by him; so that the effect thereof redound to their profit and weal: so ought the Prince to do towards his people. As the kindly father ought to see all inconveniencies and dangers that may arise towards his children, and though with the hazard of his own person press to prevent the same: so ought the King towards his people. As the father's wrath and correction upon any of his children that offendeth ought to be by a fatherly chastisement seasoned with pity, as long as there is any hope of amendment in them: so ought the King towards any of his lieges that offends in that measure.

In this work of political philosophy and practical advice about ruling, James I gives voice to a theory of patriarchy in which a hierarchy of rule descends in order from God to monarch to father, and all intersect and cohere. Within this model, femininity and women are always subordinate. It is ironic (or perhaps telling) that James had a mother who reigned in a kingdom, and that he himself inherited the power of the Scottish and English thrones from two queens, respectively Mary Queen of Scots and Elizabeth I. England had been ruled by a female monarch for forty years at the point at which James wrote this: and the memory of Elizabeth's reign remained resonant throughout James's own reign. There was a strong and increasing element of nostalgia for her person, the literary culture and the political practices of her reign, particularly after about 1608. The perception that she listened to her parliaments and courtiers more than James did, encouraged this nostalgia as a minor form of political resistance.

During Shakespeare's late career women poets began to write and publish in English for the first time: Aemilya Lanyer was the first woman poet to publish in her own name in English in the year of *The Tempest*'s first performance, 1611. *Salve Deus Rex Judeorum* (Hail to thee, King of the Jews) was a rereading of Christian history from a woman's point of view. During this period, there were also a number of legal challenges made by women to patriarchal legal authority. Lady Anne Clifford challenged the courts as a young woman in 1605 for the right to inherit her father's lands and titles as his sole surviving child: both courts and king refused this right, allowing the titles to go to a cousin. Clifford continued to challenge this decision unsuccessfully for the next forty years: but when her cousin died without an heir, was able to inherit and run the family Cumberland estates in her middle age from 1649 until her death in 1676. Another high-profile case was that of the king's cousin, Lady Arbella Stuart. She had a technical claim to the Scottish and English thrones, and James I refused to enter any negotiations for her marriage, possibly because it might strengthen a claim for the throne which would challenge either his or that of his children. Arbella Stuart married William Seymour in secret in 1610 (the year in which *The Winter's Tale* was performed and *Cymbeline* and *The Tempest* were being written), and James I imprisoned the couple for disobeying him. The couple arranged to escape, Arbella Stuart dressing as a man to facilitate this, and attempted to flee to the continent. However, they were betrayed, re-arrested and confined to the Tower. Lady Arbella Stuart died in 1615 in the Tower. She petitioned the Privy Council in 1611 with the following plea, illustrating a contemporary aristocratic woman's perception of her fundamental rights and liberty:

> Whereas I have been long restrained from my liberty which is as much to be regarded as my life, and am appointed as I understand to be removed far from these Courts of Justice where I ought to be examined and tried, and then condemned or cleared... this is to beseech your Lordships to inquire by a habeas corpus or other usual form of law what is my fault... And if your Lordships may not or will not of yourselves grant me the ordinary relief of a distressed subject then I beseech you to become humble intercessors to his Majesty that I may receive such benefit of justice as both his majesty by his oath hath promised and the laws of this realm afford to all others, those of his blood not excepted.

The two related questions of gender, (what is the place of women in a political world, and what role do arranged marriages play in political diplomacy?) are both posed and answered by each of these examples: a woman is seen as an object of exchange between men in a patriarchal political world, but not as a subject in her own right (she cannot inherit as a man can, nor negotiate her own marriage). This is particularly true for aristocratic and royal women, whose marriages were conventionally part of international and national political and economic diplomacy. Arranged marriages were the norm for these women, and arrangements included not only questions of dowry, but more importantly, debates about how marriage would cement political relationships between families or countries. When Frances Howard was married to the young Earl of Essex in 1606, the Venetian Ambassador wrote home:

> The marriage of a daughter of the Chamberlain [Suffolk] to the Earl of Essex is to be celebrated on New Year's day, and his Majesty intends to be present. ... Essex is but little the friend of Salisbury, who was the sole and governing cause of the late earl's execution. Nothing is more earnestly desired by Salisbury than not to leave this legacy of hatred to his son, for though Essex is not rich nor in enjoyment of the power Lord Salisbury wields, yet if the latter were to die his son would not succeed to the influence and authority which his father possesses, whereas Essex has an infinite number of friends all devoted to the memory of his father... Lord Salisbury hopes by creating ties of relationship to cancel the memory of ancient enmities.

Marriage was accepted as international political diplomacy. When we watch Miranda playing chess with her husband, and hear her consent to her husband's possible cheating, we watch the active role some aristocratic women did play in political marriage negotiations. Many of the married women of James I's court actively engaged in helping cement political alliances through marriage arrangements. The marriage negotiations and consequent celebration for James I's daughter Elizabeth were the most significant political events from 1611–13. Elizabeth was portrayed as a new Elizabeth Tudor, and her marriage to Frederick of Bohemia cemented political alliances with the Protestants of Germany and middle Europe. The wedding was finally celebrated in the winter of 1612–13, with *The Winter's Tale* and *The Tempest* played as part of the court celebrations.

The next question which these plays posit (what is the place of a 'natural' aristocracy?) was one debated continually by James I's upper house of parliament, and both implicit and explicit in James I's theories of 'divine right' in his political writings, including *Basilikon Doron* (1599). The revival of chivalric tournaments, particularly those supported and patronised by his eldest son Prince Henry in the period 1608–11, encouraged a cult of militaristic medieval chivalric values. These were partly linked to political pressure to become more involved in European religious politics, but representations and debates about chivalry at the time tended to conservatively celebrate ideals and ideas of a 'natural' aristocracy.

The question 'What is liberty?' is fraught with some difficulties, since conceptions of liberty vary so much between our time and the early seventeenth century. Parliamentary debates in James I's reign consistently clashed with the monarch about ideas of liberty: arguing that it was parliament which should determine taxes, not the king, the 'right' of property owners to make such decisions since the Magna Carta. Broader ideas of liberty slowly evolved during the seventeenth century: some of the radical groups of the English Civil War, such as Levellers, Ranters and Quakers began to voice ideas about the individual liberty of all people. The Civil War broke out some 26 years after Shakespeare's death, but the political and social ideas generated by his stage debates expressed many of the ideas which were fought over in that later conflict.

The concomitant question about political absolutism (is it possible or desirable?) is integral to all the late plays, engaging in a debate about a central tenet of Jacobean political theory. Parliament throughout the reign of James I and Charles I clashed with both monarchs about their insistence on the royal 'prerogative' (that he the monarch was above the law, and responsible only to God) was legally untenable. Both monarchs continued to argue that their moral and legal rights were absolute.

The ethical question about the rights and status of indigenous populations was explicitly raised by writers such as Montaigne in his *Essays* (translated into English in 1603), and by Bartolme de las Casas's *A Short Account of the Destruction of the Indies* (translated into English in 1583). Interestingly, in many of the pro-colonial writings, for example Robert Gray's *A God Speed to Virginia* (published in 1609 as the late plays are being written), explicit debates are rehearsed about why the native peoples need English rule and beliefs imposed on them. The fact that works like these, which bordered on propaganda, needed to find arguments against the 'opposite' view (that indigenous populations had rights) tells us this debate was live, and that the influence of radical and philosophical writers like Montaigne and de las Casas was significant.

Finally, it is worth mentioning three other political and social phenomena related to the reigning Stuart political family. The first was the marketing of the Stuart family: in contradistinction to Elizabeth's singular rule, a woman with no husband or dependents, the Stuart family were pictured as fertile and communal. Although James's Queen Anne kept her own household, employed her own staff, and had her own entertainments, the couple marked a departure in English iconographic traditions. The family were frequently pictured together, news of Anne's pregnancies was widely discussed, and the surviving children, Henry, Elizabeth and Charles, received popular press. What has sometimes been called 'the Stuart family romance' was in many ways enhanced by the pathos of the sudden death of Prince Henry in late 1612. Ideas of family and family leadership (integral as we have seen to James I's political philosophy) were softened and broadened through the actions and images of the whole royal family.

The second political change from Elizabeth I's reign was that James I was the first monarch to unite the countries of England and Scotland, as legitimate monarch of both. Ideas and celebrations of and about political union abounded: but equally, so did debates about the autonomy of England and Scotland and their distinctive histories and heritages. Contemporary political ideas and ideology thus encompassed some of the real complexities of political life, authority and geography which we also encounter in the late plays.

The third shift was that James I's reign saw the first formal establishment of a colony directly ruled from Westminster: the colony of Virginia. As the seventeenth century progressed, new colonies in mainland America and the West Indies islands were placed under British rule. Throughout the century annexation of land was wrought with difficulties of leadership, relationships with native populations, disputes about natural resources, and the place of slaves in the establishment and maintenance of power. By the end of the century, the colonies were wealthy communities, central to the triangular trade between England, Africa and the Americas in cotton, slaves, sugar and tobacco. The Jacobean plays are written at the opening of this history, but carry observable traces of the ethical, political and economic debates and changes to come.

Of course, we do not have to read and see the plays as forever embedded in their contextual origins. The revivals of the plays in different guises and interpretations throughout the succeeding centuries attest to the richness of their political, social, sexual and artistic attractions. The ability of each generation of readers, directors, critics and actors to find contemporary meaning and resonance in each new production or edition shows us that the text as originally produced and conceived does not have to dominate the meanings of that text through history and time. What context does give us is a more nuanced sense of the original play's connotations and origins, so we are better placed to understand how subsequent generations respond to and interpret it.

12

Sample Critical Views and Performances

Your own analyses, built up gradually through this book, will have provided you with a strong and individual interpretation of the plays. Since these are based on, and justified by, close readings of the plays, your interpretations are equal to those of critics and directors. Nevertheless, it is stimulating to read and engage with the ideas of other critics and interpreters of the plays, in the same way as it is stimulating to talk and argue with friends when we have seen a play or film. You should think about reading critics as part of the process of a developing discussion, and not to find the 'right' answer about a play. If you use critics in this way, you will be able to think about their arguments critically and thoughtfully yourself, and you will be better placed to develop your own independent thinking, arguing and writing skills.

This chapter considers both conventional literary criticism of the late plays, and some sample performances, with the aim of introducing you to some of the critical debates and approaches to Shakespeare's late plays, and of asking you to think about these in the light of our analyses in this book.

There is so much written on Shakespeare that the following cannot be representative of all possible approaches to the plays: the bibliography at the end of the book can guide you to more resources and sources on the critical debates around the late plays.

Northrop Frye

Our first critic is Northrop Frye, whose *A Natural Perspective* was first published in 1965. This work is the classic articulation of seeing the late plays as 'romances' which self-consciously create a finale to an artistic career. The work was originally given as four lectures, which explicitly argued that Shakespeare's dramatic trajectory was unified, so that the comedies of the earlier part of his career saw a fulfilment in the 'romances' of the late period ('a logical evolution towards Romance in Shakespeare's work', p. 7). Although he does not concentrate on close readings of the individual plays, he argues that patterns of imagery and plot prove a coherence and consistency of authorial ideas about how patterns of human life and experience are echoed in the structure of comedy and romance. He argues that 'recurring images and structural devices' which dominate many of Shakespeare's plays, and which culminate in the late plays lead the reader:

> from the characteristics of the individual play, the vividness of characterization, the texture of imagery, and the like, to consider what kind of a form comedy is, and what its place is in literature. Shakespeare ... does not ask his audience to accept an illusion: he asks them to listen to the story. Everything we are told in that story has equal authority.... It follows that the criticism devoted to the vividness of characterization in Shakespeare's comedies may get out of proportion if it is not kept in its context. That context is, again, like the context of characterization in a detective story: lifelike and highly individualized characters may appear, but we should never lose sight of the incidental *tour de force* involved in the skill of so presenting them. Shakespeare's technique is the opposite of say Chekhov's, where the characters seem to be prior to the plot.... Shakespeare tells a story that stylizes his characters and may force them to do quite unreasonable things
>
> (pp. 13–14).

Frye argues that Ben Jonson, Shakespeare's great contemporary, does the opposite of this: deriving plot from character, and consequently could never understand the attraction of 'mouldy tales' (self-mockingly used by the narrator Gower in *Pericles*, and the title of Frye's first chapter). The setting and plots of late plays is deliberately 'primitive' (p. 32) because:

> The logic is that of the Arabian Nights... where so uncritical a participation is demanded from us, the action cannot be lifelike: it can only be archetypal. It evokes the primitive responses from us that are evoked by popular literature: it has a hero's hairbreadth escapes, a heroine's deliverance from death and dishonour, a miraculous curing of someone apparently dead; it appeals to the horror of incest and the tearful joys of reunions. The dramatic construct, for all its symmetry, has been reduced to great simplicity and directness in order to put the strongest possible emphasis on the immediate dramatic experience itself
> (pp. 32–3).

Frye shows that comedies have a 'festive' structure, ending in a social celebration of marriage and inclusionism, and are myth-like in this formal arrangement. This festive structure is reinforced in the romances by a coincidence with providential intervention, rendering them even closer to mythical writing. In his third chapter ('The Triumph of Time'), Frye shows how comic structure involves stories of thwarted young love, a younger generation struggling to assert their identity against an older one. Comic structure has a tripartite pattern: anti-comic and irrational society blocks change; the new young lovers or younger generation conflict with the older ones and move through confusion; to a final phase of reconciliation and festive celebration. In his final chapter ('The Return from the Sea'), Frye argues that the world of comedy and romance is one which is archetypal, and deliberately and self-consciously appeals to a human desire for repeated symbols of fertility, death and rebirth. Comedy usually concentrates on young love and fertility, while romance encompasses the breadth and span of human life by including cycles of death and rebirth. For Frye the Christian story itself is the ultimate model of this archetype, and he thus places Shakespeare's late plays as great allegorical and metaphorical equivalences to the story of the life of Christ

This critical position is illuminating in a number of ways. First, it enables us to see Shakespeare's late plays as equal in status to those of his great tragedies. Second, it displays replicated imagistic and dramaturgical patterns across all of his plays. Third, it relates dramatic experiences to more general cultural, ideological and social practices. The weaknesses of Frye's approach lie in its lack of specificity: closer readings of the plays would draw us away from the generalisations he wants to make about all of the plays; and historical or contextual readings would suggest that Shakespeare's individual plays speak to a historical moment, which detracts from the mythological force he finds in the plays. Finally, as with many critics, Frye does not really discuss the performance context or effect of the plays, which could potentially strengthen his argument about the plays' mythical drama.

Leonard Tennenhouse

Our second critic is Leonard Tennenhouse, whose *Power on Display: The Politics of Shakespeare's Genres* was first published in 1986. This work takes as its starting point the premise that Shakespeare was 'political', both in the sense that 'literature' and 'politics' intersect in this period and in his adroit control of the rhetoric of power. Tennenhouse fuses an understanding of genre (in itself indebted to Frye) with political context and effect: asking how each genre represents power, and what rhetorical and dramatic strategies tragedy, comedy and romance share with political discourse to represent power? He then moves into his radical argument:

> We might have to conclude that Renaissance drama displayed its politics in its manner of idealizing or demystifying specific forms of power. It is my contention that such display and not a work's transcendence or referentiality made it aesthetically successful
>
> (p. 6).

Tennenhouse's argument is that these plays' success does not lie in their timelessness, but their effective display and articulation of seventeenth-century power. He shows that the intersection of the political and aesthetic in the seventeenth century made it impossible to separate performed drama from the political rhetoric of the day. Not only did drama have to be licensed for performance (and was therefore censored), but it was commissioned by royalty and patronised by aristocracy. Tennenhouse shares with many other critics of the 1980s and 1990s a view that renaissance drama both replicated dominant Stuart political ideologies, and were part and parcel of those ideologies. Where they might initiate oppositional and alternative views, these views were contained by the plot's action. Dramatic plots' narrative trajectory (moving from resistance to containment) replicated the rhetoric of contemporary political power, which shut down the articulation of resistance to dominant ideologies through the monarch's voice in parliament, censorship, and the explicit articulation of Stuart political philosophy in James I's own publications.

Tennenhouse argues that all genres (comedies, tragedies and history plays) share this ideological and dramaturgical function. His final chapter ('Family Rites: City Comedy, Romance and the Strategies of Patriarchalism') argues that parliamentary and religious opposition to James I engendered a need to reassert monarchical power:

> Though never a serious threat in themselves, the appearance of a coherent form of resistance in turn coalesced those ... whose interests remained firmly bound to the king. In place of the Elizabethan situation, where the threat to a centralized government appeared to come from competing patriarchs... the Jacobean court and its dependents understood the opposition as an assault on patriarchy itself. In response to the apparent threat, we find speeches, proclamations, plays, court entertainments, indeed the whole iconography that grew up around James, cooperating to produce a more conservative royal authority by portraying a world without patriarchy as a world in grave danger... city comedy and absent monarch plays participated along with dramatic romances in a struggle to rewrite the political body of the monarch. This was done not simply to revise Elizabethan patriarchy for a king, but also to meet the forms of resistance that kept rising against James's notion of patriarchy.... James saw a political advantage in claiming the strategies of a natural father in relation to the state. This figure invokes natural law as the basis for his claim to patriarchal power. Such a representation of monarchy undermined the traditional argument of the contract which was used to oppose patriarchy. Employing tropes which based political authority on the natural rights of husband and of father enabled James

to link himself to earlier monarchs in a patrilineal system of descent. It also gave him the authority of the father over all families in the realm. To describe the whole island as his wife was further to remind parliament of an earlier age when England and Scotland were joined as Britain. The ideological centre of this Jacobean theory of power can be isolated in James's treatise on *The Trew Law of Free Monarchies*
(pp. 149–150).

In the Jacobean plays Tennenhouse discusses 'so long as kinship remains the language of politics, disruption of its rules is tantamount to political chaos' (p. 169). He goes on to explain how this relates to the romances:

> This ideological matrix informs all the Jacobean dramatic genres... Unlike city comedy, however, the romances represent the aristocratic body on the stage, and, in contrast with absent monarch plays, the romances debate the politics of the family.... [they] use... the family to dramatize the need for a patriarchal figure who can reform corrupt social practices, supervise the exchange of women and insure the proper distribution of power. If they are about nothing else, the romances deliberate the relationship between family and government
> (p. 171).

Before discussing the late plays in detail, Tennenhouse analyses how the language about 'family' was significantly political. Puritans, for example, posited the family in conduct books as the site where religious knowledge and debate was located. This effectively suggested the family was a separate unit from the state, and a preacher like John Dod used the term 'governor' to describe the authority of the father within the family: 'the subversive potential of such allegorising was clear' (p. 173). By contrast, James I argued that the whole commonwealth was his family, over all of whom he was 'father'.

> The distinction between the two positions is as sharp as it is basic. Given this, the Jacobean theatre was never more political than when it staged a king as a father and a court as a household, for to do so was to consider whether the king was properly bound to the rules of the father
> (pp. 174–5)

Tennenhouse uses the death of Mamillius in *The Winter's Tale* to illustrate his points. From the initial scene, through his representation with his father in 2.1, to his sudden death in 3.2:

> He stands as a living example of the genealogical principle, and like the fate of Perdita, the disappearance of Hermione and the aberrant behaviour of Leontes, the loss of Mamillius provides the means by which the play engages a larger political argument. Such catastrophic events threaten to destroy a kingdom not simply because they mean patriarchal authority has gone awry, but because they make clear patriarchy has gone awry in a way which threatens the monarch's body; together these events eliminate the possibility of a legitimate heir to the throne... The other romances similarly stage a shocking scene in which domestic violence overturns the politics of blood
>
> (pp. 175–6).

The violence which predicates action and crisis are: the Antiochus scene in *Pericles*, the banishment of Posthumus in *Cymbeline*, and Prospero's betrayal by Sebastian in *The Tempest*. Shakespeare exaggerates the monstrous qualities of the 'natural family' (for example Cloten, Caliban, Leontes):

> With the regularity of an obsession Shakespeare unfolds the monstrous potential within the natural family only to reveal that the self-enclosed family is in fact incapable of subverting the state. Whether it is Caliban or Leontes, all that is dangerous is already contained within a figure which insures its own subordination to monarchy. Thus these monsters display the debased nature of the natural family in a way that ultimately authorizes the power of the state... these scenes of violence.... are ultimately all for show
>
> (p. 179).

Tennenhouse observes a representational shift between the Elizabethan and Jacobean Shakespeare: whereas in the earlier plays nature was a benign force ensuring continuity with narrative closure, in the romances, nature is perverted. He summarises thus:

> I have described romance in terms of two forms of dramatic display. One presents scenes of domestic violence in which the natural family

disrupts the royal line; the second announces the reappearance of patriarchy as a supernatural force. These forms display the power of the playwright, I have argued, because this is how he displays the power of the state. By scattering the natural family and then inscribing it within a metaphysical body, Shakespeare made earlier dramatic materials speak for the state against a form of resistance which opposed not only James's regressive notion of patriarchy but also displays of this authority upon the stage

(p. 181).

Thus the self-conscious artistry, spectacle and music of the last two acts of *The Winter's Tale*, for example, is an offering of how art can serve power. His finales are 'hardly subtle' (p. 182) in their representation of the recuperative power of royal blood, giving each reunited family increased territory as well as the promise of future rule. The quintessential representation of this political model is the 'trope of resurrection', most spectacularly performed in the statue scene of *The Winter's Tale*.

In ritual fashion the aristocratic body comes back to life... With the apotheosis of Hermione performed upon the stage, the aristocratic body becomes a *deus ex machina* in its own right. We might regard this as the ultimate revelation of the strategy at work in all the romances – a perfect collaboration of art and ideology

(pp. 184–5).

Tennenhouse's argument is exciting and has some tremendous strengths: it alerts us to the political context and the ways in which dramatic genre is never neutral. By analysing and showing how 'genre' is actively engaged in creating political and social meaning, Tennenhouse opens up new ways of seeing the plays. He uses Jacobean political debates and texts to show us how the plays' language and structure share rhetorical and ideological codes with political and religious texts of the period. His argument, that Shakespeare's plays both implicitly served the interests of the Jacobean royal family and actively celebrated those interests, disturbed critical views that Shakespeare and his works are above politics. The major weakness of his work (and those of other 'new historicists' as this particular trend came to be called) is that it creates a monolithic model of all drama and literature in a particular historical period. By modelling representation as a movement between resistance and containment, in which containment always dominates, both politics and drama come to be stooges of a dominant and unchallengeable power and ideology. For readers, directors and critics who find alternative ideas and representations, Tennenhouse's critical view is arguably itself too absolutist.

Janet Adelman

Our third critical work is Janet Adelman's *Suffocating Mothers*, published in 1992, which addresses the late plays from a modern feminist viewpoint, considering the texts within the context of gender and sexuality in the Jacobean court. Adelman, like Tennenhouse and Frye, places the romances within the context of all of Shakespeare's work, arguing that his imaginative creation of mothers is integral to his articulation of masculine identity. From Richard of York's characterisation of his desire for love and approval in *Henry VI part 3* (3.2.153–68) as stemming from a lack of maternal love, to Hamlet's rages against his mother, maternal power is figured as both monstrous and defining of masculine anxiety. Using a combination of close textual reading, historical documents on child-rearing and modern psychoanalytical theory, Adelman argues:

> Culturally constructed as literally dangerous to everyone, the maternal body must have seemed especially dangerous to little boys: fed *in utero* on her menstrual blood and then on the milk that was its derivative, he had too much of her blood in him. Contemporary object-relations psychoanalysis locates differentiation from the mother as a special site of anxiety for the boy-child, who must form his specifically masculine selfhood against the matrix of her overwhelming femaleness; how much more difficult and anxiety-ridden this process must have been if the period of infantile dependency – with all its pleasures and dangers – was prolonged and if the body itself in all its vulnerability, could later be understood as the inheritance from her contaminating female matter
>
> (p. 7).

Contemporary theories of how bodies worked was based on a combination of the Galenic model of humours, wherein all people were made up of a mixture of the four humours, hot, dry, moist and cold. In general, men were considered to be hot and dry (the ideal temperament), whilst women were moist and cold. Humours could vary in any one individual, and medical treatment was based on rebalancing the humours. This model of gender identity was supplemented by the Aristotelian idea that men were form and women matter, men reason and women bodies. Thus in Jacobean discussions of gender formation, it was theoretically possible for feminised humours to infect a man, and vice-versa. Adelman's discussion combines this historicised understanding of how gender is understood in Jacobean times with modern feminist psychoanalytic object-relations theories of identity formation.

In her final chapter, ('Masculine Authority and the Maternal Body: The Return to Origins in the Romances') Adelman examines the late plays within this frame. She writes:

> Within Shakespeare's career *Antony and Cleopatra* functions as a fragile pastoral moment. Its pastoral is shorn of power to bring even its modest gains back to the dominating culture: as Egypt's female pastoral is in the end contained and colonized by Rome, so *Antony and Cleopatra's* moment of festive possibility is largely contained by the surrounding texts. The generative maternal power celebrated in Cleopatra's recreation of Antony is severely curtailed in *Coriolanus*, where maternal presence is once again construed as paternal absence, where mothers are once again fatal to their sons. This construction is, I have argued, the legacy of *Hamlet*, where the mother's sexual body is itself poisonous to the father on whom the son would base his identity; its consequences are variously played out in the problem plays and tragedies that follow from *Hamlet*. Taken together, the romances can be understood as Shakespeare's final attempt to repair the damage of this legacy, in effect to reinstate the ideal parental couple lost at the beginning of *Hamlet*: the idealized mother is recovered in *Pericles* and *The Winter's Tale*, the idealized father in *Cymbeline* and *The Tempest*. But the attempt at recovery itself reinscribes the conditions of loss: in the plays of maternal recovery, the father's authority must be severely undermined and the mother herself subjected to a chastening purgation; in the plays of paternal recovery, the mother must be demonized and banished before the father's authority can be restored.

> ...If *Pericles* begins where *Hamlet* does, in the psychic world poisoned by female sexuality, *The Tempest* answers his need for a bodiless father immune to the female, able at last to control her unweeded garden. Except for a moment in *The Winter's Tale*, when the generative female space of Cleopatra's monument recurs in Paulina's own sheltering moment, the mother and father lost in *Hamlet* cannot be fully recovered together. Instead the romances oscillate between them, broadly structured by a series of gendered either/ors: either maternal or paternal authority; either female deity or male; either nature or art; either trust in processes larger than the self or the attempt to control these processes
>
> (pp. 193–4)

Adelman's analysis involves close and compelling readings of both characterisation and dramatic structure to validate her argument. The overarching argument here suggests that all the romances are finally both politically and psychically masculine and patriarchal. Adelman does, however, suggest that *The Winter's Tale* posits a more humane and female-friendly model of identity and society.

> The Hermione who awakens is thus both the creation of Leontes' renewed desire and independent of that desire: she exists at the boundary between inner and outer, self and other. Situated thus she epitomises the recovery of fruitful relatedness with the world: the relatedness.... [of] the infant's relation with its first not-me possession, the relatedness that enables creative and recreative play in the potential space that is neither self nor other. And if Leontes is brought to this place, we are brought there too. In the last moments of the play Shakespeare aligns his own theatre with Paulina's female space, where we too can 'sup' (5.2.103), where our desires can be safely fed in recreative play. For the female space of Hermione's recovery is also the space of Shakespeare's theatre: as many have noted, Hermione's aliveness alludes to the risky aliveness of theatre itself, with its moving actors, and, like Paulina, Shakespeare's is a participatory theatre in which the awakening of our faith is required...
>
> *The Winter's Tale* is, I think, an astonishing psychic achievement: through his nourishing art Shakespeare figures the loss and recovery of the world in the mother's body, returning us what we didn't know we had lost. But there are, of course, limitations to this achievement. First of all it takes place – not surprisingly – within a framework that is decidedly patriarchal. Leontes is fully restored to personal and political potency at the end; and the female agents of restoration turn out to

have been good patriarchalists all along.... Female power of all sorts is contained because it is divided; reproductivity is split between Hermione and Perdita, deflected in one and deferred in the other; and female rage is located in the safely asexual Paulina

(pp. 235–6).

The strength of Adelman's argument lies in the combination of close textual analysis, Jacobean contexts and feminist psychoanalytical theory. Adelman is sensitive to the performance feel of the plays and to how the audience respond to the representation of mothers, sons and lovers. Like Frye and Tennenhouse she considers the whole of Shakespeare's work as illustrative of an extended meditation on the place of drama and art in the social and performing world. Like them, she understands how genre has political and social meanings, and so we can see her consideration of gender as an extension and refinement of their work. Equally, she shares to some extent the ideological frame which Tennenhouse articulates, that no matter how radical staged ideas might be, they will always be 'contained' by a patriarchal and authoritarian ending. The implications of such an argument is finally conservative, assimilating literary texts to dominant ideologies.

The strength of debating all of Shakespeare's plays as a complete whole can also be a significant weakness. Adelman has a tendency to read off plays as though they are part of a continuous narration or life-story. *Hamlet* is a quite different play from *The Tempest*, *Measure for Measure* from *Cymbeline*, and subject to the playing and performance conditions and narrative specificity of their origins, rather than belonging to an uber-narrative to which all the plays are subsumed.

Gabriel Egan

Our fourth critic is Gabriel Egan whose *Green Shakespeare: From Ecopolitics to Ecocriticism* was published in 2006, and considers the late plays in the context of an emergent nationalist consciousness about land and identity, self and others, including ideas about colonial plantation.

Egan argues that we need to read Shakespeare in an entirely new context so that we can put 'new ways of thinking about humankind's relations with earth... to use... for disrupting the self-persisting habits of thought under which industrial capitalism emerged and flourished' (p. 175). He argues that by returning to the Elizabethan and Jacobean conception of the material world as one based on sets of correspondences between natural and human, and looking at the plays as expressions and engagements with those beliefs through their visual and metaphorical performances, modern audiences and readers can re-envisage a world where the natural and human worlds are analogous and connected in a way now alien to us, but wished for by those campaigning for a sustainable political and economic global world.

He discusses *The Tempest* and *The Winter's Tale* in illuminating ways: for example, he analyses a semantic and thematic emphasis on 'wood' in *The Tempest*. From the logs which Caliban and Ferdinand must haul, chop and stack, to the frequent references to the plant and natural world. 'This recurrent arboreal imagery has a very real point in the play, for Prospero's main activity since his arrival on the island has been its deforestation... What then would an early audience have understood from all this deforestation? The answer appears to be colonization' (pp. 155–7). Egan links deforestation not only to the increase in enclosures and increased vagrancy in the early modern period, but to the Elizabethan and Jacobean colonisation of Ireland and Virginia.

In an equally attentive textual reading of *The Winter's Tale*, Egan analyses how the words 'climate' and 'weather' recur: the latter and its compounds appearing six times more than in any other Shakespeare play. The wintry Sicily, counter-referentially, is destined to exist in perpetual winter, a half-light, unless 'that which is lost be... found' (3.2.134).

> In inadvertently bringing Perdita back to Sicilia, Florizel has allegorically brought the weather of spring with him. Understood... as a fertility myth... *The Winter's Tale* is archetypally Green in its insistence that human productive capacities and the Earth's are interdependent
> (p. 128).

The festive, restorative and archetypal cycles which Frye finds in the romances have now been greened.

The strengths of Egan's argument lies in the ability of new political and conceptual movements to bring us refreshed readings of old plays: although we can see traces of Frye's, Tennenhouse's and Adelman's approaches here, the Green critical engagement with Shakespeare's texts proves how these texts are continually renewed by each generation's own political and ideological concerns. Of course 'Green' is a contemporary way of understanding the world and our relationship(s) to it. However, Egan makes a strong case that the early modern period was the period when conceptions of the human relationship to the earth were shifting away from an organicist sense of connection towards a proto-capitalist model. Capitalist and scientific developments (including deforestation, the development of enclosures and early industrialisation) reconfigured the human relationship to nature as one of domination and use rather than mutuality. Shakespeare's works, whether unconsciously or not, chart the historical moment as we sever the connection between the human and the natural and animal worlds. Egan asks that we re-read and re-perform them with an eye to rediscovering and restoring an organic connection between humanity and earth.

Performances

Let us now move on to consider some performances of the plays, limiting our discussion to two performances each of those more frequently performed and studied, *The Tempest* and *The Winter's Tale*.

The Winter's Tale

Cheek-by-Jowl's touring version of *The Winter's Tale*, directed by Declan Donellan (touring 1997–9) was jointly produced and performed by the Russian Maly theatre company of St Petersburg, spoken in Russian with English surtitles. In interviews about this production Donellan has voiced a variety of rationales for this enterprise. One was to defamiliarise viewers from the language and text by forcing the English-speaking audiences to concentrate on the spectacle, visuals and bodily expressions equally with the textual meaning. However, more pragmatic reasons were that his company were sharing other repertory work with Maly in both countries, and undertaking a joint production on tour seemed a logical step. He has also argued that working with older actors on a play with significant roles for older actors was an opportunity not to be missed.

The performance's visuals referenced key Russian historical events, speaking to both its contemporary audiences on tour, and to some of the play's own Russian references. The opening scene evoked a tsarist pre-revolutionary visual ethos with Chekhovian theatrical connotations. The trial scene in its harsh lighting, spare wooden stage properties and vertical and horizontal lines, seemed to evoke the world of Stalinist show trials. The ineluctable inevitability of the trial's outcome was implicit in characterisation and delivery: Leontes did not listen, the trial was a political sham. The Russian references in the original (evoked by Hermione) are given a 'local habitation and a name' by the production. However, because the imagery of the wintry first half continued to dominate the play's second half: ideas of pastoral were represented as transitory: Perdita and Florizel's youthfulness was never represented as something strong enough to provide redemption. When Hermione's statue came alive, both she and Leontes were old and broken: the visuals and narrative were experienced more as a Beckettian-type post-apocalyptic fall rather than the promise of rebirth and restoration. This was underlined by emphasising Hermione's silence at the end of the play, showing her refusing to speak to her husband, rather than passively remaining silent. The performance also cut Leontes' marriage brokerage of Camillo and Paulina. This production's atmosphere was far removed from the idea of the late plays as redemptive romances: and consequently it foregrounded many of the problematic political and gender questions raised by the play which we have discussed in this book.

The second performance is the film version of *The Winter's Tale*, directed by Gregory Doran, with Antony Sher as Leontes (released in 1999). This is a filmed version of the Royal Shakespeare production from 1998/9, and is shot in the theatre, retaining a sense of the spatial and intimate feel of the performance in a theatre with the advantages of close-camera work. The 'look' of the production was dark and claustrophobic, with a series of raked shutters used to narrow off the stage space at key moments. Costume and gait (with some notable exceptions, to which we shall return) evoked late nineteenth-century Russia (a popular era for many RSC versions), from the sumptuous court scenes of the early part of the play, to the barer harsh stage of the finale, which reminded some critics of Tolstoy's advocacy of a pared-down simple life. Two exceptions to the periodisation were Leontes' costuming in the state events: at his initial entrance (which was a triumphal parade) and the trial scene he was gowned in red velvet and ermine; and the sheep-shearing festival was set in an industrial shearing hall. Costume and settings thus evoked Hermione's Russian background, the sense of pomp and status implicit in Leontes' function but played down the pastoral elements of Act 4, emphasising the potential attractions of court life by contrast. Costume echoed character: Hermione rich and sumptuous in maternity silk at the beginning, but in a dirty and bloody shift at her trial; Paulina in silk, velvet and furs; Leontes in a black severe bureaucrat's suit. Stage properties were used with numinous sensitivity: a shawl Hermione wears in the second scene, but discards to dance with Polixenes, was sniffed by Leontes as he starts his jealous outburst, and is folded carefully and reverently back onto a sofa at the scene's end by Polixenes. The same shawl then wraps the baby Perdita when Paulina presents her before Leontes, becoming the wrap which Antigonus fastens round her as he abandons her to the elements, and is again worn by Perdita in the final scene as she greets her mother. The dock in which Hermione stands for her trial later becomes the plinth on which her statue stands.

Antony Sher's Leontes was mesmerisingly convincing: from his early slightly nervous festive welcome to Polixenes, through his developing manic jealousy, he managed to convey a sense of Leontes' insecurities as ones shared by everyman. His hesitancies about Hermione and her love for him were explicit in his demeanour, his bureaucrat's clothing, his physical tics and clumsiness. We believe this man's crazed jealousy comes from a deep-seated insecurity about himself. This interpretation of Leontes' character strangely softened the audience towards him. His final 'hastily lead away' was spoken not as part of his old impatience, but as one grasping at a sudden hope that he can find love again. Alexandra Gilbreath's Hermione was warm, witty and welcoming in the opening scenes, and her appearance in the trial scene as physically dragged from the child-birth bed was haunting and resonant. Leontes and Hermione look physically wrecked in that scene: a reinterpretation suggesting visually that the emotional costs of Leontes' jealousy destroyed them both even before the trial and its outcome. Mamilius was played by Emily Bruni, who doubled as Perdita in the play's second half: as Mamillius she was in a wheelchair, emphasising his declining health from the beginning; as Perdita she played a rather rough shepherd girl, with country manners. The doubled part's emotional impact lay in Leontes' shocked response to her when her meets her: time really does go backwards, for here is Mamillius again.

This account makes clear that, for Doran, the play's centre was a study of Leontes and his character (echoed in the elimination of the opening scene, so Leontes' state entrance commences the play): what made him tick, why does he descend into madness, and what happens when he is redeemed? This gave a fresh feel to the production, and certainly converts audiences to a greater sympathy with Leontes than many other productions or interpretations. However, the cost of such a focus means that Paulina and Hermione's resonance is muted. Although Paulina carried a visual and moral authority in her demeanour, costume and eventual softening towards Leontes, it was Leontes' passion which dominated. The feminisation suggested by the Perdita–Paulina–Hermione axis was never quite numinous enough in the final act.

The Tempest

Let us now turn to two productions of *The Tempest*. The first is the film directed by Derek Jarman which premiered at the London film festival in 1979. Although the plot remains faithful to the original play, the film is a free adaptation that meditates on the importance of environmental politics, the decline of colonial power, and the role of the artist. Watching the film alongside a good knowledge of the play is an excellent illustration of how a director uses Shakespeare to debate contemporary and personal ideas.

Jarman alters the original's structure, for example showing us Prospero as an all-controlling magician and artist from the beginning to end, moving things round his darkened cave-like cell. The film ends on a camp celebration of Miranda and Ferdinand's wedding, with Elizabeth Welch singing 'Stormy Weather' to cast and sailors, evoking not only Hollywood musicals, but an iconic filmic showcase for African-American performers. This visual and aural combination of Shakespeare and popular filmic tradition connects the original text to twentieth-century cultural diversity as well as creating an ironic commentary on how Shakespeare's place as bard of the cultural elite narrows his dramatic, social and intellectual breadth. However, this ending also negates many of the darker elements implicit in the play's ending. The casting of both Prospero and Miranda, acted respectively by Heathcote Williams and Toyah Wilcox, was unconventional: a stage magician and a punk rock-star created character connotations far removed from the conventional characterisation of Prospero as reverend patriarch and Miranda as modest virgin. Their off-screen identities were deliberately imported into their on-screen characterisation to destabilise conventional interpretations of both characters. In addition, Prospero was portrayed as obsessively preoccupied with his magic and art, and Miranda as obsessed with images of herself and her sensuality. Thus Jarman intensified an aspect of their characterisation offered from the play (Prospero's back-story and Miranda's brief reference to her mirror). In both these examples Jarman enabled audiences to reconsider the play's artistic and political messages. Jarman added Sycorax as a playing character, balancing Prospero's male magic with that of a female witch, and enhanced Caliban's numinous connection to the natural world of the island. He cut many of the scenes with the courtiers. The film is set mainly at night, on a windswept coast, lit by candles and fires. The sound track is sensuous and varied, consisting of songs and music from eighteenth-century chamber music to popular songs and dissonant orchestration. Costumes were a fantastical hybrid combination of punk, gothic and Hollywood musical. These effects help create an other-worldly experience, analogous to the original play, but unique to the film itself. The darkness lends a more bizarre nightmarish quality to the film than any initial reading suggested by the play-text. The island, landscape and environment dominated characters and action in this film, prefiguring Egan's critical approach in *Green Shakespeare*, as well as many of the post-colonial engagements with the play from the 1980s onwards.

Finally, let us consider a recent performance directed by Rupert Goold, and starring Patrick Stewart as Prospero, performed by the

Royal Shakespeare Company in 2006. The pre-performance publicity included many reminders of Stewart's role as Captain Picard in the second series of *Star Trek:* so the production's marketing strategy was to defamiliarise potential audiences from conventional representations of Prospero, to draw in a younger audience, and to suggest *The Tempest* had some kind of connection to science fiction. Goold's setting for the play echoed this branding: the island is a cold barren place from the beginning, where characters huddle against wind and snow. The initial visual impact was reinforced by the broadcast of a BBC shipping forecast as the storm began. The arctic imagery extended to Stewart's powerful characterisation of Prospero as an aged and near-senile man. Miranda was downtrodden and ragged: a wild child. Characters and experiences evoked the heightened realism of disaster stories like *Lost*, or the alien environment evoked in the reality-TV shows such as *Big Brother* and *I'm a Celebrity Get Me Out of Here*, the 'other worlds' of science fiction, and the visual and political images from Guantanamo Bay, in which the gritty dirt and nastiness of being shut-off, marooned and isolated is laid bare and played out to a bitter end. Prospero's island in Goold's version was no magical numinous place, a potential paradise: but a hellish prison with overtones of *The Lord of the Flies*. Prospero's vicious treatment of Caliban chillingly put these visuals into play, emphasising the violence integral to the colonial settler enterprise and its dependence on slavery, but also to humans when trapped together in a closed environment.

Goold's *Tempest* is very much a story of Prospero the individual, focussing on his personal journey into a madness generated by isolation and fantasy, emphasising his threatened violence as actual to Caliban and Miranda, but as concomitant upon the environmental and inhuman conditions in which he has been placed. The play's resolution thus focuses on how Prospero changes at the end of the play, rather than on how the newer arrivals change (although they, too, are driven mad by the island). This is an interesting and valid interpretation, although in order to achieve its bleak reading, the production has to downplay some of the positive magical qualities of the island, the imagery linked to the young lovers, as well as Caliban's loving and lush descriptions of the island. The masque's gods garnered audience laughter at their self-consciously ironised evocation of 'this short-grassed green' (4.1.83), drawing attention to the actual barren island on which the characters stand, to Prospero's perceptual delusions and to the magical power of theatre itself to evoke and imagine the impossible. Ariel, played by Julian Beach, looked like a horror-movie zombie, and his appearance and concomitant actions cast a further pall over the island and its atmosphere.

This production set out to destabilise our views of the play. Here hope resides in a return to places other than the island and the play: Europe, our own lives, sanity itself. In contradistinction to many productions, Goold imagined the island as a nightmare rather than a dream, a dystopia not a utopia.

In forcing us to question how benign the island and Prospero really are, we return to the original text. Although this production made for uncomfortable viewing, refusing to offer the audience any of the play's original delights of music, sound or vision, it reminded us starkly of the harsh and brutal world which the original play also never quite lets us forget.

What each of the productions show is that Shakespeare's plays come alive with new directorial and performance perspectives, not only literally in their performance on stage, but also in enabling us to return to the plays and discover new things and new ways of seeing. Good productions are as effective as critics in enabling us to see these kinds of new perspectives: and a good textual understanding of the plays' originals enables you to judge the effectiveness of both critics and performances. All these performances have produced new insights into the plays, and in both critics and performances we can see how contemporary politics and popular culture continue to influence and engage artistic expression. This is a symbiosis which Shakespeare's Jacobean plays acknowledged, Heminge and Condell celebrated, and which keeps the plays live today.

Further Reading

Throughout this book you have engaged in detailed reading of the original texts. We have aimed to enable you to develop your own independent critical interpretations, reinforced by, and emerging from, close analytical readings. If you read and discuss a play using the approaches followed in this book you will be able to write interestingly, analytically and convincingly about the late plays. You may want to engage with other critics who have written about your chosen texts: it is best to do this after you have formed some judgments of your own. If you read critics too early, you will find it harder to develop your own responses and ideas: it also makes the process less pleasurable. It is, however, often helpful to read contextual and background accounts of Shakespeare's theatre and political and social history even before you read the plays.

The suggestions made here for further reading are necessarily curtailed: the Oxford Classics editions have good recommended reading lists, and you will find further reading in the books and articles listed below.

The Literary Context

Reading some of the plays we have referred to in the book can deepen and illuminate your own understanding of the late plays themselves: for example, look at *A Midsummer Night's Dream, As You Like It* and *Love's Labour's Lost,* as a way of understanding how pastoral and 'green worlds' function. Look at *Othello* and *Much Ado About Nothing* to consider ways in which masculinity and femininity play out in a tragedy and a comedy. Look at Fletcher's *The Faithful Shepherdess* to understand how tragicomedy works and became popular. Think about dead or damaging mothers in other plays: *All's Well That Ends Well* and *Hamlet*, for example. Reading *Antony and Cleopatra* will illuminate how Shakespeare codes classical Roman ideas with those of North Africa in the opposition between Caesar and Cleopatra: a gendered and cultural opposition which is arguably shared by the late plays. It would be very useful to read Shakespeare's 'other' late plays, those he wrote collaboratively with John Fletcher, *Henry VIII; or All is True* and *Two Noble Kinsmen*.

It can be extremely helpful to read other non-dramatic texts from the period, both literary and non-literary, to extend your understanding of contemporary fashions and concerns. Machiavelli's *The Prince*, Francis Bacon's *Essays*, Montaigne's *Essays* and Ovid's *Metamorphoses* are all popular and influential. Some sources are reprinted in ed. Kate Aughterson, *The English Renaissance: An Anthology of Sources and Documents* (Routledge, 1998).

Historical and Social Contexts

There is a plethora of very good contextual books aimed at students; these ones are particularly helpful: Julia Briggs, *This Stage-Play World: English Literature and its Background 1580–1625* (Oxford University Press, 1997); Donna Hamilton *A Concise Companion to English Renaissance Literature* (Blackwell, 2006); Lisa Hopkins, *Renaissance Literature and Culture* (Continuum, 2006); ed. Stanley Wells and Lena Cowen Orlin, *Shakespeare: An Oxford Guide* (Oxford University Press, 2003); ed. Richard Dutton, *The Oxford Handbook of Early Modern Theatre* (Oxford University Press, 2009); and ed. David Scott Kastan and Peter Stallybrass, *Staging the Renaissance: Interpretations of Elizabethan and Jacobean Drama* (Routledge1993). Three excellent and very readable books on Shakespeare, which give a brilliant contemporary feel for his work and longevity are Catherine Belsey's *Why Shakespeare?* (Palgrave, 2007), Simon Palfrey's *Doing*

Shakespeare (Arden Shakespeare, 2005), and James Shapiro's *1599: A Year in the Life of William Shakespeare* (Faber 2006). Two excellent guides to the language are ed. Sylvia Adamson et al., *Reading Shakespeare's Dramatic Language: A Guide* (Arden Shakespeare, 2001) and David Crystal's *Think on My Words: Exploring Shakespeare's Language* (Cambridge University Press, 2008)

Criticism

The critical works we discussed in Chapter 12 were: Northrop Frye, *A Natural Perspective: The Development of Shakespearean Comedy and Romance* (Columbia University Press, 1965); Leonard Tennenhouse, *Power on Display: The Politics of Shakespeare's Genres* (Routledge, 1984); Janet Adelman, *Suffocating Mothers: Fantasies of Maternal Origin in Shakespeare's Plays from Hamlet to The Tempest* (Routledge, 1992); and Gabriel Egan, *Green Shakespeare: From Ecopolitics to Ecocriticism* (Oxford University Press, 2006).

There are some excellent introductory discussions of the late plays available, from Joe Nutt's *An Introduction to Shakespeare's Late Plays* (Palgrave, 2002), to the more scholarly but stimulating Simon Palfrey's *Late Shakespeare: A New World of Words* (Clarendon Press, 2000) and Raphael Lyne's *Shakespeare's Late Work* (Oxford University Press, 2007). Collections of essays are included in ed. Kiernan Ryan, *Shakespeare: the Last Plays* (Longman, 1999); in ed. Catherine Alexander's *Cambridge Companion to Shakespeare's Last Plays* (Cambridge University Press, 2009); ed. Jennifer Richards and James Knowles, *Shakespeare's Late Plays: New Readings* (Edinburgh University Press, 1999) combines some exciting new theoretical and historical approaches to the plays; as does Alison Thorne's *Shakespeare's Romances* (New Casebook Series, Macmillan, 2002). Marjorie Garber's *Coming of Age in Shakespeare* (Routledge, 1997) is a stimulating discussion of ageing and learning in the late plays; Stephen Greenblatt's discussions of *The Tempest* in *Shakespearean Negotiations: The Circulation of Social Energy in Renaissance England* (Clarendon Press, 1990) and in *Learning to Curse: Essays in Early Modern Culture* (Routledge, 2nd edn, 2007) are densely argued but exciting and stimulating. David Bergeron's *Shakespeare's Romances and the Royal Family* (University of Kansas Press, 1985) debates the plays within the context of Stuart family politics. John Gillies, *Shakespeare and the Geography of Difference* (Cambridge University Press, 1994) is an excellent discussion of how place resonates in these plays. Frances Yates's *Shakespeare's Last plays: A New Approach* (Routledge, 1975) was groundbreaking in its incorporation of political and historical matter into a reading of the plays, although some of her chronology has since been disputed, her work remains suggestive. Leah Marcus's *Puzzling Shakespeare: Local Reading and Its Discontents* (University of California Press, 1988) links *Cymbeline* to Shakespeare's other political plays.

There are two excellent resource books on Royal Shakespeare Company performances of two of the plays, Patricia Tatspaugh *Shakespeare at Stratford: The Winter's Tale* (Arden Shakespeare, 2002) and David Lindley, *Shakespeare at Stratford: The Tempest* (Arden Shakespeare, 2003). Students should Google reviews of more recent productions. Other productions are discussed in Ronald Draper, *The Winter's Tale: Text and Performance* (Macmillan, 1985), Ros King's *The Winter's Tale: A Guide to the Text and Play in Performance* (Palgrave, 2009), and Trevor Griffiths, *The Tempest: A Guide to the Text and Play in Performance* (Palgrave, 2007) both of which provide extensive and useful bibliographies on performance.

Index

actors 18
  contract with audience 71–3, 236
  delivery 14, 18, 50, 66, 71–3, 78, 86, 91, 179
  implicit stage directions to, 2, 9, 28, 40, 152, 154
  in King's Men 220, 221, 224
  in modern productions 97, 113, 149, 247, 262
  performing text 9, 15, 71, 90, 154, 163, 185, 186, 187
Adelman, Janet 256–9, 261, 270
affect 53–4, 168, 203–6, 235, 236
America 134, 187, 247, 265
Antony and Cleopatra 1, 227, 228, 241, 257, 269
aristocracy 108, 215, 239, 240, 245, 252
art 9, 53, 59, 61, 64, 66, 70, 175, 183, 186, 190, 203, 215, 255, 258, 259, 265
artistic contract 72, 236
audience(s) 2, 9, 22, 39, 78, 83, 110, 189–92, 206
  and openings 9–11, 24–8
  contemporary 2, 14, 18, 42, 116, 161, 177, 189, 234, 249, 260, 261, 262
  direct address to, 126, 181, 198, 203, 204
  implicit 5, 15, 125, 177
  Jacobean 1, 76, 100, 136, 190, 221–2, 229, 231, 232, 234, 236, 239, 260
  on stage 22, 62–6, 77, 110, 142–3, 174, 177, 185–6, 190, 203
  as participant in action 71–3, 77, 78, 97, 148–9, 154–7
  privileged knowledge of, 93, 96, 108, 136, 139, 155, 195, 199, 203, 205, 206
  responses 43, 47, 50, 52, 62, 64, 71, 79, 90, 91, 102, 109, 112–13, 122, 136, 154, 166–9, 174, 179, 190, 189, 190, 204, 215, 238, 269
  and turning points 30, 38, 53–7
  see also affect
audience response theory 236–8
authority 16, 21, 27, 77, 83, 84, 85, 89, 94, 95, 103, 121, 124, 132, 147–8, 215, 223, 241, 243, 244, 247, 249, 252, 253, 254, 255, 257, 258, 264

Bacon, Francis (*Essays*) 269
Basilikon Doron (James I) 245
bed 31, 33, 34, 52, 100, 107, 183, 200, 263
  (as stage property) 152–7, 165–6, 167, 169

birth 21, 25, 35, 42, 68, 84, 103, 122, 124, 127, 134, 143, 148, 150, 164, 169, 172, 176, 187, 202, 215, 263
blank verse 2, 219, 237
  see also language, pentameter
Britain 73–5, 83, 155, 171, 215, 230, 253

Ceres 109
  see also The Tempest
character
  blocking of, 5, 19–21, 27, 28, 48, 56, 62, 63, 79, 102, 143, 191
  construction of, 147–9, 152, 212, 214, 229, 249
  in *Cymbeline* 75–6, 173–6
  in dialogue 132, 148
  direction of, 63, 80
  disguised 93, 146, 147
  in endings 57–80
  and music 193–5, 196
  in opening scenes 25–7
  "outsider" characters 76, 79, 147, 149, 238
  and stage directions 157, 166
  "stock" characters 101, 160, 178–82, 190, 236
  suspension of disbelief by 62, 190
  in *The Tempest* 19–23, 71–2, 96–7, 113–19, 133, 208–9, 265–6
  in turning-point scenes 30, 52–4
  in *The Winter's Tale* 10–14, 40–43, 64–7, 94, 107–13, 197–204, 238, 263–4
  see also characterisation
characterisation 3, 9, 22–3, 52, 71, 81, 85, 103–5, 108, 110, 117, 119, 126–8, 140, 146, 151, 167, 215, 256, 258, 262, 265
Charles I 242, 246
chastity 38, 42, 43, 121, 122, 125, 153, 155, 166
children 18, 40, 42, 66, 75, 78, 81, 85, 88–9, 97, 99, 103, 118, 140, 142, 145, 173, 188, 234, 242, 243, 246

Chorus 18, 22, 161, 177, 179–80, 206
Christian references 15, 66, 78, 109, 161, 176, 188, 190, 195, 196, 207, 243, 250
Civil War 221, 242, 245
civilisation 97
  see also New World, America
class 21, 27, 146, 148, 204, 210, 215, 230
  see also birth, status
colonialism 132–3, 140, 246, 259, 264, 265, 266
colonisation 136, 260
comedy 30, 31, 33, 35, 37, 39, 41, 43, 45, 47, 49, 51, 53, 54–5, 76, 93, 101, 139, 148, 165, 166, 176, 190, 222, 229, 234–8, 249, 250–53, 269, 270
The Comedy of Errors 225, 228
Comic Relief 53, 148
Condell, Henry 230–31, 231–2, 267
conservative politics 65, 76, 77, 125, 149, 187, 245, 252, 259
cuckoldry 39, 41, 87
  see also children, masculinity, maternity
Cymbeline 1, 25, 26, 29, 55, 62, 126, 148, 150, 166, 169, 176, 180, 227, 229, 238, 243, 254, 257, 259, 271
  analysis: 1.1.110–54 81–5
  analysis: 2.2.1–51 152–8
  analysis: 4.2.258–282 193–6
  analysis: 5.3.124–214 170–72
  analysis: 5.4.436–486 73–6
  Apollo 33–6, 40, 54, 110, 163, 164
  Cymbeline 74–6, 81–6, 101, 102, 103, 104, 125, 126, 148, 150, 195, 215, 227
  Giacomo 104, 148, 150, 153–7, 167, 171
  Innogen 29, 62, 75, 81–5, 102, 125, 126, 150, 152–67, 169, 171, 172, 174, 175, 192, 193, 194, 195, 196, 212, 213

Index   275

Posthumus 73–5, 81–5, 102, 104, 126, 150, 154, 156, 167, 170–77, 194, 254

daughters 81, 102, 106, 107, 109, 111, 113, 115, 117, 119, 121, 123, 125, 127, 192, 214
deus ex machina 5, 77, 79, 173, 255
discovery 53, 62, 63, 75, 179
  see also peripeteia
divine judgment 50, 176
  see also Christianity, providence
divine right 101, 245
  see also James I, political philosophy
Doran, Greg 262, 264
dynastic succession 65, 69, 75, 101–2, 148, 149

Egan, Gabriel 259–61, 270
Elizabeth I 35, 219, 223, 240, 241, 243, 245, 246
endings 53–80, 102, 106, 149, 150, 214–15, 239
Eros/thanatos 66
European identity 47–9, 71, 97, 98, 99, 101, 115–9, 132, 134, 136, 138–40, 165, 187, 241, 245, 267
  see also colonialism

fairy tales 47, 165
  see also magic, *The Winter's Tale*
faith 31, 60, 63, 66, 70, 90, 156, 165, 258
family 39, 42, 53, 65, 77, 81, 84, 94, 6161, 173, 174–7, 187, 195, 204, 213, 214, 239, 243, 246, 252–6, 271
  see also fathers, maternity, motherhood, patriarchy
family politics 204, 271
family reunions 64, 250
fantasy 24, 49, 64, 136, 150, 188, 189, 208, 266
  see also magic, romance

fate 17, 24, 45, 50, 54, 78, 156, 162, 230, 254
  see also providence, Christianity
fathers 76, 78, 81, 83, 85, 87, 89, 91, 93, 95, 97, 99, 101, 102, 103, 105, 118, 192, 206
femininity 54, 75, 150, 213, 214, 242, 269
festivity 76, 100, 125, 185, 197, 250, 257, 260, 263
Fletcher, John 229, 233, 234, 237, 238, 240, 269
freedom 10, 12, 72, 73, 115, 123, 136, 138, 139, 148, 150, 208, 209, 238
Frye, Northrop 249–51, 256, 259, 260, 261, 270

gender 25, 37, 36, 63, 85, 103, 102, 106, 116, 125, 143, 147, 148, 150, 164, 165, 179, 210, 211, 215, 230, 244, 256, 257, 258, 259, 262, 269
Gilbreath, Alexandra 263
God(s) 23, 76, 78, 85, 95, 101, 110, 112, 115, 122, 128, 143, 161, 173, 176, 177, 179, 180, 186, 187, 188, 190, 205, 234
Green world 189, 215, 259–61, 265, 267, 269, 270

Heminge, John 231, 267
Hamlet 161, 221, 226, 228, 236, 256, 257, 258, 259, 269, 270
Henry VIII 1, 35, 222, 227, 229, 269
Henry VIII 32, 222, 241
Henry, Prince of Wales 239, 242, 245, 246
husbands 25, 81–105, 140, 143, 149

idealism 73, 136, 189, 215
identity 37, 39, 49, 66, 69, 71, 102, 115, 133, 146, 147, 149, 159, 160–64, 167, 174, 176, 186, 192, 195, 198, 208, 209, 210, 212, 215, 228, 229, 250, 256, 257, 258, 259

see also birth, gender, status
illusion 11, 47, 53, 54, 62, 249
  see also magic, romance
imagery 4, 13, 22, 23, 27, 28, 41, 42, 43, 54, 55, 75, 101, 109, 110, 136, 149, 161, 187, 196, 208, 214, 215, 249, 260, 262, 266
islands 22, 26, 44, 45, 48, 49, 51, 70, 71, 72, 95, 96, 97, 99, 101, 117, 130, 131–4, 135, 139, 140, 159, 186, 187, 189, 204, 205, 206, 207, 208, 209, 247, 253, 260, 265, 266, 267
islanders 44, 136, 138
Italy 98, 171, 175, 187
  see also Naples, European identity

James I 76, 81, 83, 85, 101, 190, 219, 220, 223, 237, 238, 239, 240, 241, 242, 243, 245, 246, 247, 252, 253
  Basilikon Doron 245
  The True Law of Free Monarchies 85, 242
Jonson, Ben 229, 232, 239, 240, 241, 249
justice 30, 33, 34, 54, 74, 121, 144, 172, 200, 244
  see also God, providence

King Lear 29, 221, 227
knowledge 10, 12, 20, 21, 30, 38, 39, 42, 53, 72, 80, 103, 108, 110, 123, 133, 139, 140, 148, 151, 156, 164, 207, 253
King's Men, The 170, 191, 193, 220, 221, 229, 230, 232, 233, 234, 237

land 19, 43, 90, 133–6, 148, 162, 165, 184, 189, 215, 247, 259
law 37, 143, 148, 252
language 2, 24, 27–8, 41, 42, 78–9, 91, 129, 131, 233, 255
  and character 12, 35, 42, 49, 52–4, 89–90, 101, 102, 103, 105, 109, 112, 113, 116, 123–4, 126–8, 143, 50, 155–7, 160, 181, 230
  and colonialism 131–4, 137, 139
  and dialogue 12
  and delivery 14, 15, 21, 27, 49, 85, 143, 144
  and grammar 13, 15
  and imagery 13, 37, 40, 43, 49, 52, 55–6, 63, 72, 104, 134, 214
  and interiority 229
  and music 191–2, 211
  register 37, 38, 49, 51, 69, 147, 149, 150, 151
  as stage directions 28, 66, 91
  see also imagery, rhythm
Lanyer, Aemilia 243
liberty 72, 148, 150, 208, 240, 244, 245
Love's Labour's Lost 222, 225, 229, 268
Lucretia 155
  see also The Rape of Lucrece

Machievelli 148, 269
magic 47, 48, 51, 58, 61, 62, 63, 64, 65, 66, 68, 69, 72, 77, 78, 80, 95, 96, 97, 101, 128, 131, 159, 168, 174, 181, 185, 186, 187, 193, 194, 202, 204, 205, 208, 210, 215, 264, 265, 266, 267
male prerogative 41
  see also gender, femininity, husbands, masculinity, patriarchy
masculinity 54, 65, 75, 101, 102, 104, 106, 213, 228, 269
  see also femininity, gender, husbands, patriarchy
masques 71, 73, 100, 128, 170, 184–90, 193, 210, 212, 239–40, 266
maternity 42, 263
  see also motherhood
Measure for Measure 227, 228, 259
medieval quest narrative 47, 161
meritocracy 134, 172, 215

Index

metaphors 4, 14, 23, 24, 25, 26, 41, 43, 48, 52, 54, 55, 66, 75, 84, 89, 90, 91, 103, 109, 110, 124, 144, 164, 189, 190, 192, 207, 215, 250, 260
  see also language
Meres, Francis 222, 223
Metamorphoses 64, 136, 156, 207, 222
meta-theatricality 5, 71, 180
  see also theatricality
A Midsummer Night's Dream 189, 222, 226, 229, 268
misreading 14, 157, 164
monarchy 155, 252, 254
monsters 44, 46, 49, 50, 51, 111, 112, 202, 254, 256
Montaigne 136, 241, 246, 269
Morte D'Arthur (Thomas Malory) 47
motherhood 42, 78, 106–28, 256–9, 263, 269, 270
  see also maternity
music 5, 9, 44, 46, 48, 60, 63, 39, 95, 96, 96, 128, 170–75, 177, 181, 190, 191, 192, 193–213, 214, 229, 230, 239, 240, 255, 265, 267
myth 49, 50, 56, 64, 69, 185, 219, 231, 250, 251, 260
  see also fantasy

narrative 53, 55, 57, 75, 77, 80, 102, 152, 155, 157, 176, 262
  arc 25, 53, 54, 76, 77, 85, 101, 104, 124, 125, 149, 165, 174, 176, 192, 193, 194m 234m 252, 254
  devices 55, 75, 77, 78, 79, 95, 103, 109, 125, 161, 162, 190
  and music 192, 196, 204, 210
  story 5, 26, 35, 47, 53, 71, 77, 78, 80, 128, 147, 165, 168, 196
  tension 179
  see also plot
Natural Law 148, 171, 252
nature 21, 50, 52, 64, 76, 102, 108, 110, 117, 135, 136, 140, 145, 165, 171, 179, 187, 188, 189, 197, 208, 215, 231, 235, 242, 254, 258, 261

New World 25, 27, 45, 54, 99, 101, 118, 119, 136, 187, 207, 270
  see also civilisation, Green world, islands, Italy, land

Othello 223, 227, 228, 269
Ovid, *Metamorphoses* 64, 136, 156, 207, 222

paganism 76
pastoral 89, 94, 107, 108, 110, 136, 165, 166, 188, 189, 194, 195, 203, 204, 229, 234, 237, 257, 262, 263, 268
paternity 42, 102, 164
  see also fathers, masculinity, patriarchy
patriarchy 81, 101, 102, 228, 242, 252, 254, 255
  see also fathers, masculinity, paternity
pentameter 2–3, 38, 39, 50, 85, 133, 142, 176, 181, 187, 188, 197
  see also blank verse, language, rhythm
performance 4, 10, 15, 55, 57, 113, 117, 152, 157, 190, 214, 231, 236, 271
  of actors 21, 22, 42, 66, 110, 113, 146
  modern performances 261–7
  of music 199, 204–5, 209, 210, 212
  in Shakespeare's lifetime 9, 193, 220, 221, 223, 224, 229, 239
  on stage 51, 70, 156, 177, 184, 192, 199
  as a theme 21, 43, 51, 66, 70–72
  see also metatheatricality, music, productions, theatricality
Pericles 1, 25, 29, 55, 76, 78, 104, 125, 126, 127, 168–9, 191, 192, 213, 215, 224, 227, 249, 254, 257, 258
  analysis: Scene 5, 155–204 158–61
  analysis: Scene 19, 47–150 119–24
  analysis: Scene 22, 21–65 67–9
Marina 67–9, 119–24, 125, 127, 151, 192, 213

Pericles 67–9, 104, 127, 157–61, 167, 169, 192, 213, 215, 227
peripeteia 5, 79, 165, 167, 177, 213
plot 5,9, 26, 28, 30, 43, 68, 79, 126, 141, 143, 147, 148, 149, 159, 166, 167, 177, 179, 180, 193, 214, 237, 238, 249–50
  comic 84
  crisis points 52, 53, 55, 211
  main plot 129 139, 145, 148, 149, 190, 210
  and music 196, 202, 210, 211
  in Renaissance dramatic theory 234, 236
  resolution 24, 57, 76, 78, 177, 189, 252
  reversals 62, 125, 166
  and Shakespeare's other plays 228, 229
  sub-plots 129, 148, 149
  tragic 29, 42, 144, 145, 176, 228
  tragicomic 237–8
  see also metatheatricality
politics 15, 73, 89, 90, 102, 105, 129–51, 151, 155, 204, 245, 251, 254, 255, 259, 264, 270
political pragmatism 215
political theory 81, 246
  see also politics, rulership
productions 35, 49, 65, 80, 113, 118, 206, 210, 211, 261–7
  see also music, performance, theatricality
Proserpina 107, 109
  see also myth, nature, Ovid
providence 77, 176, 177, 190, 215
Pygmalion 64, 65, 78
  see also myth, Ovid

quest narrative 47, 161

The Rape of Lucrece 222, 225
rebirth 64, 66, 69, 76, 78, 214, 215, 250, 262
  see also narrative, nature, romance

recognition 47, 69, 71, 75, 78, 79, 159, 161, 177, 189, 213
  see also peripeteia, reconciliation
reconciliation 64, 69, 76, 77, 81, 101, 102, 104, 125, 145, 149, 189, 192, 207, 213, 214, 215, 228, 250
  see also narrative
redemption 53, 102, 187, 262
repentance 51, 53, 144
republicanism 155, 241
  see also politics
revenge 34, 50, 165, 170, 175
rhetoric 14, 20, 38, 40, 43, 55, 93, 94, 112, 123–5, 132, 147, 166, 251, 252, 255
rhyme 2–3, 55, 73, 174–6, 181, 195, 199, 202, 207, 210
rhythm 2–3, 38, 39, 50, 54, 73, 85, 86, 90, 91, 103, 142, 174–5, 195–6, 197, 199, 203, 207, 209, 210
  see also language, music, rhyme
romance 47, 54, 77, 103, 161, 165, 166, 190, 208, 210, 214, 228, 229, 234, 240, 246, 249–50, 251–8, 260, 262, 270, 271
Rome 26, 75, 104, 126, 150, 155, 157, 215, 241, 257
royal family 84, 161, 239, 246, 255, 271
  see also political theory, politics, rulership
rulership 72, 105, 134, 148, 149, 215
  see also politics, royal family

scenic structure 5, 19, 28, 37, 53, 54, 55, 56, 215, 229
  see also narrative, plot
servants 88, 129–51, 221
Shakespeare, career 219–32
  see also individual works by title
Sher, Antony 262–3
Sidney, Philip 234, 236
silence 16, 21, 31, 41, 51, 57, 58, 64, 65, 75, 80, 117, 127, 153, 156, 181, 184, 185, 186, 262

see also stage directions
slaves 129–51, 234, 235, 247
  see also colonialism, land, new world, slavery
slavery 114, 122, 124, 150, 266
Social Contract 72
  see also politics
songs 73, 147, 168, 187, 188, 193–213, 223, 265
Sonnets 222, 228
Southampton, Earl of 222
spectacle 56, 65, 78, 170–92, 193, 203, 210, 211, 212, 214, 228, 230, 233, 239, 240, 255, 261
spirituality 51, 52, 53, 63, 72, 78, 85, 206
stage directions 5, 10, 18, 20, 28, 40, 41, 48, 50, 53, 55, 63, 108, 152, 154, 157, 167, 191, 192, 193, 206, 212, 215
stage properties 48, 56, 79, 108, 110, 152–69, 214, 215, 262, 263
status 12, 20, 21, 25, 27, 63, 65, 71, 72, 83, 84, 85, 123, 124, 129, 133, 144, 146, 147, 148, 161, 173, 204, 215, 223, 263
  see also birth, class, politics
step-mothers 56, 75, 85
  see also fairy tales
Stewart, Patrick 265–6
suspension of disbelief 49, 62, 64, 69, 77, 236

The Tempest 1, 10, 15, 24, 26, 27, 28, 53, 68, 76, 79, 102, 103, 105, 125, 127, 168, 191, 193, 199, 211, 212, 215, 223, 227, 238, 243, 245, 254, 258, 259, 260, 261, 264–70, 271
  analysis: 1.1.1–68 16–23
  analysis: 1.2.306–364 129–35
  analysis: 1.2.374–404 204–7
  analysis: 1.2.388–422 95–8
  analysis: 2.1.100–133 98–9
  analysis: 2.1.141–162 135–7
  analysis: 2.2.41–75 and **154–182** 137–9
  analysis: 3.1.48–91 113–17
  analysis: 3.2.114–24 208–10
  analysis: 3.3.1–110 43–51
  analysis: 4.1.13–33 99–101
  analysis: 4.1.57–142 181–9
  analysis: 5.1.88–94 207–8
  analysis: 5.1.165–184 117–119
  analysis: 5.1.319–338 70–73
Alonso 20–21, 26, 47–9, 51–3, 71, 95, 97–99, 102, 117–19, 131, 135, 150, 208, 212
Antonio 18, 20, 21, 22, 43–4, 47, 49, 51, 53, 71, 77, 80, 98, 118, 135–6, 149–50, 208, 215
Ariel 4, 45–54, 71–3, 95–6, 100, 105, 130, 132, 134, 136, 185, 204–9, 212, 267
banquet scene 44–53, 168, 169, 185, 191, 206, 212
Boatswain 16–24, 137
Caliban 47, 49, 51, 71–2, 79, 97, 105, 129–34, 136–40, 148, 149, 150, 184, 188, 205–9, 254, 260, 265, 266
Ceres 181–9, 190, 212
Ferdinand 4, 16, 19, 46, 47, 50, 52, 53, 71, 72, 79, 95–7, 100–102, 105, 114–19, 125, 131, 134, 168, 183–9, 204–7, 260, 264
Gonzalo 16–18, 19, 20, 23, 43, 44, 45, 46, 47, 48, 49, 51, 52, 98, 99, 118, 134–6, 188
Harpy scene 43–52, 185, 191, 206, 211
Miranda 47, 53, 71, 79, 95, 96–105, 113–19, 125, 127, 128, 129, 131, 132, 133, 134, 168, 184, 185, 186, 188, 189, 205, 205, 245, 264, 265, 266
Prospero 4, 44–53, 70–73, 77, 78, 80, 95–101, 102, 105, 114, 115, 117–18, 125, 129–34, 136, 139,

140, 150, 151, 181–8, 204, 205, 208, 209, 212, 214, 254, 260, 264, 265–7
Sebastian 16–22, 43–51, 77, 98–9, 117, 135–6, 149, 150, 208, 215, 254
Tennenhouse, Leonard 251–5, 256, 259, 261
theatre 9, 18, 66, 70, 72, 73, 170, 175, 181, 189, 190, 193, 210, 219, 220, 221–3, 233, 234, 238, 239, 258, 261, 262, 267, 268, 269
see also theatricality
The Theatre 221
theatricality 5, 42, 66, 69, 71, 72, 78, 168, 170–92, 214, 233
time 18, 19, 24, 25, 27, 35, 37, 60, 61, 62, 64, 66, 68, 78, 81, 88, 90, 107, 112, 117, 127, 133, 146, 154, 157, 162, 163, 177–81, 186, 188, 189, 192, 197, 203, 215, 228, 229, 235, 236
tragicomedy 234, 237, 238, 239, 269
trauma 69, 75, 77
treachery 80, 143
see also treason
treason 31, 35, 38, 135
trial 30–43, 52, 53, 63, 65, 142, 230, 238
Twelfth Night 11, 149, 227
Two Noble Kinsmen 1, 224, 227, 229, 233, 269

unities (dramatic theory) 229
usurpation 48, 134, 150, 185, 241
utopia 24, 267
see also Green world, New World

Venus and Adonis 195, 222, 225

westerners 47
see also European identity

The Winter's Tale 1, 24, 25, 26, 29, 69, 70, 76, 77, 78, 101, 102, 103, 105, 125, 127, 148, 150, 161, 168, 192, 211, 212, 214, 215, 223, 227, 228, 229, 236, 243, 245, 254, 257, 258, 260, 261, 262, 271
analysis: 1.1.1–43 10–16
analysis: 1.2.152–209 86–91
analysis: 2.3.95–157 140–45
analysis: 3.2.1–147 30–42
analysis: 3.3.1–56 162–6
analysis: 4.1.1–32 177–81
analysis: 4.3.1–30 196–8
analysis: 4.4.97–135 106–10
analysis: 4.4.219–233 198–200
analysis: 4.4.257–317 200–203
analysis: 4.4.378–438 91–4
analysis: 4.4.724–747 145–7
analysis: 5.1.34–75 110–13
analysis: 5.3.8–155 57–66
Autolycus 145–8, 149, 150, 196–204, 210, 212
Florizel 65, 91–5, 103, 105, 107–10, 127, 146, 147, 178, 197, 198, 204, 260, 262
Hermione 2, 14, 30–43, 53–67, 78, 86–91, 105, 109, 111, 112–13, 127, 142–4, 147, 163–5, 180, 196, 238, 254, 255, 258, 259, 262–4
Leontes 2, 3, 14, 30–42, 53, 57–67, 69, 78, 86–94, 102, 105, 109, 111–13, 140–45, 150, 164, 165, 166, 178, 179, 180, 203, 228, 238, 254, 258, 262, 263–4
Mamillius 11, 14, 36, 37, 41, 42, 86–9, 105, 144, 164, 202, 238, 254, 264
Perdita 53, 58, 60, 61, 63, 64, 65, 78, 93, 94, 95, 105, 106–110, 127, 146–7, 150, 163, 165, 178, 179, 204, 254, 259, 260, 262, 263, 264
Paulina 30, 35, 36, 37, 54, 57–66, 94, 110–13, 125, 127, 140–45,

147, 148, 149, 150, 168, 214, 258, 259, 262, 263, 264
trial scene 30–43, 63, 65, 144, 164, 262–4
witchcraft 93, 94, 143, 194, 196
wives 106–28
women 25, 33, 36, 37, 53, 64, 65, 78, 88, 89, 90, 94, 100, 106, 124, 125, 127, 129, 135, 144, 149, 165, 189, 199, 203, 228, 240, 242, 244, 245, 253, 257
women's voices 78, 116, 174, 175, 202, 203, 204
women as agents of change 64–5, 214, 258
women's silence *see* silence
see also daughters, gender, wives

www.ingramcontent.com/pod-product-compliance
Lightning Source LLC
Chambersburg PA
CBHW050135240426
43673CB00043B/1681